Island of Hope

Island of Hope

MIGRATION AND SOLIDARITY
IN THE MEDITERRANEAN

Megan A. Carney

UNIVERSITY OF CALIFORNIA PRESS

University of California Press
Oakland, California

LIBRARY OF CONGRESS CATALOGING-IN-PUBLICATION DATA

Names: Carney, Megan A., 1984– author.
Title: Island of hope : migration and solidarity in the Mediterranean /
    Megan A. Carney.
Identifiers: LCCN 2020051228 (print) | LCCN 2020051229 (ebook) |
    ISBN 9780520344501 (cloth) | ISBN 9780520344518 (paperback) |
    ISBN 9780520975569 (epub)
Subjects: LCSH: Immigrants—Italy—Sicily. | Solidarity—Italy—Sicily. |
    Sicily (Italy)—Emigration and immigration.
Classification: LCC JV8139.S5 C37 2021 (print) | LCC JV8139.S5
    (ebook) | DDC 305.9/0691209458—dc23
LC record available at https://lccn.loc.gov/2020051228
LC ebook record available at https://lccn.loc.gov/2020051229

Manufactured in the United States of America

29 28 27 26 25 24 23 22 21
10 9 8 7 6 5 4 3 2 1

For my parents,
Danna J. Vedder and Edward L. Carney

Contents

Contents

Illustrations

Acknowledgments

Language opens doors. It opens doors in doing fieldwork, and it greatly enhances our ability to understand how others experience and interpret the world around us. There are two women who were instrumental to my study of the Italian language beginning some eighteen years ago, first at Villa La Pietra in Florence, Italy, and then in the Italian department at the University of California, Los Angeles. To this day, they remain in my mind not only as incredibly gifted in imparting their passion for the Italian language to others but also as two of the most caring and effective teachers that I have ever known. Valentina and Giovanna, wherever this text might find you, *grazie mille.*

This project overlapped with many major life events during which I have been fortunate to benefit from the enduring support of colleagues, family, and friends. There have been births (notably, those of my two children) and deaths, weddings (including my own), moves between states (no less than four times), and transition as well as acclimatization to four different work environments. This text has undoubtedly evolved with each of these life events, as has my perspective on doing fieldwork. In the several years that I have been returning to Sicily, each trip has meant something different. My Sicily-based friends and collaborators have observed me from the time when I was a fairly naive and nomadic freshly minted PhD to when I became a mother and an established academic. Through each life transition, they have shown unrelenting support and acceptance. This book is a labor of their love as much as my own. I want to thank everyone in Sicily who contributed in ways big and small to this project, especially Elisabetta Di Giovanni, Alessio Genovese, and Daniele Saguto. I very much look forward to our working together for years to come.

While a postdoctoral fellow in Comparative Border Studies at the School of Transborder Studies at Arizona State University (ASU) from 2013 to 2014, I had the privilege of time to embark on this work and to receive feedback from several faculty members, including Matt Garcia, Desiree Garcia, and Cecilia Menjívar, as well as fellow postdocs, Laia Soto Bermant and Holly Karibo. I found an equally supportive research environment while serving on the faculty of the University of Washington (UW) from 2014 to 2017. In particular, I benefited from exchanges with the Department of Anthropology, the Integrated Social Sciences Program, the Jackson School of International Studies, and the Center for Western European Studies. Matt Sparke (who inspired the title for this book), Katharyne Mitchell, Ricardo Gomez, and Sara Vannini were ideal collaborators and mentors. I am also very grateful to have had opportunities to present this work to students, particularly those enrolled in the Spaces of Sanctuary Seminar in winter 2017, and to have discussed it with colleagues, including Rachel Chapman, James Pfeiffer, Jenna Grant, Marieke van Ejik, Nora Kenworthy, Ann Anagnost, Jody Early, Janelle Taylor, Radhika Govindrajan, Danny Hoffman, Tony Lucero, and María Elena García.

The University of Arizona (UA) has been the ideal setting in which to complete this book, and I am especially indebted to my colleagues and students in the College of Social and Behavioral Sciences. Several faculty members in the School of Anthropology and Middle Eastern and North African Studies in particular influenced me as I put the finishing touches on the manuscript, including but not limited to Maribel Alvarez, Diane Austin, Emma Blake, Julia Clancy-Smith, Linda Green, Janelle Lamoreaux, Mark Nichter, Ivy Pike, Eric Plemons, Brian Silverstein, and Qing Zhang. My students have been a source of inspiration and have pushed me in challenging various aspects of my teaching and scholarship.

I am grateful to those who were enrolled in my spring 2018 and spring 2020 Food and Migration Seminar, fall 2018 Mediterranean Borderlands Seminar, and fall 2020 Mediterranean Migrations Seminar. I received crucial financial support to complete the fieldwork and writing phases of this project from UA Research, Discovery, and Innovation and the Udall Center for Studies in Public Policy. My year as a Tucson Public Voices Fellow with the OpEd Project also provided essential mentoring and connections that pushed the boundaries of this work.

Other crucial sources of funding for this project, from data collection to dissemination of findings, included the Institute for Humanities Research at ASU, the Center for Western European Studies at UW, the Center for Global Studies at UW, a Studio Collaboration Grant from the Simpson Center for the Humanities at UW, and the Fulbright Schuman European Union Affairs Program. The Provost's Author Support Fund at the University of Arizona helped cover expenses associated with the production of this book.

Many individuals provided feedback on various iterations of this manuscript and read it either in its entirety or in part. Thank you to participants in the panels "Shifting Climates, Everyday Solidarities, and Transpolitical Spaces of Displacement" at the 2019 Annual Meeting of the American Anthropological Association (especially Paul Silverstein), "Bodies and Their Materials: Creating and Critiquing 'Good' Care" at the 2018 Annual Meeting of the American Anthropological Association (especially Jessica Hardin, Melissa Caldwell, and Juliet McMullin), and "Health in the Time of 'Belt Tightening': An Anthropology of Austerity in Europe and Africa" at the 2015 Annual Meeting of the American Anthropological Association and at the 2016 Summer School on Migration, Democracy, and Human Rights at the University of Palermo. I am especially indebted to Melissa Caldwell, Teresa Mares, Carolyn Sargent, Bayla Ostrach, Emily Yates-Doerr, and the anonymous reviewers whose feedback has been integral to this work.

Kate Marshall has been the most supportive editor and friend. I will always sing her praises! She is steadfast in her commitment to championing a project and provides much-needed moral support. Working with her on not one but two books has been like winning the editor lottery. It was originally her suggestion that I consider developing this research into a book, and I am eternally grateful that I followed her advice. I am also grateful to the rest of the editorial team at the University of California Press, including Enrique Ochoa-Kaup.

Finally, thank you to all the friends and family whose support and encouragement helped midwife this book into being. I don't think I would have survived these past few years without the unwavering generosity and kindness of parents and grandparents, baby group friends, and nannies. I certainly would never have found the space or time to research and write without childcare support from Strauss ECE, Khalsa Montessori, Corrissa Kellett, and Evelyn Pickering. To my daughters, Hazel Marley and Nova Saoirse, you're the reason I write. It has been my biggest joy to bring you with me into the field. To my husband and best friend, Lucas Johnson, few others can hold their own among drivers in Sicily.

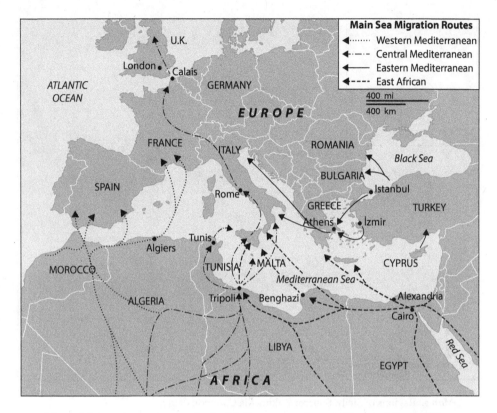

Map 1. Major migratory routes in the Mediterranean. Source: *National Geographic* (2015).

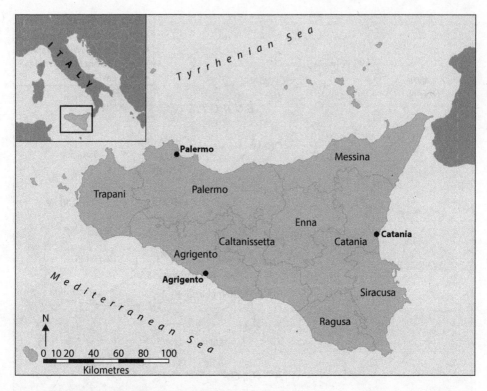

Map 2. Regions of Sicily. Source: Wikimedia Commons 2017.

Introduction

> Migration is not a crime. Saving lives is not a crime.
> Solidarity won't be stopped.
>
> —Banner displayed by the mayor and local residents marching
>   through the streets of Palermo, June 2019

IN DEFENSE OF SOLIDARITY

On June 29, 2019, thirty-one-year-old Captain Carola Rackete defied Italian authorities and risked arrest when she decided to dock her search-and-rescue boat at the Sicilian island of Lampedusa, allowing forty migrants to disembark after seventeen days of drifting at sea. Before announcing this decision on social media, Captain Rackete had made numerous attempts to solicit the sympathy of public officials who refused to grant permission to disembark. The authorities promptly arrested Rackete when her boat arrived onshore, but fortunately by then she had attained international recognition; several crowdfunding campaigns had already been organized across the European continent to pay the hefty fines that would likely be levied against her and the nongovernmental organization (NGO) for which she worked, Sea-Watch. With her arrest, protests erupted across Europe as elected officials joined demonstrators who demanded of the Italian authorities, "Free Carola!" In the Sicilian capital of Palermo, Mayor Leoluca Orlando, followed by hundreds of demonstrators, took to the streets carrying a banner that proclaimed, "Migration is not a crime. Saving lives is not a crime. Solidarity won't be stopped."

Days later, a court in the town of Agrigento on Sicily's southern coast declared Captain Rackete innocent. Sicilian officials added that Rackete's actions were justified "in the performance of a duty": to save lives at sea and to prevent migrants from being transferred to unsafe conditions at migrant detention centers in North Africa. Within hours of the court's decision, an air raid struck a migrant detention center in Libya, killing more than forty people. Rackete heralded the court's decision as "a big win for solidarity with people on the move."[1]

Between 2014 and 2018, more than two million migrants arrived by sea on the shores of Europe. Fleeing war, severe hunger and poverty, military conscription, political and social turmoil, and environmental collapse in their countries of origin, a large number of these migrants landed in Sicily.[2]

Yet Italy's government forcibly stopped migrant disembarkations in early 2018 when national elections resulted in the appointment of a far-right, populist coalition. Italy's newly appointed interior minister, Matteo Salvini—also known as "Italy's Trump" for his derisive, anti-immigrant rhetoric—had orchestrated a sea change in national immigration policies. He banned NGO ships transporting migrants from docking at Italian ports and sought to criminalize anyone providing assistance to migrants. Salvini labeled Captain Rackete a criminal and condemned her decision to dock in Lampedusa as "an act of war," as he was quoted in numerous media outlets.

Meanwhile, Rackete's actions elicited a mix of compassion and rage among Sicily's residents. Some *siciliani* praised her boldness, calling her a saint for upholding humanitarian commitments; others sided with Salvini, condemning and harboring resentment toward Rackete for ostensibly further burdening local communities with Europe-bound migration through Sicily (figure 1). Many bemoaned the fact that their island had been transformed into a de facto point of entry into the European Union (EU), or the "refugee camp of Europe," as Salvini quipped (BBC News 2018). Even *siciliani* who supported immigration believed it was unfair that their island and region should have to assume the bulk of responsibility in matters of migrant reception.

This book centers on the lived experiences of the citizens and noncitizens who have been performing various aspects of migrant solidarity work at the front lines of Europe's "migration crisis." Despite anti-immigrant

Figure 1. Public installation "Santa Carola" (Saint Carola) honoring Captain Carola Rackete by Italian street artist TVBoy in Taormina, Sicily. The painting was defaced by a supporter of Salvini within 48 hours of its debut.

and populist sentiment gaining momentum throughout Italy and much of Europe, there has been an equally robust movement for social solidarity, antiracist political action, and pro-migrant policies. *Island of Hope* underscores the threads of migrant solidarity that are coalescing with broader mobilizations for social justice at this moment in the Mediterranean. As this book illustrates, migrant solidarity is mobilized as an antidote to the effects of political, economic, and social marginalization within Europe's southern peripheries, specifically Sicily, and to more recent economic crises and neoliberal reforms that have brought about feelings of alienation and malaise in the region (Bassel and Emejulu 2017; Kersch and Mishtal 2016; Knight and Stewart 2016). This book sheds light on the forms of collective action among ordinary citizens and noncitizens that have surfaced in spite of multiple humanitarian and welfare state failures. These collective actions both advance the struggle for autonomy and dignity among *siciliani* and represent an important—but often overlooked—facet of migrant reception in the Mediterranean.

Yet defending solidarity with migrants is an increasingly criminalized enterprise in the European context, as epitomized by the case of Captain Rackete (Fekete, Webber, and Edmond-Pettit 2017). Nonetheless, the principal social actors of migrant solidarity underscore that their work is vital, especially as EU governments continue to invest in "bordering tactics" that expose migrants to heightened risks in the Mediterranean (De Genova 2017). With more than ten thousand deaths recorded between 2014 and 2018, the central Mediterranean has been deemed "the world's deadliest border," a distinction rightly decried as "disgraceful" by the anthropologist Nicholas De Genova (2017, 3).[3] Similar to systematic refusals by the US government to accept responsibility for the widespread loss of human life in the Sonoran Desert that straddles the US-Mexico border region and serves as a primary route for illicit migration (De León 2015; Holmes 2013), EU governments have routinely deployed a *politics of irresponsibility* in accounting for the death toll that has rendered the Mediterranean a "macabre deathscape" (De Genova 2017, 2). The specter of criminalization in the geopolitical contexts of both the EU and the United States has emboldened existing efforts by humanitarian groups to assist migrants and flagrantly defy state powers that consistently violate human rights. As a spokesperson for Mediterranea Saving Humans, another search-and-rescue NGO, asserted following Captain Rackete's arrest and during an interview with Italy's national news network, RAI 24, in early July 2019, "There isn't a price we wouldn't pay to save lives." This book examines the work of these humanitarian actors alongside the more grassroots and locally specific forms of politicized, collective action and mutual aid that animate contexts of migrant reception in the Mediterranean.

AUSTERITY AND THE AFFECTIVE DIMENSIONS OF NEOLIBERALISM

Shortly after Italy's "sovereign debt crisis" in 2008, the International Monetary Fund (IMF) and European political and economic institutions pressured Italy's government to implement a series of austerity measures. Italy's austerity diet consisted of more aggressive taxing and rollbacks of the nation's welfare and pension systems. Notable among these changes were increases in income and property taxes; cuts to pensions and wages; delays in the age of retirement and when individuals would be eligible to receive pensions; and widespread reductions in public spending primarily affecting the health, education, transportation, and cultural heritage sectors (see, e.g., Oxfam 2013). These austerity measures were implemented even as an economic recession plagued the fates of many Italian citizens and noncitizens.

Critical social scientists have keenly observed the colossal harm generated by austerity regimes. Rollbacks of basic public health and welfare services are often accompanied by price increases on commodities, slashes of wages, and widespread unemployment (Pfeiffer and Chapman 2010; Stuckler and Basu 2013). Direct cuts in health services and other public sectors are associated with widespread health decline, though the majority of research shows the greatest health losses are among the poor and those who are systematically marginalized because of their race, ethnicity, gender, class, citizenship, or (dis)ability (Basu, Carney, and Kenworthy 2017; Carney 2017; Sargent and Kotobi 2017; Stuckler and Basu 2013). Recent ethnographies have highlighted the pervasiveness of austerity policies in exacerbating uneven life chances and heightening social and economic precarity (e.g., Knight and Stewart 2016; Muehlebach 2016; Ostrach

2017). Speaking to these trends, the anthropologist Andrea Muehlebach (2016, 4) writes, "Europe's austerity policies have . . . not only broken stable work regimes, pensions, infrastructures, and the lives of impoverished Europeans, but the very idea of welfare as such."

Recent intensification of migration into the EU cannot be analyzed without considering the influence of certain institutions such as the IMF and the World Bank on development and markets throughout much of the African continent and the Middle East (Merrill 2014). Decades of structural adjustment programs, trade liberalization, and deregulation between the EU and its "partners" in the global South have impoverished many of today's migrant-sending countries.[4] Anthropologists in particular have engaged "upstream" and structural perspectives to illuminate how governments in the global North are actually implicated in various forms of human displacement, including through the imposition of debt, disruption to agrarian livelihoods, and privatization of basic services that have threatened the welfare of entire populations in the global South. As asserted by De Genova:

> Migrants arriving in Europe today, much as has been true for several decades, originate from places that were effectively mass-scale prison labor camps where their forebears contributed to collectively producing the greater part of the material basis for the prosperity, power, and prestige of Europe. . . . [V]irtually all migrations and refugee movements that today seek their futures in Europe have been deeply shaped by an indisputably European (colonial) past. (2017, 18)

Pro-migrant activists throughout the EU have frequently invoked the phrase, "We are here because you were there!" (Andretta and Porta 2015), indexing the centuries of colonial rule and decades of neoliberal policy making that have shaped today's patterns of migration.[5]

Akin to free trade agreements, the deregulation (or alternatively, "neo-regulation") of markets and corporations, and the privatization of public services, austerity policies are integral to neoliberal capitalist systems (Harvey 2005). Read as "a complex of opposites that can contain what appear as oppositional practices, ethics, and emotions" (Muehlebach 2012, 25), "neoliberalism" is regarded by many scholars as having a pluralistic character that encompasses manifold tensions, contradictions, and countermovements. Along these lines, recent scholarship examining solidarity movements in Southern Europe suggests that neoliberalism and solidarity are "entangled" and represent two sides of the same coin (see, e.g., Cabot 2016b; Knight and Stewart 2016; Ostrach 2017; Rakopoulos 2015). Drawing on the insights of these scholars, I examine migrant solidarity initiatives as corresponding to a *politics of becoming* that reveals important shifts in the social (and global) organization of care and meanings of citizenship and belonging as they apply to both citizens and noncitizens. I invoke the Sicilian case as an example of the ways that neoliberal projects are both made possible and challenged by specific affective dispositions that articulate with particular configurations of labor, welfare, and citizenship (Foucault 1980; Klein 2007; Parla 2019; Parvulescu 2014). Recognizing that differential subjectivities and life chances underpin and shape the politics of austerity and migration, an ethnographic analysis of recent austerity measures and responses to migration in the European context renders the biopolitics of citizenship and governmentality a necessary theoretical framework (Agamben 2005; Cole and Groes 2016; Fassin 2005; Foucault 1980; Gonzales and Chavez 2012).

For the purposes of this text, I engage empirically and analytically with research that interrogates the affective dimensions of neoliberal ideology as it pervades political-economic systems around the globe and disciplines "indebted" and "moral" subjects who are necessary to the ongoing expansion and entrenchment of neoliberal projects (Lazzarato 2012; Muehlebach 2012). Ethnographic accounts from Greece have been particularly poignant in demonstrating how austerity regimes attribute "debt" to undisciplined, "piggish" individuals and groups and prescribe a regimen of "shared sacrifice" (Brown 2015) among citizens that precedes their widespread emotional collapse and alienation (Cabot 2016; Carastathis 2015; Vavvos and Triliva 2018). I interpret neoliberalism as a mode of affective discipline that targets the body—more precisely, a person's thoughts, feelings, and aspirations—as its primary site of intervention (Carney 2013). Debt and its counterpart, austerity, are tools of affective disciplining in that they attribute material circumstances to personal, moral failings and reinforce the hegemony of markets and borders as "structures regulating what appear to be our innermost, authentic experiences of feeling and thinking" (Carastathis 2015, 109). Affective modes of discipline have the effect of relegating subjects to a self-imposed exile, inclusion by means of exclusion (see also De Genova 2017), and practices of surveillance that materialize in the form of self-policing and individual restraint.

SICILY: BOTH ITALY AND NOT ITALY

Just prior to the summer of 2012, Italian, European, and US-based media outlets reported on plans for a "Greek-style takeover of Sicily" that ostensibly had been made necessary by reckless spending in the region's public sector. These reports represented essentially nothing new. For years, Italian and global media sources had been covering politicians who disparaged Sicily as being the "Greece of Italy" and referred to the so-called economic indolence of *siciliani* as "a modern-day Greek tragedy."[6]

Italian and European political elites routinely manipulated and reframed the post-2008 economic climate as one emerging from a sovereign debt crisis—as opposed to holding the financial sector accountable for its unregulated fiscal practices (Muehlebach 2016)—and invoked essentialist discourses when both blaming this debt crisis on Sicily's "culture" and making decisions that resulted in the withholding and deprivation of material resources from Sicilian institutions. In the broader context of European economic austerity, Sicilians were being constructed as "indebted subjects" and scapegoated for Italy's economic woes.

Sicily and its people have also been routinely scapegoated when human rights organizations have alluded to "failures" in Italy's migrant reception system, as if Sicily was not a region of Italy (albeit ostensibly one of autonomous status). Responding to the accusations made against the island's inhabitants, many *siciliani* have resorted to hostile, antimigrant discourse that further displaces blame for debt and austerity away from state practices and Sicily's own citizen population and toward noncitizens, despite the fact that many of them are there because of postcolonial configurations of power that sustain and fortify European presence in places as distant and removed from so-called European borders as the Horn of Africa (Carastathis 2015; De Genova 2017). These discursive and material practices are consistent with the colonial dynamics that have historically defined relations between the Italian nation-state and the region of Sicily and constitute both structural and epistemic forms of violence. Similar to trends in Greece, austerity measures in Sicily are representative of "an ongoing global, economic and colonial project" (Vavvos and Triliva 2018, 317) that largely operates to undermine the region's autonomy.

While the question of formal belonging for migrants is perpetually suspended throughout many parts of the global North, warranted for discussion here is Sicily's liminality as being situated on the margins of belonging with respect to the Italian nation-state and Italy's position of liminality with respect to the EU. Sicily is and is not Italy, just as Italy is and is not Europe (Albahari 2015; Soto Bermant 2017). The anthropologist Maurizio Albahari (2015, 17) notes, "As part of southern and Mediterranean Europe, [Italy] is also reproached for its people's alleged *moral* deficit and ensuing Continental financial crisis" (original emphasis). Meanwhile, Italy, among other Southern European countries, has been "made responsible for guarding an idea and an entity," namely, Europe, "to which it was not clear that they themselves belonged" (Soto Bermant 2017, 134). The anthropologist Laia Soto Bermant (2017, 134) underscores how the "'European-ness' of Southern Europe" has been consistently "called into question." She adds that "the repeated threat of withdrawal of European-ness during the [2008] crisis, along with the EU's endorsement (or, perhaps more accurately, imposition) of budget cuts and austerity measures, [has] taken a toll on the legitimacy of the European Union in Southern European countries" (134–35).

Dissent and skepticism, particularly among Southern European countries, about the "European project" have attained heightened visibility in recent years and have amplified existing discordance among all European countries —from east to west and north to south—regarding any singular "idea of Europe" (Parvulescu 2014). In the case of Sicily—an island whose history has been shaped by many different phases of colonization and settlement (see chapter 2)—many native-born *siciliani* do not think of themselves as Italian or European.[7] As one nonprofit director explained to me, "We *siciliani* have no interest in policing those migrants arriving and serving as the border guard for Europe. Because, in our heart of hearts, we are not really European."

MIGRANT SOLIDARITY: RECONFIGURING THE SOCIAL ORGANIZATION OF CARE

This book contributes to the rich ethnographic body of literature on migration in Europe and intervenes in debates central to recent, complementary scholarship on institutional arrangements and social relations surrounding care in neoliberal capitalist societies (see, e.g., Boris and Parreñas 2010; Cabot 2016b; Caldwell 2004, 2007; Cole and Groes 2016; Degiuli 2016; Fassin 2005; Feldman-Savelsberg 2016; Giordano 2014; Mol et al. 2010; Muehlebach 2012; Pine 2013; Ticktin 2011; Zimmerman et al. 2006).

To the extent that anti-austerity mobilizations have intersected with deepening hostilities toward migrants perceived as "drains" on the welfare state (Andretta 2017; Carastathis 2015), anti-austerity sentiment has also inspired ordinary citizens' expressions of compassion and migrant solidarity. Whereas migrants are frequently relegated to the marginalized spaces of "illegality" and "abjectivity" (De Genova 2002; Willen 2007) and constructed as undeserving beneficiaries, the aspirational project of migrant solidarity seeks to transform migrants from passive to active subjects endowed with the resources and capacity to integrate with society. Migrants can "choose," or not, to participate, attesting to the paradoxical aspects of solidarity work in both emancipating and individualizing the citizenship project. Migrant solidarity initiatives explicitly call for the active participation of noncitizens in the performance of solidarity work and in solidarity as an aspirational politics. Although the vast majority of migrants living in Italy today remain excluded from the realm of political citizenship—and denied the terms of formal belonging—they are often enlisted in the making of alternative forms of citizenship.

Throughout this book, I examine how meaningful connections shared among citizens and noncitizens and the cultivation of social capital among them may reveal a "will to wellness" (Ticktin 2011, 26) in combating the effects of economic austerity and the myriad forms of violence enacted against migrants. As evidenced by research in the medical social sciences, social capital defined as "the resources to which individuals have access through their social networks" (Moore and Kawachi 2017, 513) has important implications for health across the life course and between generations. Access to a broad support system often serves as a buffer against health decline (Arce and Long 2000; Carter and Reardon 2014). Social scientists have probed the relationship between social capital and mortality arguably since Émile Durkheim's ([1897] 1951) classic investigation of suicide and its connection to something he named "anomie" in reference to social disintegration. Individuals with more social capital are believed to possess greater capacity for resilience: the ability to adjust emotionally and function socially following exposure to crisis (Panter-Brick 2014). When connections are rich in social capital, epidemiologists argue, communities are able to engage in collective action, or *collective efficacy* (Moore and Kawachi 2017). Communities displaying higher levels of resilience when faced with disasters (Aldrich 2012; Hikichi et al. 2017; Inoue et al. 2013) serve as prominent examples of how stronger degrees of social capital may improve collective health outcomes and support longer life expectancy. Importantly, however, "social capital is not identical with solidarity, because social capital refers to those resources or ingredients that need to be mobilized into acts of solidarity" (Lahusen and Grasso 2018, 9). Nonetheless, for these reasons, scholars claim that "solidarity is one of the key phenomena studied in the social sciences" (e.g., Lahusen and Grasso 2018, 4; see also Glick Schiller 2016 and Rodotà 2004).

In contrast to affective discipline, affective resistance may be observed in practices that aspire to nourish affective ties (social healing), disrupt and replace hegemonic market-based systems of value (people over profits), and improve subjective and collective well-being. I contend that the aspirational project of migrant solidarity is animated by affective resistance and, comprising one affective dimension of neoliberalism, indexes a politics of becoming wherein differential belonging is always present and the struggle for justice remains as such: a process that knows no end (see also Caldwell 2017).

This book marshals the concept of solidarity work in reference to a form of caring labor that attends to collective psychosocial and material well-being by mobilizing an alternative economy of affects (Ahmed 2004; Caldwell 2017), strengthening social relations, and contesting broader inequalities exacerbated by processes of neoliberalization. Jacquelyn Litt and Christine Bose (2006, 3) define *caring labor* as "the multifaceted labor that produces the daily living conditions that make basic human health and well-being possible." Solidarity work is caring labor radically politicized to usurp the status quo. In other words, it seeks to disrupt the very conditions that have made such forms of caring labor necessary for the reproduction of society (Boris and Parreñas 2010). The work itself is generally performed in the context of "'solidarity groups[,]' [which] might be informal cliques, formal organizations, or full-fledged nation-states, but all of them will be based on the idea that membership is tied to the expectations of mutual support, even if these expectations might range from informal to formalized, from voluntary to binding rights and obligations" (Lahusen and Grasso 2018, 5).

Andrea Muehlebach's (2012) concept of the moral neoliberal is particularly germane to developing a theory of solidarity work. The moral neoliberal "hinges on a particular ethical subject[;] . . . it feels (cares about) and acts (cares for others) at the same time" (7–8). Italian citizens have been enlisted in the project of ethical citizenship vis-à-vis voluntarism through appeals by state institutions such as the Italian Ministry of Labor and Social Politics that identify "loneliness as a new challenge" (34) that Italy must overcome and aim to address a crisis of relational, rather than material, poverty. Ethical citizenship corresponds to the sphere of practices characterized by the unwaged, relational labor performed by volunteers administering "care" on which the Italian nation-state depends for guaranteeing the "welfare" of its population. Muehlebach argues that morality is not in opposition but rather "indispensable . . . to market orders" (6). It is also part of the "unremunerated labor regime" in which citizenship is reconfigured as "something one does not simply have but must constantly attempt to attain and keep. Citizenship in the ethical labor regime is a form of work" (138). Attention to the moral neoliberal, she explains, "lets us explore [the limits of neoliberal projects], the unexpected ways in which new kinds of collective living may emerge out of, and despite, new forms of difference and inequality" (8). Solidarity work might be understood as one permutation of the moral neoliberal. As broader declines in psychosocial well-being constitute a significant threat to the reproduction of society, the material and agentive aspects of migrant solidarity represent a form of care of citizens and noncitizens. Solidarity work in this context entails reckoning with feelings of abject isolation and despair made mundane by a precarious political and economic environment in the Mediterranean region.

The aspirational project of migrant solidarity assumes that caring labor is a necessary ingredient in the project of citizenship and belonging. Migrant solidarity efforts simultaneously articulate with and subvert neoliberal logics in that they contest the arrangements of power that necessitate both austerity policies and migration while paradoxically restricting the latter (Oliveri 2015). Solidarity work is "work" because it is embedded in and articulates with market forces and responds to the conditions of neoliberal capitalism. Subsequently, the benefits and costs of solidarity work are distributed differentially among disparate social actors, particularly citizens and noncitizens. Similar to regimes of stratified reproduction wherein the burden of social reproduction and provisioning of care is displaced on the most vulnerable members (and nonmembers) of society, solidarity work is not always entirely virtuous in practice (Colen 1995; Mullings 1995). Transformations in the global division of caring labor have also necessitated migration and conscripted the dispossessed and displaced in an arrangement of stratified reproduction. This book is thus a contribution to the burgeoning literature that examines how social reproduction is increasingly stratified both within and across societies, even in the context of social movements that seek to prove themselves as transformative (Carney 2015; Cheng 2006; Glenn 2012).

OVERVIEW OF CHAPTERS

Chapter 1, "Austerity and Migration as Mediterranean 'Questions,'" chronicles Sicilian—and to some extent, Italian—experiences with austerity and its antecedents in the economic restructuring of the Italian nation-state. It also analyzes how these experiences have intersected with recent migration to Europe. Scholars have debated the "questions" of Europe and migration while also claiming that one question is inextricable from the other. Intervening in this debate, I contend that austerity has also emerged as a "question" in the Mediterranean, particularly in the Sicilian context. As a recent experiment conducted primarily on the people of Europe's southern peripheries, austerity has proven highly detrimental. This climate of austerity is crucial to understanding local contexts of migrant reception in Southern Europe. In the Sicilian case, the persistence of these questions—austerity, migration, and Europe—sustains and compounds the island's social, economic, and political marginalization in Italy and the EU.

Chapter 2, "There Is a Lot of Creativity on This Island," examines Sicily's history and present as a site of colonization, asymmetrical development, emigration, and im/migration. The chapter highlights instances in which *siciliani* have been essentialized, blamed, and made responsible for complex social problems such as poverty and corruption in politics as well as migration. This imposition of "responsibility" alongside "hospitality" as modes of affective disciplining implies myriad moral failings of *siciliani*, that is, as indebted, irresponsible subjects, that also operates to dehumanize and alienate them from Italy and the rest of Europe. I argue that sociohistorical and political-economic conditions underlying present-day material and affective realities in Sicily distinguish migrant solidarity work in this setting, particularly in coalescing with the island's history of struggles for dignity and autonomy.

Chapter 3, "The Reception Apparatus," provides an overview of Italy's (and by extension, Sicily's) migrant reception system, colloquially referred to by Italian officials, social workers, activists, and other local actors as *accoglienza*. The first half of the chapter illustrates the *politics of irresponsibility* that animate state practices of migrant reception characterized by privatization and increased responsibility on nongovernmental actors. In the second half of the chapter, I shift my focus to the less formal, street-level configurations of *accoglienza*. Using ethnographic vignettes and individual narratives, I illustrate how from the moment that migrants disembark on the shores of Europe, anxieties seep in about how much support they will receive, what form(s) this support will take, and how long any form of support will last. I argue that state abandonment and a tattered street-level safety net precipitate the aspirational project of migrant solidarity.

Chapter 4, "Migrant Solidarity Work," examines solidarity work as a particular configuration of caring labor. Drawing from ethnographic observations and interviews, I explore how solidarity work surfaces in the narratives of charismatic individuals, social relations among ordinary citizens and noncitizens, and physical spaces throughout Sicily but primarily based in Palermo, "the city of solidarity."

Chapter 5, "Edible Solidarities," introduces forms of social solidarity with migrants enacted through and around the forging of fusion cuisines. The chapter features interviews and ethnographic observations from two case studies, Moltivolti, a "multiethnic kitchen" and co-working space in Palermo's Ballarò neighborhood that opened in 2014, and Ginger, a similar "intercultural" restaurant in Agrigento that opened in 2016. Combining culinary practices from throughout Africa, the Middle East, and Sicily, these food establishments seek to transform the material, affective, and political possibilities of both citizens and noncitizens and explicitly marshal models of migrant integration that are also focused on rejecting the logics of austerity and debt regimes. In focusing on these businesses and the broader web of social and economic relationships in which they are embedded, this chapter engages with the emergent body of scholarship on solidarity economies.

Chapter 6, "Caring for the Future," brings attention to the specific experiences of younger generations of migrants and how they are being (un) accounted for in the work of migrant solidarity. Drawing on interviews and ethnographic observations pertaining to migrant youth's experiences of arriving in Italy and street-level *accoglienza*, I discuss the complicated ways that solidarity is mobilized both *for* and *with* migrant youth. This chapter also analyzes the temporal dimensions of solidarity work in its potential to connect present-day and future generations.

While this book does not foreground migrant narratives for reasons that I think the text itself will elucidate, it does not explicitly exclude these narratives as they are essential to describing the dynamics of migrant reception and solidarity work and developing more humane and just responses to migration. The systematic omission of migrants' perspectives is both a crucial shortcoming in current approaches to developing im/migration policies and operates as a form of epistemic violence that compounds with other forms of violence to which most of today's globally displaced persons are always already subjected (Agamben 2003).

MIGRANT SOLIDARITY AS ANTHROPOLOGICAL METHOD

This book draws on several phases of field research that I conducted from 2014 through 2019 (February and March 2014, June 2016, April and May

2017, and May 2019) on the everyday dynamics of migrant reception and solidarity in Sicily.[8] My fieldwork entailed methods of participant observation, semistructured interviews, and informal interviews at NGOs and grassroots organizations that provide a range of services to migrants such as Italian-language instruction, meals, bathing facilities, clothing, job training, and legal assistance; migrant disembarkations at seaside ports; reception centers for adults and also migrant youth; offices of social workers as they met with individual clients; public protests and demonstrations in support of Italy's migrant population; ceremonies, including burials, mourning the thousands of migrant lives that have been lost at sea; film screenings and art exhibitions showcasing the plight of migrants; health clinics predominantly serving migrants; restaurants and cafés promoting community building around fusion cuisines; fund-raisers to support humanitarian organizations engaged in some aspect of migrant reception; and conferences focused on collaborative approaches to ameliorating migrant reception conditions. I conducted more than one hundred semistructured and informal interviews with migrants, social workers (both inside and outside state institutions in Italy), Italian officials and authorities (coast guard, military police, local police), volunteers at charitable and humanitarian organizations, clinicians, medical interpreters, members of the clergy, attorneys, university professors, students, business owners, and grassroots organizers. While Italian served as the primary language for my interactions with *siciliani*, other Italian citizens, and many migrants who had been living in Italy for longer than one year and had thus acquired a basic knowledge of the native language, in situations and encounters that involved many recently arrived migrants, interactions proceeded in English or a combination of the two languages.[9] Often, I was informally solicited as an interpreter for interactions between Italian citizens and recently arrived migrants.

While away from the field, I utilized virtual ethnographic methods that included analysis of photos, videos, and other content shared by the administrators and followers on different social media platforms (Oiarazabal and Reips 2012).[10] Since embarking on this project, I have also been tracing the discourses on "migration" and "crisis" as they appear in Italian media. I subscribe to Google alerts for different keywords ("austerity," "migrants in Italy"), listen daily to Italian news programming, and follow several Italy- and Sicily-based organizations and news outlets on social media. Because of the hostile environment that has made them vulnerable to public scrutiny, violence, and criminalization, for the purposes of this book I have altered the names of some individuals and groups.

It is worthwhile naming the spaces that I was *unable to access* during fieldwork for one reason or another but that almost always related to my positionality as a white American scholar and mother of very young children (one of whom I carried in utero during a research trip in 2017). Access, as it corresponds to ethical and methodological decision making in the field, is always politicized (Rozakou 2017). Inaccessible sites in this project included many reception centers, migrant "camps," sites of migrant labor, and boats at sea intercepting or transporting rescued migrants. While my inability to access such sites might filter into a discussion of "limitations" of the study, and thus somehow reflect my own individual failing, I reconceptualize them here as part and parcel of the broader structural conditions that shape researcher possibilities (and rewards). That the gendering, class, and racialization of social spaces makes certain types of research agendas possible only for the privileged few who can access them is a pressing concern for the field of anthropology. We should be wary of a discipline and broader public that rewards "bold and daring" ethnographers, often at the expense of generating hostile environments both in the field and in the office for women, gender and sexual minorities, Black and Indigenous communities, and people of color (Berry et al. 2017). The inability to fulfill certain expectations in the field and within academia relates to rules about individual comportment and mobility across both settings that deserve revision.[11] Moreover, it is questionable the extent to which grand acts of ethnographic heroism help advance the struggles of our interlocutors in the field.

In writing this book, I have been inspired by those writing in the feminist anthropological tradition and especially by the contributions of Black and Indigenous scholars who have been theorizing and advancing an abolitionist, decolonizing, and radical orientation to ethnographic fieldwork and to critiquing racial capitalism (Gilmore 2007; Hawthorne 2017; Hoover 2017; Mohanty 2003; Perry 2009, 2014; Reese 2019; Tuhiwai Smith 1999). As such, in engaging with migrant solidarity both empirically and analytically, I seek to align with the struggles of my interlocutors and their political projects in fighting against structures of oppression that are upheld primarily by white supremacy: "the interlocking systems of racism, patriarchy, homophobia, ultranationalism, xenophobia, anti-Semitism, and religious fundamentalism that create a complex matrix of oppressions as a tenacious ideology in practice" (Davis 2019, 27; also citing Washington 2008). Yet I remain cognizant of how such an endeavor is also an aspirational project, as "even research with emancipatory intentions is inevitably troubled with unequal power relations" (Oparah and Okazawa-Rey 2009, 3). Beyond the life of this book, I continue to search for ways to strengthen transnational ties of solidarity between myself and like-minded scholars and the grassroots activists laboring on the ground in Sicily and in the Mediterranean.

Although this book engages with various usages of the term "crisis," it simultaneously pushes back against the "normalization" of crises linked to neoliberal policy making (Carney 2020; Comaroff and Comaroff 2011) and concomitant claims of "exceptionality" (Rakopoulos 2014). Instead, I attend to neoliberal ideology and governance as a crisis and to the ways in which this crisis has manifested in the quotidian lives of citizens and noncitizens in producing seemingly intractable and colossal inequalities. Anthropologists extol the potential of ethnography in drawing "attention to people's grounded responses to crisis" (Rakopolous 2014, 192), "the multiple ways in which people make sense of their experience of living with austerity" (Knight and Stewart 2016, 13), and "ordinary peoples' struggles to create coherence in the midst of out-of-syncness" (Muehlebach 2016, 2). I follow these scholars' insights on crisis to denaturalize and demystify the "violences of abstraction" (Muehlebach 2016) enacted through neoliberal policies and the imposition of debts and deficits as "technical fixes" that ultimately benefit few at the cost of many (Heyman 2016a). The lack of formal response to the "migration crisis" by the EU and its member governments has often meant that in practice, humanitarian organizations, NGOs, civil society, Italian citizens, and migrants are burdened with the responsibility of tending to immediate circumstances (Cabot 2016a; Narotzky 2013; Rakopoulos 2015). In other words, while EU officials debate existing regulations and plans for sharing the burden of the "migration crisis" and enforcing austerity measures, local communities have had no other option but to *respond to* and *care for* the circumstances immediately before them. While "being in motion, ambiguous, and contradictory," the aspirational project of migrant solidarity, and its corollary ethnographic form(s), underscores the politics and potentials of "human becomings: people learning to live, living on, not learning to accept death, resisting death in all possible forms" (Biehl [2005] 2013, 394).

1 Austerity and Migration as Mediterranean "Questions"

The economic crisis in Europe has pushed society, and above all, politicians, to demonize migrants.

—Reception center director, June 2018

The once triumphant ethos of a united Europe with open internal borders, and a commitment to liberal, social democratic politics that has shaped Europe since the Second World War is everywhere in retreat. There is a growing Euro-scepticism sweeping the continent.... [T]he European project is under pressure because of the perception (propagated through the media and by varied populist politicians) of an overwhelming "wave" of migrants coming into the continent from North Africa and the Middle East that is flowing across Europe's open internal borders.

—Teresa Fiore and Ernest Ialongo, "Introduction: Italy and the Euro-Mediterranean 'Migrant Crisis'"

"ITALIANS FIRST!"

According to a national survey conducted in 2017, levels of hostility toward migrants in Italy were at a record high and mounting. One in two Italians perceived migrants as a threat to society that should be expelled (Camilli 2018). The victors of Italy's 2018 national election ascended to office championing "Prima gli italiani!" (Italians first!) and "Aiutiamoli a

21

casa loro!" (Let's send them home!) as campaign slogans. "Italians first!" resonated with Italian voters both for eschewing migrants, who were perceived as competing with Italian citizens for limited public resources, and for deeming austerity an unfair sacrifice being made by Italians to benefit other nations within the EU. In his 2018 inaugural speech, Italy's newly appointed prime minister, Giuseppe Conte, restated his promise to enforce a "tough line" on migrants and to reject economic austerity (Agence France-Presse 2018).[1]

Stoking economic and nativist anxieties, Italy's far-right politicians have been actively campaigning against migration for years and with demonstrable results. Social media platforms especially have enabled far-right populists to disseminate "disinformazione" (disinformation)—as noted by my interlocutors—that reframes Italy's economic woes as the result of "a migrant invasion." According to many of those I interviewed over the span of five years in which a period of stringent austerity measures and record migrant arrivals in the Mediterranean overlapped, these politicians were responsible for cultivating "un clima d'odio" (a climate of hate) among the Italian public and reinforcing race-based (white) claims to Italian citizenship. References to Italy's declining fertility rate, for instance, had amplified decades-long concerns about the very idea of Italianness (and Europeanness more generally) as being under siege by foreign, nonwhite Others (De Genova 2016, 2018; Hawthorne 2017; Krause 2005; Krause and Marchesi 2007; New Keywords Collective 2016).[2] Far-right, populist parties had even resorted to exploiting the voices of migrants themselves in campaign propaganda to underscore the hardships that migrants would encounter in coming to Europe. A controversial video released in 2014 and commissioned by Angelo Ciocca, a candidate for the EU Parliament campaigning with the far-right political party Lega Nord, epitomized such efforts. The video, recorded in several languages with Italian subtitles, featured five immigrants from Pakistan, India, Sri Lanka, Angola, and North Africa warning their compatriots, "Don't come to Italy," because of the difficult economic conditions. As described by one of the video's protagonists, "Italy, along with Spain and Greece, is one of the poorest countries in Europe. So don't delude yourselves: now Italy can't offer anything to anyone. Don't come here because you will be sentenced to hunger."[3]

Today's global migration trends and economic systems are indeed intertwined, but the reality is significantly more complex than typically acknowledged by far-right politicians and mainstream media. This chapter is focused, in part, on probing this relationship and showing how experiences of austerity in the European context—and particularly in Sicily—have articulated with political and economic transformations in both Italy's welfare state and globally over the past few decades. As a starting point, I concur with the claim that "the question of Europe itself has become inextricable from the question of migration" (De Genova 2017, 22) and offer a revision: both "questions"—of Europe and of migration—have become inextricable from austerity politics. Although this chapter foregrounds the experiences of austerity primarily as they registered in Sicily, I align with recent anthropological scholarship that views these experiences as connecting more broadly to what is often imagined or described as the "Mediterranean" or "Southern Europe." As described by Knight and Stewart (2016, 2), "The imposition of austerity measures . . . has had the effect of converting this Southern part of the European Union into an area unified by shared problems, emergencies, and exigencies. The study of the Mediterranean . . . analyses how societies in this region negotiate the structural violence (economic and political) to which they are all now subject." Following my discussion of austerity's permutations in Sicily as well as at the national level in Italy, I pivot to examining the question of migration in the Mediterranean, particularly Sicilian and Italian, contexts. I bring these questions—of austerity and of migration—together to show how Sicilians, and to some extent Italians as well as migrants, have been conditioned toward specific ways of being—and feeling—in the world that facilitate both the further entrenchment of neoliberal projects and the possibilities for alternatives.

"GREEK-STYLE TAKEOVER" OF SICILY

> Headline: "Monti plans 'Greek-style' takeover of Sicily to avert default—Italian premier Mario Monti is mulling emergency action to take direct control of Sicily's regional government before the island spirals into a full-blown financial crisis, fearing contagion to the rest of Italy."
> —*Daily Telegraph*, July 18, 2012

Headline: "Italy Worries Sicily's Woes Could Have Ripple
Effect"
—National Public Radio, July 31, 2012

In July 2012, prominent Italian, European, and US-based media outlets unilaterally speculated about Sicily's culpability in an impending financial crisis of national proportions. They cited Sicily's €7 billion deficit that put the region in danger of default if the national government were to fail to impose sweeping cuts. Interviewed by a correspondent with US-based National Public Radio (NPR), one of Sicily's public officials who had been appointed to trim the fat from the region's budget warned of a monetary nightmare on the island: "I'm afraid we will soon no longer be able to pay civil servants' salaries."[4]

Alluding to a "Greek-style takeover," these media reports made much reference to antiquated practices of clientelism and to ostensibly lavish spending in Sicily's public sector. They described the regional government's headquarters in Palermo's Palazzo dei Normanni as being "grossly overmanned, with a bigger staff than Downing Street,"[5] mainly explained by practices of hiring and promotion predicated not on merit but rather on political favors. Sicily was also being scrutinized by the EU, which was demanding that €600 million be returned due to alleged misuse of funds for frivolous projects such as couscous festivals and other cultural events on the island. For these reasons, Rome was "dictating tough bailout conditions on Sicily" similar to those "imposed on Greece";[6] it explicitly sought to penalize the island's political elites whose decision making had been corrupted by relations of patronage and clientelism (Chubb 1982; Cole 1997; Orlando 2015). Similar arguments had been made to justify sweeping cuts in the recent past, as with the national economic crisis in the early 1990s, when Italy terminated the "*Cassa per il Mezzogiorno*, or Development Fund for the South, caricatured as having squandered valuable resources" (Schneider and Schneider 2003, 232).[7] Moving to resist yet another attempt by Italy's north to legitimize its political control of the south (see also Giordano 2014), Palermo's public sector workers led citywide protests demanding that Italy "keep [its] hands off Sicily." "We want to be our own master," they proclaimed.[8]

At the same time, these media reports also acknowledged the role of drastic austerity measures in rendering Sicily's debt. As one of Italy's poorest regions, Sicily's economy has long centered on public sector jobs and subsidies from the north. Summarized by one Sicilian journalist, and reiterated in various ways by my interlocutors, Sicilian municipalities (*comuni*) "live essentially by state and regional funds." According to this journalist's research, Sicilian municipalities received 61 percent of their funding from federal and regional sources, compared to the national average of 39 percent; local taxes accounted for only 28 percent of available funds, compared to the national average of 40 percent. He also noted vast discrepancies in the Italian state's spending on Sicily versus other regions; while elected officials in Rome allocated €170 per capita to Sicily, the rest of Italy received an average of €380 per capita. Anticipating imminent cuts to public spending and slashes to Sicily's budget, an editorial in Sicily's regional newspaper noted that "those who pay will be the poor, the sick, and the marginalized" and mocked decision makers in Rome and Brussels: "There will not be development at this rate of Italian spending that is 'excessive,' 'redundant,' and 'wasteful.' "[9]

"WE SICILIANI WERE ALREADY POOR"

"Sicily resisted [*ha resistito*] the effects of the [2008] economic crisis. Northern Italians suffered much worse," a Palermo-based social worker told me. "We *siciliani* were already poor." Aside from recalling that some family-owned businesses such as barber shops, beauty parlors, and clothing stores were forced to close due to increased belt tightening among consumers, my Sicilian interlocutors do not associate the 2008 crisis with widespread economic devastation. Instead, they allude to seasoned practices of intergenerational wealth transfer, resource pooling among kin and within communities, diversified income strategies of individuals and households, and transnational familial networks. In the case of this particular social worker, she had been sharing part of her income with her retired, pensioner parents and with her adult daughter. She also had a sister permanently living in the United States from whom she could ask for financial support, and her own family was deeply embedded in the local community owing to their *palermitano* heritage that traced back several generations.

While *siciliani* by and large related to me that they were generally unscathed by the 2008 global financial crisis, they have not managed to evade economic austerity. During the past decade, municipalities throughout Sicily have absorbed substantial cuts to budgets for public school systems (including school staff, meals, and bus service), clinics, information and communication technology systems, public health, city sanitation, street lighting and other infrastructure, and postal services. During the earlier years of my fieldwork, it was very common to overhear patrons at the local *bar* or *gelateria* grumbling about these cuts and speculating on their corollaries. Most *siciliani* I have come to know feel that Sicily has been (erroneously) blamed for problems that are endemic to the very existence of an Italian nation-state. They are also acutely aware of their unfavorable reputation among those in the north. Arguing that Sicily had unduly endured the worst of the worst, a 2011 editorial in *Giornale di Sicilia* underscored that state-mandated budget cuts were further evidence that northern Italians viewed Sicily as "the nation's black sheep."

Some weeks prior to my first visit to Sicily in 2014, I had been in contact with faculty members in the social sciences at the University of Palermo who I hoped to meet with and from whom I sought advice regarding lodging and transportation. In one email, a faculty member forewarned me about relying on public transportation from the Falcone-Borsellino airport to the center of Palermo, a distance of about 30 kilometers. While there was a passenger train that serviced this relatively short route, the number of daily departures had been significantly reduced and the trains rarely operated on schedule. As I learned through a multitude of conversations and my own direct experience over the course of my stay, such characterizations extended to all forms of public transportation. Tired of worrying about making it on time to meetings with individuals and organizations generous enough to indulge my research questions, I did as *palermitani* who were without access to a car, or *motorino*, elected to do: walk. Some days I walked for hours at a time, meandering my way through labyrinthine networks of streets that led me from the university to hospitals, clinics, and charitable assistance programs scattered throughout the city.

As any experienced ethnographer knows, these walks were immensely instructive in revealing the material and human dimensions of a debt-ridden society. Not a single piazza or busy street corner I passed in

Figure 2. Condemned buildings surround a Palermo piazza. Photo by author.

Palermo was without its share of residents holding signs that revealed some details of their calamitous fate(s) and pleading for help. With the exception of a few secluded, wealthier neighborhoods, most streets were littered with garbage, partly because dumpsters and receptacles had not been serviced in weeks, if not months, and were overflowing. Many build-ings were in obvious disrepair, especially in the historic center where there was extensive scaffolding but rarely any work crews (figure 2). Cuts to public spending had stalled many of the city's renovation efforts. I later learned that much of the structural damage in this part of the city had been caused by airstrikes during World War II. In short, local residents had initially been quite excited about plans for renovation finally com-ing to fruition. Sometimes this damage extended to buildings covering an entire city block. Nonetheless, these properties were not entirely vacant. The city's poorest residents, along with the city's thriving population of stray cats and dogs, often squatted there. Rather than simply vestiges of an economic crisis or traces of austerity's gruesome toll, these aspects of

Palermo's cityscape revealed a deeper history of poverty, one distinctly embedded in claims by *siciliani* that "we were already poor."

When I would finally arrive at my destination at one of Palermo's hospitals and clinics, I was particularly struck by the absence of any intake personnel. Aside from being stopped by a security guard who manned the front entrance of one of Palermo's largest medical facilities, I usually proceeded straight to the offices of physicians I was scheduled to interview, often passing exam rooms along the way and overhearing fragments of conversations between health providers and their patients. This was yet another effect of austerity: the eradication of "superfluous" personnel in the healthcare sector.

It was also during this visit that I observed some of the effects of austerity on universities, particularly the University of Palermo. Arriving at campus on a bitter cold midwinter morning, my hosts apologized for the lack of heat: the heating system had been shut down. Over the next hour, I huddled together with a small group of faculty and students as we spoke about budget cuts through occasionally chattering teeth while wearing our coats and scarves. Many of them feared succumbing on graduation to the path followed by too many of their peers who held degrees in sophisticated subjects such as engineering and art history but were now working in northern Italy or somewhere abroad. Or possibly worse, they would end up working part-time at their family's laundromat, hotel, or restaurant that only generated revenue during the peak tourist season. Most of their parents were struggling, having to care for their own parents—mostly retired *pensionati* who had seen their pensions cut by nearly 25 percent and were drawing from whatever limited savings they had to make up the difference—and for their children, many of whom were still living at home. A graduate student who was a mother and looking for employment as a teacher lambasted recent cuts to public education. She cited reduced spending on special education in public schools and rising costs for university students while resources for them were dwindling: "It's true that people have been trying to leave Sicily, but it's difficult to transfer one's entire family. Meanwhile, schools have been receiving almost no money from the state, so we must fund-raise and be as creative as we can. The schools must find their own sources of funding. The schools don't even have enough money to provide toilet paper." This young woman was describing some of the effects of the Decreto Brunetta (Decree Law 112/2008), which cut €8 billion from Italy's public schools and resulted in higher student-to-teacher ratios and fewer nonteaching personnel. Schools with a student population of a thousand or less were either closed or coerced into merging with other schools; in Sicily, two-thirds of schools underwent such mergers (Nastasi and Palmisano 2015).

Palermo's university students have been among the most vocal opponents of austerity. On December 6, 2012, thousands of students and striking metalworkers declared "Blocchiamo tutto Day" (Block Everything Day), during which they paralyzed (*paralizzato*) city traffic surrounding Palermo's Piazza Politeama and the piazza overlooking Palermo's marina. One of the student organizers was quoted the day of the event in the *Giornale di Sicilia:* "Today, coinciding with the metalworker's strike, we bring attention to our struggle by connecting with the struggles and daily lives of others that have been brought down by the weight of a crisis and a politics of austerity." Nearly one year later, on November 22, 2013, thousands of students flooded the streets of Palermo again, demanding secure schools and job opportunities while using the slogan, "The schools are crumbling" (*Le scuole crollano*). Media outlets covering the protest affirmed that austerity politics were at the center of students' grievances; they decried "the bleeding out of the public school system, the killing of culture, and the consequences for the future of younger generations."[10] Long-term or permanent displacement of these youth from their native region of Sicily ranks high among such consequences. Northward migration by younger generations due to lack of economic opportunity locally has been particularly disconcerting for public officials, who, like the president of Palermo's Confcommercio chapter—representing the largest business association in Italy—bemoan, "Young people leaving Sicily inexorably contributes to the decline and impoverishment of our society."

These conditions corresponded to broader trends in Italy, where "the government passed around 51 emergency law decrees with almost no parliamentary input since 2008, all of which directly impact public finance and provisioning" (Muehlebach 2016, 12). A report commissioned by the Committee on Civil Rights, Justice and Home Affairs within the European Parliament (Nastasi and Palmisano 2015) showed how Italy's austerity policies proved especially destructive for the education and healthcare sectors as well as the pension system.

Italy's National Health Service (NHS) (Servizio sanitario nazionale), established in 1978, ensures equal access to healthcare for all of its citizens, or nearly 60 million people (Palese et al. 2014, 170). Although health spending grew by an average of 6 percent annually between 2000 and 2007, it declined to 2.3 percent between 2008 and 2010 (CENSIS 2012). Notably, NHS spending decreased for the first time ever in 2013, from €107.8 billion to €106.8 billion (CENSIS 2012). All Italian regions subsequently cut their health spending by 5 percent following the adjustment to NHS spending in 2013 (Vicarelli and Pavolini 2015). Higher user fees proved a deterrence from utilizing services; for example, in 2011, more than nine million individuals reported economic barriers to accessing healthcare (Bocci and Tonacci 2013).

With fewer resources at their disposal, many regions initiated hiring and salary freezes for healthcare professionals as well as changes to hospital procedures (Vicarelli and Pavolini 2015, 1611). One study examined the effects of cost containment interventions as perceived by Italian nurses, who reported "(1) increased stress levels, (2) increased number of patients with social problems, and (3) increased nursing workloads" (Palese et al. 2014, 168). In the span of only a few years, Italy shifted from having a shortage of nurses in the healthcare system to widespread unemployment of nurses; while in 2007, 94 percent of nurses had a job one year after graduation, this number dropped to 63 percent in 2012, creating a brain drain effect in the nation's healthcare sector (Vicarelli and Pavolini 2015). To absorb budget cuts, many hospitals reportedly reduced the number of beds on site, admitted fewer patients, and shortened lengths of stay (McKee et al. 2012).

Considering recent estimates that over 50 percent of Italy's total social protection expenditure goes to funding pensions (Muehlebach 2012), austerity measures that targeted the pension system registered across wide swaths of the population. The Save Italy Decree 201/2011 (Decreto Salva Italia) altered "the age and contribution requirements for retirement, as well as the methodology for calculating the amount of retirement pensions" (Andretta 2017, 207). The pension reform of 2010 (L. 122/2010) introduced stricter requirements regarding age and contributions and periodic adjustments to benefits (Nastasi and Palmisano 2015).

Within a few years of the post-2008 wave of austerity measures, research from public health was already revealing striking downward trends in overall population health and well-being (e.g., Arie 2013a, 2013b; Ayuso-Mateos, Barros, and Gusmao 2013; Brand et al. 2013; McKee et al. 2012; Pearce 2013; Porter 2013; Stuckler and Basu 2013). In Italy, as in Greece, a spike in suicides was among the most tragic and immediate of these austerity-related health consequences. Across Italian regions, Sicily showed the highest positive correlation between unemployment and suicides (De Vogli and Owusu 2015). One study also found that the fall of GDP per capita and the rise of unemployment triggered a sharp increase in deaths related to mental and behavioral disorders (De Vogli, Vieno, and Lenzi 2013). In 2012, global media outlets covered the high-profile suicide of a seventy-eight-year-old woman in Gela, Sicily, who threw herself from the balcony of her third-floor apartment after she had received a cut in her monthly pension. They reported that she was "worried about how to make ends meet." Her son elaborated, "The government is making us all poorer, apart from the wealthy, who they don't touch, in contrast with us workers and small businessmen who are struggling with heavy debts."[11] There was also the story of the fifty-four-year-old plumber from the Sicilian town of Caltanissetta who immolated himself after reportedly struggling with depression after many months without work.[12] The local chapter of the Confederazione generale italiana dell'artigianato (GCIA), an association of artisans and small businessmen, shared in mid-2012 that "thirty-two businesspeople have taken their own lives since the beginning of 2012, mostly over problems due to the recession and painful austerity measures."

ITALY'S "NEOLIBERAL TURN"

While considerably more aggressive than reforms of the recent past, the post-2008 austerity measures mapped onto a longer trajectory of increasingly "neoliberal" reforms in Italy. Muehlebach (2012, 105) notes that since the early 1990s, Italy has undergone a "radical reversal" from its post-

World War II expansion of the welfare state. Former prime minister Silvio Berlusconi is widely blamed by Italian citizens for enacting a "merciless US-style form of deregulation and privatization," resulting in "the flexibilization of Italy's labor market, the birth of a new stratum of poor, and the dismantling of welfare" (Muehlebach 2012, 5). As related to me by one of my Palermo-based friends who was in his forties, "We had twenty ugly years of Berlusconi, the results you see today, because in that twenty years there were massive changes spanning the familial, cultural, educational, and economic realms."

It was also during Berlusconi's reign that Italy shifted its currency from the lira to the euro, an event that many of my informants underscored as particularly significant in the collective memory of Italians. "It was possible [before the euro] to feed a family of four, because salaries were high enough to cover rent and utilities. But with the introduction of the euro, prices doubled while wages remained stagnant," recalled one *palermitano* who was just coming of age and preparing to enter the labor market at the time. With wages stagnant, he explained, "people started to panic. We were buying things at a discount and being as economical as possible. And those who had bought cars or houses with loans were not able to make their payments. Many people lost their homes to the banks because they couldn't pay their mortgages. Those with money in savings experienced a sudden devaluation."

In 2016, the Italian National Institute of Statistics (ISTAT) found that a staggering one-third of Italy's population was living in poverty (23.1 percent in "relative poverty" and 7.6 percent in "absolute poverty"). The same report also emphasized that Italy had not seen a poverty rate so high since 2005. Shortly after the publication of these findings, the International Monetary Fund released more troublesome news: Italy was at risk of a protracted recession that could last through the year 2023 (IMF 2016).

Reflecting on Italy's rising rates of poverty and inequality, scholars often allude to the nation's precarious labor market that has resulted in the proliferation of "flexible workers," or *precari* (i.e., those without work contracts) (Degiuli 2016; Molè 2012; Muehlebach 2012). The anthropologist Noelle Molè (2012, 374) observes that labor market changes in the past thirty years have contributed to the production of such workers whose work lives are characterized by "ambiguity, unpredictability, organizational malfunctions, rapidly fluctuating work responsibilities, solitary labor, and higher rates of job transfer." The features of this flexible labor regime were revealed to me firsthand through the accounts of many Italian friends and peers who have been living from one short-term contract to the next and for whom the prospect of settling down and having children appears economically nonviable. Unlike their parents or grandparents, they do not foresee ever accumulating enough wealth to buy a home or to retire with the security of a pension. A survey conducted by Gallup in 2013 corroborates the prevalence of these sentiments: "66 percent of Italians are rather pessimistic about the future of young people in Europe: as many as 92 percent believe that young people will have fewer opportunities than their parents' generation to have a secure job; 87 percent a satisfying job; 93 percent a secure pension; 92 percent a high salary; and 54 percent a comfortable accommodation" (Andretta 2017, 208). The proliferation of *precari*, or the emergence of a class of precarious workers in Italy, Molè (2012) argues, has crippled the organizing capacities of workers, foreclosed "affective possibilities" such as feelings of solidarity among workers, and intensified feelings of loneliness and social isolation to such an extent that the Italian Ministry of Labor and Social Politics "singled out loneliness" as a national priority (Muehlebach 2012, 34). Muehlebach (2012, 70) explains that Italians have been mourning "the loss of work for its capacity to create the conditions for social belonging."

Meanwhile, national and regional figures for unemployment are sobering and make aspirations of cultivating belonging in the context of work seem like a rather lofty goal. Unemployment in Italy is widespread and has prompted increased emigration to other parts of the EU (IOM 2010). Yet southern Italy and younger generations have been disproportionately affected. Southern Italy's unemployment rate peaked at 17.2 percent in 2012; the rate of unemployment among people under the age of twenty-four in Sicily has hovered above 40 percent since 2008 (ISTAT 2015).

In recent years, far-right politicians have frequently appealed to Italy's economic conditions and diminishing work opportunities to juxtapose them—though in highly generalized and manipulated terms—to the "question" of migration.

MIGRATION TRENDS IN EUROPE

In "Migration and Immigrants in Europe: A Historical and Demographic Perspective" (2016), Christof Van Mol and Helga de Valk outline three periods of migration to and within Europe since the 1950s. The first period, ranging roughly from the early 1950s to the early 1970s, they explain, "was characterized by steady economic growth and development and deployment of guest worker schemes, (return) migration from former colonies to motherlands, and refugee migration" (32). Following World War II, the countries of Northwestern Europe were booming economically. As citizens of these countries sought education and expanded their possibilities for upward mobility, "local workers could not fill the vacancies, as labor reservoirs were limited" (32). Vacancies were gradually filled with labor migrants from Southern European countries: "Estimates of the numbers of individuals that left Italy, Spain, Greece and Portugal between 1950 and 1970 vary from 7 to 10 million" (33). There was also limited migration from North Africa and Eastern Europe during this time.

These flows of labor migration were brought to a halt during what Van Mol and de Valk (2016) describe as the second period of migration to and within Europe. Beginning with the 1973 oil crisis and ending in the late 1980s with the end of the Cold War, this period was characterized by "increasing unemployment levels due to the economic recession [that] fueled hostility, racism, and xenophobia towards certain 'visible' groups of resident migrants" (Van Mol and de Valk 2016, 35). Western European governments implemented restrictive immigration policies that limited entry to individuals for family reunification purposes. It was at this time that Italy developed its reputation for being a potential "backdoor" into Europe. As explained by the anthropologist Francesca Degiuli (2016, 47), "Until the early 1990s, border controls in Italy were not as strict as those of Northern European countries and its geographic configuration made it possible to reach it by water, making it particularly attractive for im/migrants coming from Northern Africa and Eastern Europe." The third period, spanning from the end of the Cold war to today, has been characterized by "increasing EU influence and control of migration from third countries into the EU" (Van Mol and de Valk 2016, 31). Beginning in the 1990s, migration to Southern Europe increased from North, West, and Central Africa and Eastern Europe, as well as from Latin America and Asia.

Although Eastern Europe has been "a crucial reserve of migrant labor" (De Genova 2017, 19) for the rest of Europe arguably since the Cold War, it was not until the fall of the Berlin Wall and the subsequent collapse of the Soviet Union in 1991 that migration from this region became particularly pronounced. Scholars attribute much of this migration to the transition from socialist to free market economies and political instability in formerly Soviet states such as Albania (to Greece and Italy predominantly), Poland, Romania, the former Yugoslavia, Moldova, Ukraine, Lithuania, and Estonia (Caldwell 2004; Degiuli 2016). As described by Van Mol and de Valk (2016, 37), "Between 1989 and 1992, for example, asylum applications increased from 320,000 to 695,000, to decline to 455,000 by the end of the decade and increase again to 471,000 in 2001." Many of those seeking asylum fled to Northern Europe, especially Germany (Doomernik and Bruquetas-Callejo 2016). Doomernik and Bruquetas-Callejo (2016, 62) write that "policymakers across Europe shared a fear of an imminent 'invasion' of Central and Eastern European migrants." While the 1992 Maastricht Treaty facilitated the freedom of movement between EU member-states, stricter border controls were enforced to regulate entry into the EU and prompted an increase in irregular migration (Van Mol and de Valk 2016). A Palermo-based friend who was a language instructor and originally from the southern Italian region of Puglia, recalled events surrounding the so-called invasion of Albanian asylum seekers in the early 1990s.

> I was working for a local radio station at the time that the first boat arrived. The prefecture required us to make an appeal to residents asking them to host these people. Around two hundred had arrived, so hotels, families, and churches were being asked to help find a place for them all, and to provide food and clothing. But the boat arrivals then became a daily event, and more and more asylum seekers arrived. I remember that police in the city of Bari closed the local stadium where they put nearly four hundred people but without access to any bathrooms, no sunlight, no food, no water, and it was hot as hell.... Consider that they had escaped a war, or some horrible situation, and now they were living in a prison.

Despite the fact that the vast majority of asylum seekers who were arriving in Italy by sea at this time had viewed it as a transit country (Albahari 2015), those who stayed in Southern Europe primarily filtered into the low-wage labor market consisting of domestic work, including caregiving, necessitated by "the Mediterranean welfare regime" (Doomernik and Bruquetas-Callejo 2016, 62). Parvulescu (2014, 2, 7) observes how this segmentation of the labor market precipitates "the gender-specific circulation of East European women in West Europe.... One becomes a domestic worker in Italy on account of being *from* Romania. It is the fact of *being from* East Europe that qualifies women for certain occupations" (original emphasis).

The "Crisis" of Migration from Africa

Contrary to the popular belief that migration from the African continent to Europe is a recent phenomenon, as reinforced by the spectacle of boat arrivals, Jennifer Cole and Christian Groes (2016) provide ample evidence of the "long history of entanglement" between the regions resulting from European colonization. This entanglement was initially forged by "practices ranging from forced labor and tax collection to concubinage, domestic employment, and conscription into colonial armies, and their relationships sometimes brought Africans to Europe" (2). Even in the years following decolonization, many Africans traveled to Europe to study or to work and sustained transnational family ties.

It is only in the past few decades that European governments have made concerted attempts to restrict African mobility into Europe, as summarized by Cole and Groes (2016, 2–3): "New political and economic arrangements associated with the growing pervasiveness of neoliberal capitalism have shifted the terms of interaction." Structural adjustment programs in particular, consisting of austerity measures and implemented in the second half of the twentieth century, facilitated these new political and economic arrangements. Cole and Groes explain:

> Instituted by the World Bank and the International Monetary Fund in response to the debt crisis in Latin America, these economic policies sought to reduce African debt and minimize state control of the economy so as to encourage foreign investment. To do so, they compelled African countries to enact severe austerity measures to qualify for loans. As a result of these measures, states drastically reduced the value of local currencies and withdrew from public projects, including housing and schooling. In Senegal, Cameroon, and Madagascar...household revenues dropped by almost 50 percent between 1961 and 1991, while the gross national product declined by about 38 percent during roughly the same period.... Today in Ethiopia,

unemployment rates for youth with a secondary education hover at around 50 percent, and some estimates place youth unemployment in Mozambique at close to 60 percent. (2016, 10)

Other changes associated with structural adjustment programs in Africa included "privatization of corporations and industries, cuts in public spending, the introduction of user fees for education and health, and the removal of subsidies on particular food items and agricultural inputs" (Kea 2016, 83). Reductions in public spending combined with difficult economic conditions have also prompted an increase in internal displacement and migration within the African continent (Feldman-Savelsberg 2016).

In 2017, the most reported countries of origin during disembarkations at Italian ports were Nigeria (18,158, or 15.2 percent), Guinea (9,701), and Côte d'Ivoire (9,507) (Osservatorio migrazione 2018). As explained by a Palermo-based nonprofit volunteer who regularly helped migrants complete their asylum paperwork, increased migration from the African continent in recent years could be attributed to "the situation in their countries: wars and conflicts that have created myriad challenges, so much so that they cannot make lives for themselves. There is no work. They are seeking a better life." As of the latest figures from EUROSTAT (2020), EU member-states with the highest number of asylum applications included, in descending order, Germany, Italy, France, Greece, the United Kingdom, and Spain.

THE MIGRATION "QUESTION" IN EUROPE'S SOUTHERN PERIPHERIES

> [The] borders of Europe are simultaneously entangled with a global (postcolonial) politics of race that redraws the proverbial color line and refortifies European-ness as a racial formation of whiteness, and a comparably global (neoliberal) politics of transnational mobility and capitalist labor subordination that produces such spatialized (and racialized) differences, above all, to capitalize upon them.
>
> —Nicholas De Genova, "Introduction: The Borders of 'Europe' and the European Question"

In present-day Europe, the racialization of immigrants in general and the construction of African migrants in particular as an illegitimate social group (Ticktin 2011) compounds with migrants' experiences of illegality. Defined as a form of subjectivity, illegality relegates migrants to the fringes of society where they are vulnerable to the crippling effects of institutional and social abandonment (Biehl [2005] 2013), confinement (Carney 2014; Coutin 2010), discrimination, and social exclusion (Coutin 2010; De Genova 2002; Gonzales and Chavez 2012; Menjívar and Kanstroom 2014; Willen 2007). In reference to state practices of migrant surveillance, detention, and deportation, Gonzales and Chavez (2012) theorize the biopolitics of citizenship and governmentality and demonstrate how the migrant body is a key site for constructing "subjective understanding" of what it means to be considered "illegal." Compounding with processes of racialization, illegality thus often acts on one's feelings, thoughts, and emotions, yielding to an internalization and acceptance of one's suffering as "natural and deserved" (Carney 2015; Greenhalgh and Carney 2014). In Italy, as in much of Southern Europe, intersecting and layered experiences of racism, precarious legal status, economic marginalization, and compromised health status are intimately intertwined (Calavita 2004). Migrant workers living in a state of illegality rarely if ever find the means to contest the conditions of their labor. While studies of more established immigrant communities in other parts of the global North show that extended social networks, generational advancement, and socioeconomic mobility may help as a buffer against attempts by the state to exploit and affectively discipline migrants (Vélez-Ibañez 1996), access to these forms of social support and advancement is extremely limited and uneven in the Sicilian context.

The concept of deportability (De Genova 2002) is particularly salient for speaking to the genuine interests of those in power who decide the terms of migration in the Mediterranean. As a subjectivity, deportability indexes the ever present possibility of one's deportation that is reinforced through practices of surveillance, detention, and, of course, deportation. From the perspective of power, the imposition of deportability as a way of being in the world secures a source of exploitable, surplus labor. European governments, including far-right anti-immigrant leaders, do not necessarily seek to eradicate migration entirely but rather to preserve deportability of migrants that will ensure the accumulation of capital. Relatedly, it should not be discounted how changes to Italy's labor market and broader trends in favor of increased privatization and deregulation of markets have necessitated migrant labor. Evidence from ethnographic and demographic research reveals how migrants are instrumental to buttressing Italy's tattered safety net. For instance, with Italy's aging population and declining government support for eldercare, many migrants, usually women, are recruited or solicited by families for domestic services in private homes (Degiuli 2016; Fullin and Reyneri 2011; Muehlebach 2012).[13] As stated by one social worker I interviewed in Palermo, and reiterated on various occasions by others with direct experience assisting migrants, "They take the hardest jobs, which in part also uphold Italy's welfare system. They are the only ones who are willing to work as janitors, domestics, service workers. They are completely exploited." At the same time, research shows that migrants' fiscal contributions to Italy's welfare system as workers outpace their use of this system (Osservatorio Migrazioni 2018). Marshalling a *politics of visibility* to denounce racialized Others (African migrants especially) alongside a *politics of invisibility* to preserve this pool of surplus labor, the presence of unauthorized migrants (Mares 2019) has allowed the state to officially maintain an anti-immigration stance. Migrants are the scapegoats for a vast array of social afflictions while their labor is mercilessly extracted.

Often deemed a latecomer to matters of im/migration in comparison to much of Western Europe, Italy did not introduce its first legislation dealing with im/migration until the late 1980s (no. 943, December 30, 1986) (Zincone 2006, 18). Alluding to the fact that "Italy has never even had a debate on whether it is, or is not, becoming a country of immigration," Costanza Hermanin (2017, 9) suggests that the nation's history with emigration may provide some explanation. From 1860 to 1985, more than 30 million Italians (mostly from Italy's south) emigrated to the Americas and other parts of Europe; it was not until the mid-1970s that Italy slowly shifted from being a "country of out-migration to a country of immigration": "From around 300,000 at the beginning of the 1980s, the immigrant population grew to almost 2 million in 2004 and reached 4.4 million at the beginning of 2013" (Degiuli 2016, 45, 46). Today, Italian law differentiates among the categories "migrazione regolare" (regular migration), "asilo" (asylum), "migrazione irregolare" (irregular migration), and "migrazione clandestine" (illegal or clandestine migration).

Italy's vacillation between more restrictive and less restrictive immigration policies has dovetailed with economic conditions and labor shortages (Degiuli 2016). The Bossi-Fini law that once criminalized Italian citizens who assisted *irregolari* (irregular migrants), recalled by one of my informants as "a policy that prohibited hospitals from caring for migrants without documents and put doctors and nurses at risk of imprisonment," as well as the more recent *decreto sicurezza* serve as prominent examples of restrictive immigration policies that have gone into effect in the past two decades. Degiuli (2016, 48) explains that Italian immigration laws frequently tie regularization processes and legality to labor due to "acknowledging the important role of im/migrant labor not only in providing a cheap and flexible workforce, but also in providing a solution to the growing need for care." Tuckett (2018, 6–7) adds that "the domestic work and agricultural sectors are overwhelmingly dominated by migrants based on pre-Fordist employment relations, yet exist in a context of post-Fordist globalized economy where the principle of flexibility—or precarity[—]rules." Italy's Istituto nazionale della previdenza sociale (INPS), which collects data on workers, reported that nearly seventy thousand migrants were formally employed in Sicily's agricultural and fishing sectors (38 percent) and as domestic workers (30 percent); meanwhile, almost the same number were unemployed or underemployed as *flessibili* (flexible) workers.[14]

Migrants who enter Italy through authorized channels with visas or work contracts or successfully obtain a *permesso di soggiorno* (residence permit) are considered *regolari*. The *decreto flussi* (flow decree) allows employers to bring workers over from abroad (Chauvin et al. 2013). However, many employers require that migrants present proof of residence prior to extending work contracts or else risk falling into "irregular" status, a form of illegality.

As summarized to me by a cultural mediator working inside one of Sicily's migrant reception centers, "The problem is that migrants don't always find work because many Italians don't have much trust in them. But then, without a job, a migrant cannot apply for a residency permit. It's like a dog who bites his own tail: without a residency permit, one cannot find a job." This configuration linking work to residency—as well as to race or ethnicity, as reflected in the discourse of "trust" referenced by this cultural mediator—and vice versa often acts as a double-edged sword for many migrants. As explained by Tuckett (2016, 115), "Regardless of how many years one has lived in the country, losing one's job or being employed unofficially in the 'black market' can result in the loss of legal status." The lack of formal status hinders migrants from negotiating with their employers.

While Italian law states that asylum applications will be processed within thirty days of submission, most applicants I met during the course of my fieldwork had been waiting for much longer, sometimes up to eighteen months, for a decision. If asylum seekers remain in Italy after a petition for asylum has been denied, they shift to the category "irregular migrants."[15] Similar to individuals of undocumented or unauthorized status in the United States, irregular migrants descend into indeterminate states of illegality that exclude them from a range of public services, compromise their ability to attain work and housing, and exacerbate social isolation from fear of being apprehended by authorities. As an Italian journalist who also works periodically in special operations with the military told me, "For the most part, the people who we receive here in Italy, after a year, or two or three, they find themselves of 'irregular' status, without documents, leaving the country or working in the black market. It is a situation completely out of control, owing to the fact that it is a system based on a logic of 'emergency' rather than long-term solutions."

Social workers with whom I interacted throughout Sicily related similar frustrations with Italy's immigration system. Elena, a social worker who had been assisting migrants since 2007, possessed extensive knowledge of Italian laws, regularly citing specific codes and ordinances over the course of our conversations. Like many of her peers, she deeply resented the decision-making practices of bureaucrats who overemphasized nationality in categorizing migrants as either genuine "refugees" or "economic migrants" and also alluded to the fluidity of these categories as people could conceivably move in and out of them over time, depending on how criteria changed.

Someone who has just arrived is identified either as an economic migrant—someone who comes from a place that is not at war—or as an asylum seeker who can request protection. I contest the fact that this decision hinges on one's nationality. There are so many variables that should be taken into account: age, sex, origin. Not only one's country, because you cannot say you come from Syria, so you're a refugee, or you come from Gambia, so you're not a refugee. You could be a minor from Gambia, trafficked; so you don't qualify for protection? Or a woman under these circumstances doesn't qualify for protection? It's not a simple issue. It requires the utmost care.

My few encounters with Italian officials suggested that they routinely subscribed to this logic as they colloquially referred to Syrians and Iraqis as genuine refugees and to persons from Africa as economic migrants.[16] Yet Eritreans, for example, who represent one of the largest groups of migrants in Italy, have been fleeing military conscription for years, and the UN has accused Eritrea of crimes against humanity. Despite pleas by Elena and others like her working to ensure the human rights of migrants, a person's nationality frequently served as shorthand for their worth and invoked a range of stereotypes, as lamented by one Palermo-based nonprofit director: "These stereotypes correspond to religion, poverty, ignorance or lack of education, food even. The worst are those stereotypes that connote class and race with level of education or knowledge."

"IT'S ALL CONNECTED": TRACING THE BOUNDARIES OF BELONGING

In February 2014, I met the director of the Palermo chapter of Caritas for morning tea at her office close to Palermo's central train station. After being introduced to a number of her chapter's staff and volunteers, some of whom were in the process of seeking asylum, we began discussing the multifaceted nature of charity work in her city particularly as *palermitani* coped with the effects of austerity and as Palermo was receiving record numbers of asylum seekers. As she was underscoring how the need for charitable assistance among *palermitani* had spiked in recent years to rival the needs of migrants, she paused and, carefully considering her words, told me, "Tutto è legato" (It's all connected). She then launched into an elaborate narrative through which she sought to elucidate the linkages between Italy's political system and the broader global economy to transnational migration as well as to cycles of unemployment, homelessness, and sickness that plagued the lives of both citizens and migrants in her community.

Between 2014 and 2017, and in the rawness of austerity's aftermath, an estimated 624,747 migrants arrived in Italy, primarily through Sicily, while "13,457 were lost along the way to its shores" (Fiore and Ialongo 2018, 482). Based on records maintained by the Italian Ministry of the Interior, the majority of those arriving had begun their journeys from countries in Africa and the Middle East. European leaders and mainstream media outlets made declarations of a refugee crisis and a humanitarian emergency, with their discourse—as well as the EU's—later shifting to reframe the situation as one of a "migration crisis" (De Genova 2017).

In meeting with fellow EU member-states, Italian leaders frequently underscore the burden of receiving EU-bound refugees and asylum seekers on Italian shores. Prior to terminating its own state-sponsored search and rescue operation, Mare Nostrum, which had been in effect from 2013 to 2014, former Italian prime minister Matteo Renzi called on EU member-states to share in its costs: "Mare Nostrum cannot just be 'nostrum' [ours] and, if Europe has a heart, it must understand dignity is being challenged in the Mediterranean" (ANSAmed 2014b). Meanwhile, Italy's migrant reception system and broader immigration bureaucracy had also been the targets of derision by human rights advocates. Overcrowding and unsanitary reception conditions in Italy, grossly understaffed Italian immigration offices charged with handling asylum applications, and lengthy bureaucratic delays in meeting the basic needs of migrants such as access to housing and healthcare suggested failures to uphold basic human rights. Yet Italy's political leaders countered these attacks by alluding to how migration should not be mistaken as a uniquely "Italian problem" simply because many consider it the backdoor into Europe.

Italy's citizenship project and enforcement of its borders have been sites of struggle arguably since the mid-eighteenth century, with its "relatively late and turbulent entrance into nationhood" (Giordano 2014, 19). Stymied by "deep fracture[s] (socioeconomic at best, racial at worst) between north and south" (Giordano 2014, 19), Italy was never quite able to realize a complete and total unification of its territories and population. Seeking modernity and subsequently a position "among the great Western powers," its leaders attempted to cultivate "national subjects who would be capable of carrying Italy toward the modernity it so longed for" (Giordano 2014, 19).

Citizenship in Italy, as in much of Europe, is based on *jus sanguinis* (right of blood) rather than *jus soli* (birthright) or *jus culturae* (right of culture). The descent-based criterion of jus sanguinis dates to the 1865 Civil Code. Zincone (2006, 6) describes how blood relation as the primary criterion has been preserved for the "retention and reacquisition of nationality for expatriates and their descendants." Expatriates, Zincone asserts, "were considered a vital vehicle for [Italy's] economic and strategic interests in the international arena... to allow expatriates to maintain their legal status as citizens [as] a way of maintaining these desirable ties" (6–7). This is the myth of L'altra Italia, or "the belief that the 'diaspora' of immigrant descendants mostly includes people who are still culturally very close to their homeland" (12). In stark contrast to the descendants of these expatriates, the children of foreign-born individuals who have grown up in Italy, speak fluent Italian, and know no other country as their own are routinely excluded from the terms of formal belonging in the context of the Italian nation-state.

The *seconda generazione*—the offspring of foreign-born parents— encounters institutional and everyday racism as its members are viewed by far-right political factions as threats to white Italianness and Italy's citizenship project (Bianchi 2011; Frissina and Hawthorne 2018; Hawthorne 2017; see also Fleming 2017). Meanwhile, Italian citizens living abroad who enjoy the privilege of citizenship because of their ancestral heritage are able to participate in elections and shape the fate of a country in which they do not reside. Tuckett (2016, 103) argues that "the increasing presence of young ethnically diverse people speaking with strong regional Italian accents, who dress, move, and gesticulate identically to their 'native' peers, undermine these seemingly restricted categories of identity."[17] Scholars have concluded that the current configuration of laws governing immigration and citizenship in Italy guarantees the state a supply of cheap labor by maintaining migration as a "crisis" or "emergency" and perpetuating the systematic and racialized exclusion of migrants (Calavita 2005; Cole and Booth 2007; Tuckett 2018, 14; Zincone 2006).

Structural adjustment programs as one set of neoliberal economic policies that "transformed everyday life and the ability to earn livelihoods" in migrant-sending communities (Cole and Groes 2016, 10) intersect in important ways with the imprint of austerity on the lifeworlds of ordinary citizens throughout the Mediterranean (Knight and Stewart 2016; Kersh and Mishtal 2016). As Heath Cabot (2016b, 29) has observed, "The steady dismantling of citizens' rights on Europe's borders, alongside the crisis with regard to the reception of refugees, attests to the increasing precaritization of the terrain of rights as they apply to both citizens and refugees in Europe." She thus argues that in examining local responses to austerity, "it is crucial to hold in the same field of vision the predicaments of both citizens and refugees on the margins" (32). This statement particularly resonates in the Sicilian context, where the boundaries of belonging as demarcated by the Italian nation-state have historically excluded *siciliani* from realizing the rights and privileges afforded to their northern counterparts and where there is considerable pushback against the notion of Italian and EU citizenship. Fissures between Sicily and Italy also intersect and compound with prevailing anxieties about how to maintain a robust citizenry amid Italy's aging population and near-stagnant population growth (Degiuli 2016; Krause 2005). Thus, dissenting, semiautonomous regions of Italy, and Sicily in particular, with its fair share of citizens who endorse separatist aspirations, pose threats to Italy's citizenship project in myriad ways. In exercising its power over the people and territory of Sicily by withholding various rights and entitlements, the Italian nation-state has maintained Sicily's (and much of southern Italy's) subordinate status in the larger context of the Italian nation-state, explicit themes of the next chapter.

2 "There Is a Lot of Creativity on This Island"

In Sicily, everything is possible and impossible.

—Native resident of Mondello, province of Palermo

Dark smoke obstructs our view outside the aircraft as we begin the descent to Punta Raisi airport. Our pilot makes one final announcement to explain that strong winds today will make for a turbulent landing. Stepping off the plane and onto the tarmac twenty minutes later, an inferno of dense, hot air enshrouds us. We breathe in fumes of things unnatural, unfathomable, being engulfed by flames. The scene is eerily reminiscent of what Marcelle Padovani and Leonardo Sciascia describe in *La Sicilia come metafora* (Sicily as Metaphor): "The traveler disembarking in Palermo is immediately assaulted by an atmosphere of violence[,] ... [t]he violence of the *scirocco*, the red wind blowing from Africa, which squeezes your head in a fiery vise" (quoted in Keahey 2011, 92).

As we barrel toward Palermo on Highway E90, the scene turns from slightly ominous to veritably apocalyptic. Small fires, too many to count, dot both sides of the road and extend onto the hillside (figure 3). Flames from surrounding brush and highway debris jump dangerously close to our compact rental car as we weave through rush-hour traffic.

We have arrived in Sicily during a state of emergency, but nobody seems all that panicked. Our fellow commuters push on with typical imprudence through Palermo traffic, honking at one another and yelling the occasional

Figure 3. Palermo on fire. Photo by author.

obscenity. Some of them casually toss spent cigarettes onto the arid landscape, possibly sparking more small fires.

We continue our harrowing drive across the center of the island. Much
larger fires, encompassing entire fields and hillsides, rage on without a
living soul in sight. Five hours later, we finally arrive at our destination in
Ragusa.

The following afternoon's news broadcast highlights this "incubo
incendio" (fire nightmare) that swept the island. Friends tell me that they
attribute the fires to a perfect storm of Saharan winds and excessively hot
temperatures combined with a historic drought that has plagued much

of the central Mediterranean. The drought-affected region extends into North Africa, where in recent years tens of thousands of farmers and pastoralists across the African continent have been displaced by the effects of desertification (Gettleman 2017).

One friend asks if I happen to know the cause—or more accurately, culprit—of Sicily's fires. Clearly amused by my ignorance, he smirks and says, "There is a lot of creativity on this island." He then explains that it is common knowledge that those charged with extinguishing Sicily's fires are also the ones who ignite them. This is an enterprising strategy for Sicily's otherwise underemployed firefighters, despite the inherent riskiness of this practice with hotter summers. I cannot help but connect my friend's explanation to the anthropologist Shannon Speed's (2016) concept of neoliberal multicriminalism, through which she interprets how the proliferation of illicit, income-generating activities are made possible, and even necessary, by the expansion and entrenchment of neoliberal capitalism (see also Guthman and DuPuis 2006). This "creativity" alluded to by my friend, so it would seem, holds the potential to both articulate with and subvert neoliberal logics.

My informants seldom fail to remind me of Sicily's reputation as a land of antagonisms, opposites, and contradictions. They invoke a rhetoric akin to the epigraph of this chapter: "In Sicily, everything is possible and impossible." The implication is that well-being and suffering represent two sides of the same coin. It is a place where on any given day I might meet a man from Trapani whose son recently migrated to London in search of work while his family picks up odd jobs and pieces together whatever earnings they can to survive, or I might find myself chatting with young couples destined for an afternoon of wine tasting as they mingle with the chic Sunday brunch crowd at the popular Bar Turismo, overlooking the glittering *lungomare* in the upscale seaside Palermo suburb of Mondello. Where there is hope, there is also despair; where there is scarcity, there is also abundance; where there is corruption, there is also benevolence; where there is cooperation, there is also dissonance and conflict. Sicily is a land of bourgeois wealth as well as working-class struggles and abject poverty.

Sicily is both Italy and not Italy.

In this chapter, I examine the significance of Sicily's position on the front lines of migration to Europe. First, I briefly allude to the deeper history of the island, including centuries of colonization and occupation; extraction of labor and asymmetrical development compared to the rest of the Italian nation-state; and land dispossession, displacement, and emigration of *siciliani*. Second, I argue that these historical conditions and the more recent onset of neoliberal economic policies in the form of austerity regimes articulate with particular affective states—ways of feeling—that precede local acts of solidarity with migrants. I provide examples of repeated attempts to "responsibilize" *siciliani* to attend to social problems that have afflicted the island for decades, such as poverty and corruption in politics, as well as to respond to more recent migration. As modes of affective disciplining, these processes have ascribed a set of moral failings to *siciliani*—conceived as indebted, irresponsible subjects—that also operates to dehumanize and alienate them from Italy and the rest of Europe.

ANCIENT SICILY AND ITS "HISTORY OF DEFEATS"

> Historically, we [*siciliani*] have experienced various dominations, thus I feel—with respect to my culture and my genetic heritage—the presence of Normans, Arabs, Spanish. Our land was a crossroads. I recognize an affinity with North Africa and Spain. So I feel the history of our land is one of a borderlands. We are at the center of the Mediterranean, and this is reflected in my culture. This is what Sicily represents to me, this is its richness [*richezza*].
> —Valentina, a thirty-something mother and hotel worker in Agrigento

Most *siciliani*, irrespective of their political views or moral stances on im/migration, believe that the history of their island has been shaped by the confluence of diverse migratory flows, violent invasions, and internal conflicts unfolding over several millennia. Sicily forms part of what many scholars conceptualize as the Mediterranean borderlands: both as a geography—the sea and lands surrounding it, from Southern Europe to the Maghreb and Levant, which collectively index "layered zones of contact" and varying "exchange densities" (Ben-Yehoyada 2017; Clancy-Smith 2010, 11; Giglioli 2017)—and as an excess space, that is, "a site of accumulation of discourses largely revolving around Italy-Europe, among others" (Proglio 2018, 408). Although it is the case throughout much of Italy, among Sicilians regional identity supersedes allegiance to the Italian state (Pratt 2002; Stanley 2008).[1] Regional identity among *siciliani* is especially pronounced, as other outsiders have observed: "Sicily may be *part* of Italy, a political subdivision, an autonomous region, but its people are not *of* Italy.... Sicilians might be viewed in America and elsewhere as 'Italians,' but in their hearts and souls they are Siciliani" (Keahey 2011, 92–93; original emphasis). So-called *sicilitudine*, a concept coined by the acclaimed Sicilian author and intellectual Leonardo Sciascia (1921–89), refers to the idea of Sicily as separate from Italy. Alluding to their Arab ancestry, many of my friends and research collaborators from the provinces of Palermo and Agrigento like to remind me of how much more they identify socially and culturally with North Africa or even Spain than they do with the Italian mainland.[2] In Sicily's urban areas especially, I frequently spot younger generations sporting iconoclastic shirts and hats that appeal to this sentiment, with Sicily being redrawn as an extension of the map of North Africa and no longer an appendage to mainland Europe.

Archaeological evidence suggests that humans were inhabiting the island of Sicily as early as 12,000 BC. Since these very early settlements, the island has undergone numerous phases of colonization and occupation: Phoenician (ca. 1000 BC), Greek (ca. 800–264 BC and again ca. AD 535), Carthaginian (500–264 BC), Roman (264 BC–AD 500), Arab (827–1061), Norman (1061–1190), French (1266–82), Spanish (1282–mid-1800s), and finally Italian (1860 to the present) (Regione Siciliana 2020). Traces of these earlier occupations continue to permeate multiple features of Sicily's landscape, architecture, cultural practices, linguistic diversity, religious ceremonies and festivals, and culinary traditions. Chiara Mazzucchelli (2007) asserts that this history forms the basis of *sicilitudine* as a subjectivity, or way of being, steeped in "the inescapable condition of a population marked by a 'history of defeats.'" Leonardo Sciascia devoted much of his career to examining how struggles for power and sovereignty throughout Sicily's history had been internalized by the island's inhabitants and manifested as insecurity and distrust among *siciliani* toward outsiders.

In summarizing some of Sciascia's many contributions, Keahey (2011, 97) infers that "forced colonization and the inability of [Sicily's] inhabitants to follow a course of self-determination metaphorically imprinted insecurity on Sicilian DNA." But contrasting with some of these claims about the effects of colonization on Sicilian habitus, many of my informants remained optimistic about the history of their island as a "crossroads" and place of cultural hybridity. As evidenced by Valentina's reference to this history as a source of "richness," they exhibited a certain pride about the connotation of "Sicilianness" as belonging to a historically significant frontier.

Sicily joined the Kingdom of Italy in 1861 during the period that historians refer to as Il Risorgimento (the Unification). Scholars have characterized Sicily's relationship with the rest of Italy since the Risorgimento as "colonial." As critiqued by Antonio Gramsci (1978), Sicily represented one of the newly formed nation-state's "exploitable colonies" in that it provided a source of cheap exports (primarily grain) and surplus labor in exchange for manufactured goods from the north (Fiume 2006). Keahey (2011, 12) quips that "northern Italians did not offer much to the South, except the draft to fight Italy's wars.... [I]ndustry was largely kept in the North."[3] This arrangement in which northern Italy served as the locus of production and manufacturing and southern Italy as the "state-subsidized consumer" was cemented at the end of World War II, coincidentally when the region of Sicily was also granted its "autonomous" status.

Sicilians are still reckoning with the implications of the Risorgimento and the formation of the Italian nation-state more than a century and a half later. In contemplating present-day economic struggles on the island, the director of a cooperative in Agrigento remarked, "I think that Italy's unification for us in the south was not advantageous because from that moment on history changed. We went from being economically significant—speaking of before the 1800s and the millennia preceding—to being treated as the dregs of Italy and then the world. But one does not simply become a dreg. The process is much more complex. Unfortunately, we are still paying for it." He suggested that much of this "payment" was happening within the registers of cultural memory and identity: "Sicily is a very important place in the history of Western societies. Sadly, it seems that some of us have lost awareness of this immense history and of our immense cultural heritage, perhaps one of the richest and most unique in the world."

ASYMMETRICAL DEVELOPMENT AND EMIGRATION OF SICILIANI

Lack of investment by Italy post-unification and extractive practices orchestrated from the north precipitated more than a century of land dispossession and migration of *siciliani* from their homeland. Fleeing poverty and control by the Mafia, Keahey (2011, 147) explains, "the great diaspora of the late nineteenth and early twentieth centuries took millions of disenchanted, hungry Sicilians and southern Italians to North and South America." In the first decade of the twentieth century, nearly two million southern Italians, including Sicilians, emigrated and often faced violent persecution in the United States (Barbata Jackson 2020; Guglielmo and Salerno 2003).

While Sicilian separatists were hopeful about the promise of sovereignty and seceding from mainland Italy following World War II, they "eventually were silenced with the Italian government's offer to make the islands into autonomous, self-governing regions" (Keahey 2011, 4). Instead of gaining independence, a period of modernization and consumerism ensued, one that "enforced an unequal relationship of exploitation [with Italy], and brought changes to the standard of living[;]...there are a great many more automobiles, emigrants' savings have financed construction and education, the population has become 'urbanized' and 'Italianized' in language" (Fiume 2006, 44). With modernization, emigration and unemployment soared, as did, paradoxically, an obsession with consumer goods. In recounting the "rapid urbanization of Sicily after World War II," Schneider and Schneider (2003, 14) attest to how "land reform and resultant mechanization of agriculture created a massive peasant exodus." Many of those displaced from rural livelihoods first migrated to Palermo but were met with "an inability of urban industries to absorb them" (Schneider and Schneider 2003, 232). Exceeding the numbers that made up the "great diaspora" of the early twentieth century, between 1951 and 1971, southern Italy, including Sicily, "lost over four million people out of a total population of a little over eighteen million" (Robb 2007, 157), many of them continuing to the Americas, northern Italy, or other parts of Europe. In his book, *Midnight in Sicily: On Art, Food, History, Travel and la Cosa Nostra,* Peter Robb recounts how this wave of emigration exacerbated disparities between Italy's north and south:

> The southern economy plunged into crisis as the prices of oil, wine and wool dived, setting off the huge turn-of-the-century emigration to the Americas. Through all this, and though it was poorer, [southern Italy] was still paying higher taxes and getting less back in public expenditure and capital investment than Italy's northern regions. The savings of the south, and the money sent home by emigrants, were sucked toward the north and the gulf widened between developed and underdeveloped Italy. (2007, 155)

Much of the Baroque center in Palermo that was bombed during World War II, for instance, remains in ruins and virtually untouched. In the heart of the city, many buildings are abandoned or remain in a quasi-reconstructed state: "Balconies on both occupied and unoccupied buildings are closed off and shrouded in heavy netting to keep pieces of stone and rusted iron railing from falling onto passersby below" (Keahey 2011, 7). Robb (2007, 4) elaborates on the scene in Palermo, speaking to the absurdity of its stunted reconstruction: "Other European cities had been bombed in the forties, and much worse than Palermo. What was unique to Palermo was the ruins of the old city were still ruins, thirty years, fifty years on. Staircases still led nowhere, sky shone out of the windows, clumps of weed lodged in the walls, wooden roof beams jutted toward the sky like the ribs of rotting carcasses." Nonetheless, these ruins have attracted inhabitants, including many immigrants from throughout Africa and Asia, who over the past few decades have moved into previously condemned buildings. Describing the postwar context, Schneider and Schneider (2003, 15) recount that "cloisters and courtyards were turned into parking lots, depots for construction materials and stolen goods, or artisans' noisy workshops; and empty quarters of all kinds lent themselves to prostitution and the retail sale of drugs." Despite the ingenuity of *palermitani* in the reclaiming and repurposing of formerly abandoned spaces, epitomizing the lack of investment in Sicily by its neighbors to the north is the central Italian government's routine neglect of the reconstruction of Palermo.

"SICILY IS RESPONSIBLE FOR ITS OWN PROBLEMS"

> Let us go, then. Away from abhorred Etna, and the Ionian
> sea, and these great stars in the water, and the almond trees
> in bud, and the orange trees heavy with red fruit, and these
> maddening, exasperating, impossible Sicilians, who never
> knew what truth was and have long lost all notion of what a
> human being is. A sort of sulphureous demons.... But let me
> confess... that I am not at all sure whether I don't really
> prefer these demons to our sanctified humanity.
> —D. H. Lawrence, *Sea and Sardinia* (1921)

Across a variety of literary and media genres—from classic literature to mafiosi-centric films and television series—depictions of *siciliani* are rarely dignified. Invariably, popular representations of Sicily and its people (re)produce the criminalizing trope of *sicilianismo* through which "Sicilianness" is equated with cultural backwardness, apathy, and moral corruption. Sicily has been described as boasting "a tenacious catalogue of stereotypes[:]...historic poverty and economic underdevelopment, engagement in a clientelistic style of politics, and cultural support for patriarchal gender relations and for various manifestations of organized crime" (Schneider 1998, 1). These stereotypes are not reserved to the realm of cultural media production but also intersect with the history of modern Europe and the cultivation of "modern," white European subjects. In the late 1800s, for instance, European criminologists and eugenicists regularly spoke to the genetic "inferiority" of southern Italians, Sicilians in particular, and discouraged marriage between Northern Europeans and those from Italy's south (Schneider and Schneider 2003). These stereotypes also endure in the realm of Italian national politics, as frequently highlighted for me by my interlocutors, to whom I regularly pleaded for more explanation as to why the Italian central government did not invest more in the region. The response of a migrant reception manager working in Palermo seemed particularly insightful: "Why would Italy help us? They think that Sicily is responsible for its own problems."

Conversely, Sicily's role as a prime tourist destination for northern Italians and Europeans has been reinforced by myths that romanticize life on the island. Tourists arrive in droves, especially during the summer months, to bask in Sicily's seductive beaches, bucolic landscapes, and abundance of famous archaeological and ancient sites. They exude their enthusiasm for Sicilian "hospitality." This is the "exotic" and salvaged Sicily, devoured by foreigners who are only minimally cognizant of the extreme poverty that afflicts almost half the local population.

Working in tandem, these essentialized representations of Sicily—as "a paradise inhabited by devils" (Fiume 2006, 54)—tend to obscure that present-day problems faced by many *siciliani*, from poverty to corruption in politics, are an artifact of extractive practices and colonial dynamics imposed by Italy and its Northern European neighbors (Ribeiro 2004). Countering political and media discourses that blame these problems on Sicily's "culture," scholars like Giovanna Fiume (2006, 54) call for anti-essentialist approaches that acknowledge Sicily as "a place like any other, with peculiar dynamics of modernization and resistance to modernization." This primarily ethnographic body of work attempts to debunk such essentialisms and underscore how broader political-economic forces have articulated with historical struggles for autonomy and dignity among *siciliani*.

Despite Sicily's autonomous status, local material realities and everyday possibilities for the island's inhabitants are tethered to the larger Italian nation-state and to the European Union. Levels of poverty and unemployment in Sicily have been comparatively worse than those in the rest of Italy. With a population of over five million people—representing about 8 percent of Italy's total population—and a surface area of more than 9,000 square miles, Sicily is the largest and most populated island in the Mediterranean. According to the Italian National Institute for Statistics, more than half of Sicily's population was "at risk for poverty" in 2016, almost double the national average (23.1 percent) (ISTAT 2016; see also EURES 2019). In the same year, unemployment in Sicily was 22 percent, compared to 11 percent in central and northern Italy, and youth unemployment was at a record high, with estimates hovering around 50 percent.[4] Tourism, agriculture, and construction are among the island's leading industries, with labor demands fluctuating seasonally. These economic conditions have continued to prompt emigration of *siciliani*, especially younger generations, and southern Italians to other parts of

Europe in search of better opportunities (IOM 2010). Despite often holding university degrees, younger generations of *siciliani* struggle to secure
stable employment near or close to home. They string together temporary,
informal, and contract-based forms of employment, juggle multiple entrepreneurial activities, or labor seasonally in their family-owned businesses
that cater predominantly to tourists such as hotels and restaurants. I frequently rented an apartment from one of Palermo's many unemployed
architects who was in his thirties and living in an adjacent unit with his
wife and child. In addition to managing several Palermo-based properties
on vacation rental websites, he organized authentic dining experiences for
tourists out of his mother's home, coordinated with small tourism com-
panies to offer day tours, and occasionally consulted on building projects.

Conversely, I also encountered a sense of optimism among younger
generations that Sicily could seize this economic moment and bypass its
history of being a "consumer" and beneficiary of the Italian nation-state.
As elaborated by a young man who had graduated from college only a few
years before and was managing short-term vacation rentals and volunteering for a number of migrant-serving organizations in Palermo, "There
is an opportunity to shift our collective psychology. Instead of looking to
Italy for support, we can go directly to institutions throughout Europe.
This is already happening to some extent and a new sector of [social]
entrepreneurship is emerging. We can continue to develop it if we want.
Sicily offers much opportunity, and the market is totally open. There is
much reason to invest here."

Like many southern Italians, *siciliani* display strong distrust of the
central Italian government that has kept them a "question" demanding intervention and rehabilitation. Fiume (2006, 39) explains, "From
the time of Italian unification, in 1860, the south has been considered
a 'question', to be confronted alternatively either as a problem of public
order requiring police measures, or as a social problem with a program
of reforms and public works." *Siciliani* are acutely aware of the Italian
government's role in perpetuating orientalist discourses that marginalize
the south. References to the south by politicians and northern Italian citizens as il Mezzogiorno—a pejorative term that translates as "midday" and
implies backwardness and delayed development—serve as a prominent
example (Schneider 1998). As the owner of a co-working space in Palermo

once said to me, "We in Sicily and the Mezzogiorno are habituated to this treatment by Italy, because we have always received funds from the central government. They consider us 'victims of our own wrongdoing.' For fifty years, after the war, we have been 'helped.'"

Ironically, it was the general absence and unwillingness of the state to invest or help to dispute local affairs that scholars connect to the origins and continued operations of the Mafia. As Jane Schneider and Peter Schneider (2004, 505) contend, "Clearly, had the liberal Italian state been motivated to create order in Sicily, the Mafiosi who intervened would have been redundant. Instead the state relied on them, only pretending to police their unauthorized use of violence." They note that "contrary to the conviction of many, the Mafia is both a recent social formation, dating only to the nineteenth century, and separable as a subculture from its surrounding milieu" (Schneider and Schneider 2003, 4). Nonetheless, mafiosi filled "gaps between national politics and local exigencies" and "delegated the use of violence to maintain order in and control of rural areas, because the central government was weak" (Fiume 2006, 39–40). Challenging the notion of Cosa Nostra (the term used by its own members in alluding to the Sicilian Mafia) as "an expression of disorder," Fiume (2006, 40) characterizes them as "an instrument of management." The colonial relationship of Sicily to Italy arguably made fertile conditions for mafiosi to thrive. Schneider and Schneider (2003, 46) describe Sicilian mafiosi as mediating "illegal traffics or us[ing] illegal means, including violence, to gain a foothold in legal activities. To operate in this fashion they have to be entrepreneurial, opportunistic, aggressive, capable of violence."

Scholars have traced the early foundations of the anti-Mafia movement to the University of Palermo in the late 1960s. Decades later, organizers of the movement galvanized around their collective moral outrage that followed the murders in 1992 of Judges Paolo Borsellino and Giovanni Falcone, who along with today's mayor of Palermo, Leoluca Orlando, had instigated investigations of Cosa Nostra and sought to dismantle the criminal organization. In the late 1980s, Mafia leaders had condemned Orlando to death, along with Falcone and Borsellino. As the only remaining survivor, Orlando has served three times as mayor: 1985 to 1990, 1993 to 2000, and 2012 to the present. Refusing to accept the Mafia as Sicily's "irreversible destiny," "police and judicial repression and a Palermo-centered anti-mafia social movement joined together in a concerted effort to reverse what seemed inevitable" (Schneider and Schneider 2003, 3). In the words of Orlando, Palermo as the "capital of the Mafia" was being reclaimed as "the capital of the anti-Mafia." Fiume (2006, 46) notes that organizers of the anti-Mafia movement were "prevalently educated, professional, and urban, and in open contrast to the Mafia culture itself" and wanted to bring an end to Mafia influence in national, regional, and local politics. While the presence of the Mafia is indisputably less pronounced than it was in the 1980s, recent ethnographic work has shown how Cosa Nostra still animates various aspects of Sicilian lifeworlds (Rakopoulos 2017).

The morphing presence of organized crime in this setting and the enterprising, though not necessarily legal, activities of other *siciliani* who are desperate to earn a living provide further evidence of the ways in which *siciliani* have had to adapt to structural constraints associated with their historically marginalized status within Italy and to exercise a form of "creativity" that transcends the boundary between legality and illegality (Speed 2016). Cosa Nostra has represented another form of control over the local population from which *siciliani* have struggled to extricate themselves and to overcome.

"SICILY IS RESPONSIBLE FOR MIGRANT RECEPTION"

> We confront this emergency alone. The Italian government
> could take responsibility, but it doesn't. Neither does Europe.
> All other European governments are uninterested and have
> left the onus on us.
> —NGO volunteer in Agrigento

> Europe and Italy have completely abandoned Sicily.
> —Director of a youth reception center in Palermo

As of mid-2019, 29 percent of Italy's asylum seekers were residing in Sicily (down from 40 percent in 2018).[5] Italy's Ministry of Interior reports that between 2011 and 2015, Sicily "was the region hosting the highest number of migrants seeking asylum and humanitarian protection," and in 2017, nearly 120,000 migrants disembarked at Sicilian ports (IOM 2018; Osservatorio migrazioni 2018). Yet my interlocutors were not surprised that the most recent "migration crisis"—one that had rendered Sicily on the front lines—elicited minimal investment by Italy's central government. They perceived actions by Italy and the EU as a whole as "extremely delayed and insufficient," sending the message, as summarized by a recent college graduate who was volunteering with a number of migrant-serving organizations in Palermo, that "Sicily is 'responsible' for migrant reception[,] ... that Sicily should 'take care of the situation.'" For example, following the disembarkation of two hundred migrants in Syracuse, the mayor was quoted as saying, "It's like a tap that you can't turn off—every day there are more.... Am I wrong, or is this Europe's frontier, as well as Italy's? So isn't this Europe's problem and not just ours?"[6] From coordinating search and rescue operations and disembarkations to shuttling new arrivals to one of Sicily's reception centers or identifying other options when such centers were full—a regular phenomenon—local government officials, humanitarian organizations, and social workers had come to regard these activities as rather mundane. Nonetheless, they shared the sentiments of Syracuse's mayor: these quotidian activities required investment of (limited) local resources, and there was too much uncertainty at the national and international levels about who should assume responsibility.

Yet interventions by either Italy or the EU in matters of migration were viewed with some skepticism among those involved with reception processes. In recalling the early years of the "migration crisis," back when it was still being framed as a "refugee and humanitarian crisis," my Sicilian informants often alluded to an influx of money that arrived from both the Italian central government and the EU. This "infuso di denaro" (infusion of money), as one social worker put it, was responsible for supporting new jobs among *siciliani* and is the reason that many still believe that migrant reception is one of few "industries" that have been expanding in the region. A worker for UNICEF and regular volunteer with migrant disembarkations explained feeling some ambivalence in this regard: "We're aware but also denounce that today the only source of work, for new graduates, is in reception centers. If these centers did not exist, there would be an extremely high rate of unemployment, higher than it is now. The only thriving economy is thanks to migrants, so we need migrants." In light of the unemployment rate among fifteen- to twenty-four-year-olds, which had been above 40 percent for several years, younger generations of *siciliani* I spoke with were relieved to find jobs as humanitarian workers, translators and *mediatori culturali* (cultural mediators), administrative staff, and legal advocates that allowed them to live with or closer to their families and wider social networks rather than having to migrate north. However, Italy's investment in this industry would soon prove short-lived.

On November 28, 2018, the Italian government voted in favor of Decree Law 113/2018, also known as the security decree, introduced by former interior minister, Matteo Salvini. A restrictive policy that seeks to deter more immigrants from coming and to limit the freedom to stay of those who have already arrived, the security decree significantly decreased funding to hundreds of migrant reception centers and to cultural mediators and legal advocates who were working in these settings. Following implementation of the decree, most reception centers were forced to carry out widespread layoffs or close entirely. In addition, the decree eliminated most forms of humanitarian protection for asylum seekers. Individuals who previously would have been eligible to petition for asylum were instead pushed into "irregular" status.[7] Finally, the law prohibited asylum seekers from obtaining residency permits, thereby blocking them from access to healthcare. This retraction of funds for reception centers and NGOs providing assistance to migrants yielded the *doppia crisi* (double crisis), characterized for me by my Sicilian contacts as the confluence of increased unemployment among *siciliani* and precaritization of migrants.

Sicily as Authority on Migrant Reception

Despite the sense of agitation regarding the government that resonated among those involved with Sicily's migrant reception apparatus, many had derived pleasure and pride in being looked to as authorities in this line of work, locally, of course, but especially on a national and global level. During each of my research trips, a number of conferences and seminars were taking place focused on different aspects of migration and migrant reception. Usually sponsored or cosponsored by the University of Palermo or another local academic institution, these events featured social workers, government officials, scholars, health practitioners, and attorneys who had direct experience working on migration. As I observed by attending many of these events myself or reviewing their programs, the majority of presenters originated from Sicily while their audiences had traveled from northern Italy and, in some cases, other parts of the EU. These gatherings yielded both practical advice and skills to those seeking to assist migrants as well as evidence-based critiques of Italy's reception system and immigration laws.

In May 2019, for instance, I attended an all-day seminar hosted by Clinica legale per i diritti umani dell'Universita' di Palermo (CLEDU), or Legal Clinic for Human Rights, titled "Reception, Protection, and New Procedures in Light of Law 132/2018" (Accoglienza, protezione e nuove procedure alla luce della L. 132/2018) at Ex Cinema Edison, a theater turned classroom space, on the perimeter of Palermo's Ballarò neighborhood. The seminar was mostly geared to attorneys and law students and included a roundtable discussion on new practices of solidarity in the present context of negated rights with participants from the search-and-rescue NGO Mediterranea Saving Humans, among a number of locally based NGOs, community-based associations, and small businesses. Participants voiced their concerns about Salvini's security decree, noting that it "abrogated humanitarian protection and put an entire generation of migrants at higher risk because they are now living in illegality." A panel of attorneys spoke to Italy's "fragmentation of laws, statuses, and corresponding entitlements" and observed that migrants who previously would have qualified for humanitarian protection were now "un po' fuori di tutto" (a little outside of everything). Attorneys explained how they were helping migrants find options while navigating restrictive laws. Alluding to how recent legislative changes had implications for citizens as well as noncitizens, they implored seminar participants to ask themselves, "What does it mean to live in a society that offers no humanitarian protection?" A representative from the human rights monitoring and advocacy group Borderline Sicily remarked that the Italian government was authorizing a "sistema di non accoglienza" (system of nonreception), adding, "It's not just this government. The problems with reception have been present for years, especially in perpetuating the invisibility of migrants and lack of opportunities for them." Representatives of community-based associations expressed how they fought "to help each person feel part of a community" by strengthening the social safety net and making people feel heard. They lamented that

Salvini had given a green light to "atti di violenza e razzismo nella città'"
(acts of violence and racism in the city), leaving migrants especially feeling
"insultata e minacciata" (insulted and menaced).

Less than a week before this event, the University of Palermo also
hosted the weeklong "Migrare" (whose name is the Italian verb for "to
migrate") conference. One notable outcome of the conference was a collectively authored petition, "Appeal to the Europe of Enlightenment"
(Appello all'Europa della Conoscenza), in which participants outlined an
agenda for migrant solidarity in Europe. The statement read as follows:

> We are a group of researchers, workers and students, women and men based
> at the University of Palermo, and this document is a call for members of
> other European universities to contribute towards the construction of a
> space dedicated to observing and proposing action in contexts involving
> human rights and equality, in particular of migrants today, but also with an
> eye towards the rights of future generations. It is important for us to start
> this initiative in Palermo as Sicily has been and is still today a major centre
> of both emigration and immigration. We are conscious of and indignant
> about the grave violations of human rights and dignity to which thousands
> of men, women and children are subjected during their attempt to reach
> our shores, and often even after their arrival here in Europe. We are also
> sadly aware that many, far too many, young people are migrating away from
> the South of Italy towards any place, even outside Europe, that might seem
> to offer a quality of life that is simply not possible in the place where they
> were born. The Mediterranean Sea is in many ways one of the central nodes
> which will determine many aspects of our future, and not just the future
> of Europe.... The validity of migrant policies depends on the reasoning
> behind them, on the facts they take, or do not take, into consideration, their
> respect of inviolable human rights and, last but not least, their effective-
> ness in promoting acceptance and integration. This is also the best way to
> foster the integration of young people in Southern Europe and everywhere
> in the world.... In our view a global discussion aimed at producing global
> policies can be postponed no longer.... Migration must be seen as part of a
> larger context which includes: climate change; the reduction or disappear-
> ance of non-renewable resources such as land and water; the insufficiency
> of sustainable food resources; the dominance of financial transactions over
> the real economy; the appearance of authoritarian organisations and parties
> threatening democracy and freedom. In this scenario...the recognition of
> the right of people to migrate would be a significant contribution towards
> the reaffirmation of democracy and freedom today and for future genera-
> tions. (UNIPA 2019)

Among its many insights, the statement traced and strategically linked migration from outside the EU and across the Mediterranean with the broader struggles and displacement of *siciliani*. As an appeal to the European community, the statement provided a platform for Sicily-based university faculty, staff, students, and others involved with its production to assert a position of leadership in democratic decision making through which they could actively inform practices and policies dealing with migration.

Ospitalità siciliana

> In these troubled times, Palermo, a veritable port, an open
> and hospitable city, continues to receive the men, women,
> and children who have been saved at sea.... Together we are
> constructing, little by little, a means of dialogue and cordial
> friendship.
> —Corrado Lorefice

In the summer of 2016, a season that had been marked by the landmark Brexit vote and by Pope Francis calling for every European to take in "one family of refugees," the above words from Palermo's archbishop were published in *InComune*, the city's "intercultural magazine." Consistent with local media outlets that were regularly reporting on the Sicilian-style "hospitality" (*ospitalitá siciliana*) and cooperation displayed by those involved with migrant reception activities, the archbishop commended efforts by Palermo's residents to extend welcome and show compassion toward those arriving.

The theme of hospitality as an obligation and affective orientation had surfaced numerous times in my fieldwork and elicited praise from a wide range of social actors, including government officials, social workers, members of the clergy, health practitioners, and volunteers. Yet "ospitalità siciliana" is not merely a gesture; it indexes an important tradition, as my Sicilian friends like to remind me when politely refusing my offers to pay for outings together. "Ospitalità siciliana" is also a form of emotional, affective labor.

Elena, a Palermo-based social worker, underscored hospitality as an obligation—reflected in the practice of *accoglienza* (migrant reception)—

in alluding to recent *sbarco* (disembarkation) events in Palermo: "We've been very pressed recently with these events you've most certainly read about, no? All of the *sbarchi*. I believe that...each of us who works in *accoglienza* has the responsibility to do good, to figure out how to make things better and to participate actively." Elena continued to elaborate on the complexity of *sbarchi* events. The coast guard monitored maritime traffic and alerted volunteers and professional aid groups days or sometimes only hours before a ship transporting migrants arrived in port. Aid workers, health officials, and local government staff set up tents and first aid stations where they would then receive and compile personal data on each arriving migrant while also distributing clothes, shoes, water, and food. Migrant reception events at Sicily's ports indexed a civic responsibility; like many of her fellow *palermitani*, Elena deemed a spirit of welcome toward migrants as intrinsic to the city's heritage and identity. Practices of *accoglienza*, she noted, were also important in forging feelings of social cohesion among de facto first responders, many of whom were migrants themselves. She explained:

> Prior to working on the *sbarchi*, we [i.e., social workers, volunteers, public servants, and NGO workers] didn't interact much. You should consider that each of us comes from a different institution: there's the police, the municipality, the health department, the international organizations like IOM, Save the Children....So we didn't really know each other until we began working together. Gradually, we started to salute each other and form friendships. We exchanged information, etc., and now we have a sense of working together. When we meet at the *sbarchi*, we are collaborating.

A volunteer who regularly participated in *sbarchi* events echoed this sentiment of social cohesion and juxtaposed it to the ongoing tragedy of migrant deaths off the shores of Sicily: "The hope is that social cohesion will emerge, that all will be well, because it hasn't been that way. Death is constant. It is a weight that we [*siciliani*] carry with us."

Hospitality as an affective orientation of Sicilians was largely reflected in migrants' perceptions of and experiences with the local population. Most migrants I met related positive impressions of *siciliani*, invoking adjectives such as *caldi* (warm) and *amichevoli* (friendly), as well as phrases such as "ti accolgono bene" (they receive you well). There was a belief among both migrants and their hosts that, compared to other parts of Italy and Europe, migrants tend to integrate fairly easily in Sicily.

During the years of my fieldwork, Palermo in particular had received international acclaim for being a "city of migrants."[8] Mayor Orlando was regularly heralded by global media outlets for his welcoming attitude toward migrants and solicited invitations from cities throughout Europe to help inform their reception and integration policies. At the time of this writing, Orlando had just recently returned from a trip to Berlin, where, speaking to a crowd, he proclaimed that the only way to ensure security is to respect human rights, making explicit reference and expressing his objections to the EU's policy of militarizing and securitizing its borders. In a direct challenge to Salvini and his security decree, Orlando refused to comply with orders to close Italian ports and emphasized that Palermo remained an "open port" to boats carrying migrants. He also issued city identification cards after Salvini had eliminated most forms of international protection, arguing that European migration policies erroneously maintained the "irregular" status of many migrants and thereby enabled the Mafia to exploit this population as laborers in the black market (van der Zee 2017). As such, Orlando's stake in defending the rights of migrants has coalesced in notable ways with his role in the anti-Mafia movement.[9]

Hospitality as Anathema

> The more entrenched our sense of poverty, the stronger the feelings of hostility toward migrants. Political parties like Lega Nord are tapping into this anger *and* this poverty. There is a wave of resentment toward migrants that is building. People who are dealing with great poverty in our town show much antipathy against migrants—I've overheard their conversations. They feel invaded. They applaud Salvini when he says, "The [Italian] people have lost their homes, meanwhile migrants are put up in four-star hotels."
> —Resident of Agrigento

As much as Sicily has been lauded for its hospitality to migrants, it has also been the site of burgeoning hostilities. These hostilities to hospitality had been made increasingly visible with the rising success of populist politicians in Italy, as noted by the above informant. Toward the last phases of my fieldwork, and especially with Italy's newly elected government in 2018, many of my research participants recounted their own stories of horror, which included racist attacks in everyday settings such as on buses and other modes of public transportation, or on the street, and in the form of protests led by white supremacist groups such as Casa Pound outside their places of work. Warranting discussion is how these hostilities have articulated with the class- and geographic-specific dimensions of the affective and political orientations of *siciliani* and other residents of the island.

Political orientations in Sicily tend to assemble around the island's rural/urban divide, as I learned both in traveling between major ports and in the island's interior and vis-à-vis the observations of several of my interlocutors who had spent significant time across these settings. A friend from Agrigento, who had left the small town in which she was born and raised to enroll at the University of Palermo, elaborated on the differences that constituted this divide.

> The most culturally backward places are in the interior [of the island], where there are few encounters with outsiders. These communities are not inclined toward any sort of activism. But they're also afforded so few opportunities for cultural enrichment—they likely don't have theaters, community associations, concerts, everything that enables the development of ideas and critical thinking. Since I grew up in a small town and moved to a large metropolis like Palermo, I've had the privilege to note this difference.

While she believed that Sicily's rural communities were the most fervently opposed to im/migration, she also described how anxieties about and hostilities toward migrants manifested in more urban contexts and overlapped with class divisions. As an example, she cited widespread practices of surveillance among poorer residents of her town: "We've seen that the folks living below us, who have a very basic level of education, they're afraid. Right across from us there is a [migrant] reception center. Our neighbors have filled the balcony and windows with surveillance cameras because they're afraid that migrants might break in and burglarize their home." A business owner in Palermo's Ballarò neighborhood similarly alluded to class divisions in explaining hostilities toward migrants, but he also contextualized this hostility within the broader politics of urban gentrification and inequality: "There are three categories of people living together in this part of the city: locals, or the *palermitani* who have always lived here; 'new arrivals' who are migrants; and 'new arrivals' or those gentrifying who represent a supremely wealthy class of *palermitani* and are restoring old palaces in which to lead their lives of opulence. These groups are in total conflict because each wants to stake claims on this space."

As narrated by my informants, hospitality and hostility toward migrants corresponded to fundamentally different ontological orientations that articulated with class and geography. A position of hostility in this setting emanated from assumptions that migrants were to blame for economic decline and an overall sense of insecurity; hospitality was anathema for its ostensible failures to protect from an "invasion."

The concept of hospitality has elicited considerable attention and debate among scholars of migration. The anthropologist Katerina Rozakou (2012, 563, 565), for instance, "reflect[s] on the asymmetrical aspects of hospitality," wherein "hospitable practices symbolically place the host in a hierarchically superior position and the guest in moral debt and an inferior position." Hospitality is often conceived of "as the privilege of the citizen performed on the noncitizen" (Rozakou 2012, 573). Cabot (2016, 159) adds that hospitality is "flexible and wide-ranging, reflecting models of social support as well as larger paradigms of social relationships." In her study of the refugee management system in Greece, Rozakou (2012, 563) observes that in reception centers "the refugee was produced as the receiver of humanitarian generosity, as having limited agency," whereas on the street, refugees are "cast as hosts[,] ... attributed the power and agency that they are typically denied in institutional aid contexts." Rozakou's findings attest to the "shifting" nature of hospitality (Herzfeld 1987).

Tourists visiting from other parts of Italy and the EU have often remarked to me their pleasant surprise at the hospitality exhibited by *siciliani*. Yet this praise has always struck me as a commentary on the presumed backwardness and immorality of island residents (see also Herzfeld 1987). In this context, hospitality is a facade, one that obscures the structural constraints shaping the material and agentive possibilities of *siciliani*. It can also be viewed as a "technology of the self" (Foucault 1980) through which *siciliani* practice self-restraint in interactions with northern Italians and other tourists who come to experience (or consume) the "authentic" Sicily.

Thus, I conclude this chapter by interrogating the ways that hospitality operates as a discourse that seeks to affectively discipline its subjects toward particular (docile) ways of being. Importantly, hospitality is a form of giving. Yet giving always implies a relation of debt (Mauss 1990). Notably, Sicilians do not perform this emotional, affective labor for one another; rather it is reserved for outsiders. How does the performance of hospitality then reinforce Sicilians as "indebted" subjects? Is hospitality one of the virtues that make *siciliani* desirable subjects, worthy of citizenship and formal belonging but nonetheless indefinitely excluded from this belonging and interminably indebted? Are those who are less docile and refuse to perform hospitality in this setting at risk of being further ostracized and dehumanized in the broader contexts of the Italian nation-state and the EU? How is Sicilian indebtedness reconciled (if at all) or transferred when *siciliani* perform hospitality for migrants arriving from places such as North Africa or the Middle East?

Migrant solidarity work challenges the structural inequalities animating these duplicitous—and potentially dangerous—relations of hospitality (Herzfeld 1987). The set of historical conditions shaping present-day material realities in Sicily are important to understanding the emergence of solidarity work in this particular setting and for contrasting it with other expressions of migrant solidarity in Italy and the EU. As stated in this book's introduction, the aspirational project of migrant solidarity is equally important for the struggle of *siciliani* for autonomy and dignity, especially as their belonging to and integration with the European project is perpetually held in question.

Siciliani deeply familiar with the migrant reception process have lamented how they "feel frustrated being at the behest of erratic Italian politics" that have allowed for the perpetuation of migration as a crisis or emergency. They accuse Italy's political system, rather than migration, of being "the real emergency" threatening their material security and collective well-being. The next chapter examines Sicily's—and more broadly, Italy's—system of migrant reception as it spans from state-sponsored institutions to more locally governed, grassroots spaces. Ironically, Sicily is routinely blamed for migrant reception "failures" even as those working in the realm of migrant reception attribute problems within the reception system to Italy's shirking of responsibility.

3 The Reception Apparatus

Italy does not have a system of reception [*accoglienza*].
We have a system of nonreception [*non accoglienza*].

—Migrant reception volunteer and activist

A POLITICS OF IRRESPONSIBILITY

In June 2016, I attended a roundtable discussion on *ricerca e salvataggio* (search and rescue) operations at a Palermo-based community center overseen by the local Catholic parish. That year had been the deadliest on record for migrants crossing the central Mediterranean—IOM (2016) reported 4,699 deaths by the end of 2016—and community members were demanding a coordinated response. They pieced together the circumstances surrounding these deaths: termination of Operation Mare Nostrum, which intercepted over a hundred thousand migrants between February and October 2014; the unfounded accusations by far-right politicians that Mare Nostrum was using Italian taxpayer euros to finance a "taxi service" from Africa to Europe; revamped investment by the EU to apprehend human smugglers using its own naval force and its concomitant inattention to saving lives; rumors of a bilateral agreement with Libya to apprehend migrants at sea and return them to detention centers in Africa; and the increasingly necessary role of nongovernmental and humanitarian organizations such as Mediterranea Saving Humans and Sea-Watch in search and rescue operations at sea.[1] Surrounding those of us in the auditorium were several murals depicting scenes from the Bible. My eyes locked on one mural of a passenger boat in distress, riding turbulent waters.

The trope of a biblical exodus has been invoked numerous times in Italian as well as European media and politics both to describe the specter of increased migrant arrivals in the central Mediterranean and to position state actors and institutions as powerless against a phenomenon only comparable to divine intervention. As the anthropologists Seth Holmes and Heide Castañeda (2016, 12, 13) observe, such media and political representations index a "struggle over meaning, legitimization, and power" and also shape "how various actors respond to [migrants]."[2] In the case of Italy, framing recent migration through the central Mediterranean as an exceptional event, one whose analogue dwells in divine scripture, corresponds to a politics of irresponsibility that has characterized state-sponsored interventions and has necessitated a willingness to act among ordinary citizens and noncitizens living on the front lines of migration.

This chapter delineates Italy's migrant reception apparatus, or alternatively, its system of (non)reception as framed by some activists. This apparatus includes search and rescue operations, disembarkations (*sbarchi*), transfer to and housing at reception centers, release from centers, and health and social services administered to migrants. First, I examine the realm of institutional and state-sponsored reception, primarily disembarkations and initial centers of reception where the mobility of migrants is restrained. These sites of state-sponsored *accoglienza* (migrant reception but the word that most Italians use for these activities, translated roughly as "hospitality") are increasingly being privatized and overseen by nongovernmental actors. Second, I discuss forms of "street-level *accoglienza*" enacted by social workers, volunteers, healthcare professionals, and other service providers in daily, routine contact with migrants. I have adapted this concept from Michael Lipsky's (2010) "street-level bureaucrats," referring to the frontline actors who implement, enforce, and "make" policy through everyday discretionary behaviors constrained by broader political-economic structures (see also Magaña 2003). Similar to street-level bureaucrats as being "gatekeepers" of vital forms of social, political, and material capital, those enacting and performing street-level *accoglienza* are complex social beings with particular beliefs, values, attitudes, and experiences (Portillo 2010, 2011; Schneider and Ingram 1993). Their actions potentially obstruct or facilitate the integration and life chances of migrants (Alpes and Spire 2014; Carney, Menjívar, and Soto Bermant n.d.; Levin 2009). Nonetheless, their commitment to and versatility in responding to the needs of Italy's migrant population demonstrate a devolution of care within the reception apparatus from state institutions to the street level.

Lo sbarco: *Visibility and Invisibility in the Reception Apparatus*

FIELD NOTES, MAY 9, 2017. A friend with whom I've been discussing the possibility of volunteering at disembarkations texts me this morning to say that a *sbarco* is under way at the port of Palermo. I quickly get dressed, grab a hat and my notebook, and begin the walk from the apartment I've been renting with my husband and two-year-old daughter in the historic district of Palermo to the waterfront, a distance of a few kilometers. Arriving at the waterfront area some thirty minutes later, I navigate past several large cruise ships, lines of tour buses, and bustling souvenir shops as my eyes scan the area for the pier number I've been given. The cavalcade of police and carabinieri (military police) vehicles in the distance seems like an obvious indication. I walk over to one of the carabinieri and explain that I'm there to volunteer at the *sbarco*. He gives my pregnant body a disapproving look and strongly advises me to leave. After I politely dismiss his concern and promise to take proper precautions, he reluctantly gestures with his hand to the reception area. I then proceed to find my friend at the volunteer station that is stocked with hundreds of individually bagged meal kits containing two bottles of water, marmalade and baguette sandwiches, and apples. We are told to begin distributing these items as soon as those who were rescued at sea are allowed to disembark.

Frontex (European Border and Coast Guard Agency) officials arrive to conduct an initial assessment of some six hundred passengers on board the British naval ship docked before us. Meanwhile, the passengers wait anxiously on the ship's back deck, appearing mesmerized by the impromptu village of white tents and reception personnel, some of whom are capturing photos and video on their smart phones. Many of the *sbarco* health inspection personnel wear hospital scrubs, rubber gloves, and face masks.

Once the inspection has concluded some two hours later, officials escort two pregnant women off the boat in wheelchairs. Then, about every hour for the next several hours, groups of thirty to fifty individuals are allowed to disembark. Most of the disembarking passengers are young men or adolescents; they proceed barefoot down the ramp to the dock, some of them wearing matching dark blue coveralls borrowed from the naval ship's surplus. They are directed to tables for shoes (imitation Crocs), clothes, and food and then to tents erected by UNHCR, Save the Children, and IOM, where they encounter dozens of interpreters and cultural mediators. The Red Cross administers first aid and assists local health authorities with rapid health checks before sending disembarking migrants to be interviewed by government officials. I recalled the director of Italy's National Institute of Health, Migration, and Poverty (NIHMP) explaining during my 2014 visit to his headquarters in Rome that first responders focused on addressing thirst, hunger, the need for rest, and acute health issues incurred during the journey at sea such as fractures, fever, vomiting, and disorientation.

I help distribute bags of water and food while overhearing representatives from Save the Children conduct orientations with unaccompanied minors. Journalists with cameramen in tow document the scene as they are also told to keep away from these youth. The sun beats down on all of us, with only an occasional reprieve offered by the light breeze and sparse cloud cover. There is a strong stench of seawater and sweat.

After about four hours, only one-third of the passengers have disembarked. Complaining that these events move too slowly, reception volunteers tell me that *sbarco* procedures have improved to be more comprehensive and efficient but have also been complicated and thus prolonged by stricter regulations. The *sbarco* does not conclude until several hours later, well past dark. New arrivals are led to a tent behind the disembarkation area where they will sleep on large pieces of cardboard for the night, until they are transported to a reception center the next day. They are among the luckier ones.

Tonight's Italian newscast features the tragic story of two boats colliding and capsizing as they were transporting migrants along the central Mediterranean route. It is estimated that more than two hundred people drowned, most of them adolescents and children.

Figure 4. Sbarco at the port of Palermo in May 2017. Photo by author.

 . . .

In the late spring and summer months of 2017, close to 120,000 migrants disembarked on Italian shores. Sicilian ports were a regular site of these disembarkations; Palermo's port alone was the site of multiple migrant disembarkations each month (figure 4). As I learned through my interest in volunteering at a *sbarco*, Italy's Guardia Costiera (Coast Guard) considered the size and location of boats in making swift decisions about where to direct ships, thereby affording minimal time to local communities to prepare for such events.[3] Once a port had been assigned, the coast guard usually sent alerts, often by text message, days—sometimes only hours— in advance to local police, municipalities, health authorities, and international organizations such as IOM and Save the Children, which proceeded to coordinate reception activities.

Social workers and volunteers often alluded to the *flussi misti* (mixed flows) in explaining the legal and bureaucratic procedures that prolonged the disembarkation process. "Flussi misti" refers to the heterogeneity among arriving migrants as reflected in nationalities declared at landings. In 2014, for instance, these included Eritrean (27 percent), Nigerian (13 percent), Somali (8 percent), Sudanese (6 percent), Syrian (5 percent), Gambian (5 percent), Bangladeshi (4 percent), Malian (4 percent), Ghanian (3 percent), Senegalese (3 percent), and "other" (22 percent) (MOI 2015). Local authorities collected the personal, identifying information of disembarking migrants as well as fingerprints during the *verbale* (intake report) in part to determine one's eligibility for asylum or humanitarian protection. In return, migrants received an *attestato* (certificate) that served as a form of identification with details listing a person's country of origin, date of birth, date of arrival, and reasons for migrating.

Workers and volunteers in Italy's reception apparatus acknowledged that migrants often viewed Italy as a "transit country," which discouraged them from registering with Italian authorities. One volunteer guessed that "50 percent of migrants, maybe more, are only here to pass through, maybe to learn a little Italian. They want to go north, because in Sicily there's nothing. No work. They're right." A health worker added:

> What does the Dublin [Convention] say? If you enter the EU, you must be identified and request status in the first country you entered. It so happens that Italy is that first country, but nobody wants to stay in Italy. So, for years now, Italian institutions have done basically nothing, and migrants journey north on trains, on small buses, and head to Sweden, France, Germany, Norway. Places where they have relatives or other connections.

For reasons related to the Dublin Convention, as noted by this health worker, applying for asylum or any form of legal status in Italy could compromise one's aspirations to pursue economic prospects or to connect with kin or social networks in other EU destinations. Acutely aware of Italy's high rejection rate, reception workers and volunteers displayed some ambivalence about whether or not migrants should initiate the asylum process in Italy. As of 2017, Italy rejected nearly 60 percent of asylum applications, with some applicants waiting up to two years for a final determination (EUROSTAT 2016). Alessio D'Angelo (2019, 2215) notes that "the vast majority of those entering Italy by sea—mostly black African young men—are seen as coming from 'safe' countries and thus, by definition economic migrants." He cites recognition rates by nationality, based on 2016 data from EUROSTAT: "Amongst Nigerians, the recognition rate was only 24%, and 34% for citizens of Guinea and Gambia, 32% for Mali and 29% for Senegal" (2215). The economists Timothy J. Hatton and Jeffrey G. Williamson (2006, 13) rightly indicate that those who are arriving often "prefer instead to remain underground than to risk rejection and removal.... [L]ow wages and uncertain employment in the EU are better than the conditions they would face in their country of origin."[4]

These variations in the desired visibility and invisibility of migrants were pronounced during the *sbarco* and continued to intensify in other realms of Italy's reception apparatus. Giordano (2018) explains that "the *sbarco* simultaneously enables forms of legal identification that can lead to papers and access to rights, and forms of escape into alternative undocumented forms of life." These "alternative undocumented forms of life" in the Italian context resonate with what João Biehl ([2005] 2013, 4) names zones of social abandonment wherein "authorities and institutions direct the unwanted to the zones, where these individuals are sure to become unknowables, with no human rights and with no one accountable for their condition." From the moment that migrants disembarked on the shores of Italy, anxieties seeped in about how much support they would receive, what form(s) that support would take, and the duration of support. Noting Italy's "closed ports" policy that was enforced under Salvini in 2018, my interlocutors emphasized the symbolism of the *sbarco* event, in both its relative presence and its absence, revealing a broader politics of irresponsibility that animated wavering commitments by Italy and other EU governments to human welfare, human rights, and asylum accords.[5]

"Rescued," Then "Abandoned": The Problems with Reception Centers

> Italy saves us then abandons us.... Italy certainly deserves
> credit for its search-and-rescue operations at sea with its
> navy and coast guard. What happens afterwards is the
> problem.
> —ANSAmed, "Immigration: 'Italy Saves Us Then Abandons Us'
>   Activist Says"

While being interviewed in 2014, Tareke Brhane, who is originally from Eritrea and who also led the October 3 committee that formed in the aftermath of one of the deadliest shipwrecks in recent history in the central Mediterranean, reflected on more than a decade of organizing to improve the rights of migrants in Italy. At the time, Italy was still coordinating search and rescue operations; less than one year later, humanitarian organizations would be tending to the void left behind by the termination of Operation Mare Nostrum. Brhane commended these previous efforts by the Italian government, primarily its military, but emphasized that its obligations did not stop with search and rescue and disembarkations: the state should be doing more to receive migrants, uphold their rights, and facilitate a path to integration.

Italian law stipulates that migrants arriving by sea be transferred to centers of reception or detention once they have been intercepted and identified (IOM 2013). Because Italy's new government, elected in 2018, had vowed to overhaul its network of reception centers, I discuss the network here as it was known during the time of my fieldwork: first aid reception centers (Centri di primo soccorso ed accoglienza [CSPAs]), reception centers (Centri di accoglienza [CDAs]), reception centers for asylum seekers (Centri di accoglienza per richiedenti asilo [CARAs]), identification and expulsion centers (Centri di identificazione ed espulsione [CIEs]), and centers for longer-term residence for asylum seekers and refugees (Sistema di protezione per richiedenti asilo e rifugiati [SPRAR]) (IOM 2013). The suite of center designations ostensibly corresponded to the different functions of each, but as D'Angelo (2019, 2217) notes, "Over the years, regional variations, short-term changes of function, closures and reopenings have been the norm, rather than the exception" (see also Vassallo Paleologo 2012). CSPAs, most recently rebranded as "hotspots," were charged with swiftly identifying, registering, and fingerprinting migrants and, when necessary, administering medical care. CDAs and CARAs provided longer stays to applicants for international protection and asylum. CIEs detained individuals who had been issued deportation orders and were awaiting deportation. SPRARs permitted extended stays to asylum seekers and refugees. In 2015, the Ministry of Interior tallied 3,090 temporary reception centers (CSPAs and CDAs), 13 CARAs, 7 CIEs, and 430 SPRAR projects throughout Italy, altogether accounting for about a hundred thousand migrants.[6]

A constant ebb and flow of migrant arrivals, combined with the opening or closure of reception facilities, posed a number of practical challenges for center operations. Center personnel and management struggled to uphold the reception system according to its official configuration, which shifted for reasons beyond their control. One explanation they provided related to changes in immigration policies that affected the number of migrants arriving and, relatedly, the capacity of centers. For example, the director of one youth reception center in Palermo explained that they were "at capacity and overflowing in 2017," while occupancy dropped by 40 percent in 2018 because of Italy's "closed ports" policy. This inconsistency in vacancies often translated into longer stays in centers and contributed to a lack of uniformity in reception procedures across all of Italy (IOM 2013; Kersch and Mishtal 2016), as I also observed through my conversations with center directors and personnel. Extended stays were often permitted, especially for minors or residents who had no other reasonable alternative for housing. I learned that instead of filtering migrants by age or asylum status, among other important factors, placements in centers were often arbitrary and reception standards were difficult to enforce.

Social workers and migrants themselves informed me of numerous failures to comply with government-issued standards because of inadequate institutional support and increased privatization of the system.[7] The director of Italy's asylum protection agency, Daniela Di Capua, acknowledged this fact: "First assistance to new migrants is still lacking. It's true that we're unprepared, but we're unprepared because there is no planning. Italy keeps trying to keep up with an emergency that has become ordinary" (Povoledo 2014). Even Italy's own Ministry of Interior admitted:

> Undoubtedly there have been various problems [with reception] in our country, problems related to the often-imperfect functioning of an extraordinarily complex and intricate mechanism presided over by the Ministry [of Interior], but also involving the local authorities, the communities in the reception areas, with their own characteristics and problems, and dozens and dozens of different migrant communities, also having their own specific characteristics and problems. (MOI 2015, 102)

A particularly egregious example that my interlocutors frequently alluded to was the CARA in the Sicilian town of Mineo that had been collecting millions of euros annually from the Italian government and providing substandard reception conditions while hosting four thousand residents, double its official capacity (Tondo 2016).[8]

Although I was unable to access any of Sicily's "hotspots," the few reception centers I was able to access I observed functioning essentially as nonprofits or private charities. They could not reasonably depend on the government to provide financial reimbursements in a timely manner. More than one center director lamented having to wait several months before government reimbursements arrived. The director of a Palermo-based CDA noted that it was having "to get creative with fund-raising" and solicit local donations. In theory, centers were expected to provide housing, food, clothing, pocket money, phone cards, and cigarettes, as well as medical, legal, social, and psychological support. Most current and former residents I spoke with confirmed being fed and provided with a decent place to sleep, but almost all swore that they had never or seldom received pocket money and had experienced varying degrees of access to some of these other resources. While residents frequently blamed center management or staff for withholding resources, they seemed unaware that chronic delays in government reimbursements were often to blame.

Increasing privatization of reception centers yielded a number of challenges to guaranteeing the rights of residents. Anthropologists have documented the lack of independent oversight in centers that are housing or detaining migrants, belonging to the now-globalized "network of detention structures" (Fassin 2011; see also De Genova and Peutz 2010), and, relatedly, lack of knowledge and resources among residents about their rights and the mechanisms for reporting grievances. As Maurizio Albahari (2015, 47) noted from his fieldwork in Apulia, "No institutionalized mechanisms allowed migrants to denounce potential ill treatment by the management, staff, fellow detainees, or armed forces." In their study of a CSPA in Sicily, the anthropologists Adam Kersch and Joanna Mishtal reported:

> No migrant I spoke to was aware of his or her legal situation while in [the center]. Migrants were usually told on the day of their transfer that they would be moved to another camp, but had no prior warning, making it difficult to inform loved ones, make preparations, or notify the physician that a particular refugee was to be transferred. Additionally, the migrants I spoke to who had filed a claim for asylum did not receive any formal documentation or receipts that could show that their claim was in fact pending. (2016, 103–4)

Social workers I interviewed largely agreed that more needed to be done to educate migrants about their rights and provide them with legal counsel. However, even when residents were informed of their rights and the services available to them at reception centers, often printed in large font and displayed in a central location, they were still unclear about procedures for reporting infractions. Similar to the system of privatized immigrant detention in the United States and elsewhere, I found that reception center guidelines often registered as "voluntary" and were rarely accompanied by mechanisms for enforcement (Carney 2013; De Genova and Peutz 2010).

Center management I spoke with frequently lamented lacking the resources to support on-site staff that included social workers, attorneys, and mental health specialists—individuals whose expertise was essential to migrants attaining any modicum of stability once living outside of Italy's reception centers. This absence of on-site support was not helped by the physical isolation of many reception centers. Drawing on her study of CARAs in western Sicily, for instance, the anthropologist Barbara Pinelli (2015, 13) observed that most centers were located "at the margins of urban areas," thereby posing many practical barriers to residents trying to identify possible work opportunities and access basic social services. Albahari (2015, 122) suggests that placing these centers outside of urban areas allows authorities to "physically exclude detainees from citizens' critical eye, and from a potential web of legal, political, and social interventions."

The Italian Ministry of Interior (2015, 33) ascertained that the SPRAR system was "not just any model of 'hospitality'" but rather one that "involve[d] the orientation to creating autonomous post-reception processes ... [and included] a process facilitating emancipation and the reconstruction of a life plan for the persons in the country of arrival." The SPRAR system relied on the involvement of NGOs and regional authorities to volunteer the construction and management of facilities and programs. The Ministry of Interior framed this "voluntary" aspect of the SPRAR system as intentional, "so that the setting up of a centre [was] not experienced as an imposition" (32). Independently funded, SPRARs were expected to provide Italian-language instruction, healthcare, legal counseling, and education about asylum rights, with the assistance of trained volunteers and professionals.

Figure 5. Gardens at SPRAR Casa San Francesco. Photo by author.

In the summer of 2016, I had the opportunity to accompany others on a group tour of a SPRAR that had recently opened in Palermo's Ballarò neighborhood. Ebrahim, a nineteen-year-old asylum seeker from Gambia, who had arrived in Italy almost two years before and was currently residing at SPRAR Casa San Francesco, served as our guide. Housed within an old palazzo that had been recently restored, the center's first floor included a lounging space with a television, a kitchen area, also equipped with a television, and a site to drop off and pick up laundry. Residents shared bedrooms on the second and third floors of the building and sometimes ventured onto the third floor's sundeck where it was possible to appreciate panoramic views of the mountains and coastline surrounding Palermo. From the sun deck, Ebrahim gestured to the *orto* (vegetable garden) visible below, which he described as a space for "healing and enjoyment" among residents (figure 5).

During a previous trip to Sicily in 2014, Palermo did not have a SPRAR, a matter of serious concern as conveyed to me by several prominent nonprofit leaders. Subsequently, many rejoiced in the opening of Casa San Francesco; however, less than two years into its operation, there were already rumors of its impending closure. When I inquired about these rumors with local residents, they cited pushback in the surrounding neighborhood as well as some financial problems. In lieu of government funding or in some cases delayed reimbursements, many SPRARS, both in Sicily and elsewhere in Italy, were struggling to stay afloat during the time of my research, with personnel sometimes waiting months before receiving wages and directors paying resident stipends out of their own pockets (Casati 2017).

Notably, Sicily was often scapegoated in national policy circles and media coverage for "failures" in Italy's reception system, despite the ways that the Italian government had outsourced and devolved much of the responsibility for management of this system to private, nongovernmental actors. For instance, Sicily's reputation, "marked by shipwrecks, scandals concerning the management of reception centres and media outrages on the living conditions of migrants," came under increased scrutiny following the introduction of the hotspot approach (D'Angelo 2019, 2214). Implemented rather rapidly in Sicily, the hotspot approach yielded "intended and unintended consequences," including practices "that many deem illegal by both national and international standards" (2214). However, counter-critiques such as those argued by Kersch and Mishtal (2016, 105) call attention to the fact that "Sicily simply lacks the resources to provide mandated services for the ever-increasing numbers of arriving migrants. In the absence of a stronger political will to remedy this situation, both of these factors are likely to work synergistically in perpetuating a situation of resource scarcity for local refugees." Some of my informants expressed concern about and disdain for accusations of and investigations into possible corruption within reception centers, complaining that this incited more hostility toward migrants and reflected poorly on Sicilian people and institutions. A resident of Agrigento, for instance, recollected hearing about her local magistrate "starting to investigate some of the nongovernmental organizations [operating centers], some people within these organizations." "For example," she continued, "some volunteers with Médecins Sans Frontières were even being investigated because it was suspected that they were enabling migration and conspiring with smug-

Figure 6. Demonstrators protest the CIE system outside Ponte Galeria. Photo by author.

glers. These types of investigations, perhaps they have a glimmer of truth because there are certainly some corrupt people here, but they risk generating more hate toward migrants."

On February 15, 2014, I attended "Mai più Cie" (No More CIEs), a public demonstration that had been organized at CIE Ponte Galeria, one of the largest CIEs in Italy and located some 20 kilometers outside the center of Rome. Less than one month before, detainees at Ponte Galeria attracted global media attention to "la protesta delle bocche cucite," a hunger strike during which they used fishing wire to sew their mouths shut. The demonstration "No More CIEs" drew a crowd of nearly ten thousand, including activists, social workers, and students (figure 6). Displaying banners that proclaimed, "Close the center!" and "Open borders!," demonstrators marched toward the entrance of the CIE, only to be stopped some minutes later by an armed line of carabinieri. Sensing that further escalation was imminent, my friend who had accompanied me suggested that we head home. Rome's newspaper *La Repubblica* later reported that demonstrators had fled the scene after being assaulted with tear gas.

Most of the estimated eight thousand detainees being held annually at one of Italy's CIEs during the years of this project were individuals whose residence permits had expired or who had a criminal record and were awaiting deportation. The documentary *EU 013 The Last Frontier*, by the Italian filmmakers Alessio Genovese and Raffaella Cosentino, revealing living conditions inside these centers, was screened for Italian parliament members as well as at several CIEs in an effort to galvanize public and political support for dismantling the CIE network. Human rights advocates along with former detainees described CIEs as "jail-like confinement areas" that severely restricted the mobility of detainees. The narratives of former detainees convey "the emptiness of waiting, the void of months passing, the exasperation that sometimes erupts into violence, degenerates into depression and attempts at suicide, or sparks dramatic protest actions" (Borsati 2014). While technically separate from Italy's reception system, general disdain for CIEs served as an important site for political mobilization and strengthening alliances among citizens and noncitizens. As D'Angelo (2019, 2219) argues in discussing CIEs along with other aspects of the Italian reception system, "The boundaries between reception and 'accoglienza' (hospitality) on the one hand and detention and policing on the other are problematically blurred."

STREET-LEVEL ACCOGLIENZA

Where did you leave from?
Gambia.
Nigeria.
Eritrea.
Mali.
Sudan.
My parents were killed.
There were no jobs. I couldn't support my family.
We lost our crop one year after the next.

Did you come alone?

Yes.

My brothers came with me, but they drowned at sea.

How did you come?

We came through the desert, first to Libya. Then things got bad there and I had to leave.

We were robbed in the desert.

I was put in a prison in Libya. The guards tried to get money out of my family.

You know those guards sell migrants to be slaves?

Such details regularly surface in migrants' narratives of the conditions and journeys that preceded their arrival in Italy. While I never explicitly sought to excavate these details myself, heeding the anthropological wisdom that migrants' narratives should perhaps remain "impenetrable" (Giordano 2014, 35) because of their retraumatizing potential, I indeed witnessed countless exchanges in which migrants were asked to name the severe circumstances they were fleeing and the forms of violence and criminality that they endured along their migratory journeys. They alluded to negotiations with smugglers in crossing the Sahara and arranging their passage to Europe. They described encounters with swindlers and thieves. They expressed their doubts about the boats into which they were loaded and sent off to sea. They spoke of the fear and anxiety of drifting at sea, knowing that they were as likely to die as they were to survive. They complained of having nightmares of being stuck on the boat, of crippling thirst, and of watching the desperation of others around them. It was also in this context that migrants verbalized their experiences with problems in Italy's reception apparatus, from rescue at sea to release from a center. Despite being haunted by these experiences, migrants were implored to circulate these narratives as a form of currency in their petitions for legal status and in soliciting the sympathy of institutional and street-level actors who may have connected them with housing, food, work, education, and healthcare.

Yet workers and volunteers within the realm of street-level *accoglienza* sought these narratives from migrants in part because they too were expected to reproduce them. In advocating for access to essential resources and the provision of care to migrants, they justified migrants' "deservingness" by narrating the innumerable forms of exploitation and violence that characterized their journeys across the Mediterranean: torture in one's home country; injuries committed by human smugglers in the desert; inhumane conditions at detention centers in Libya; trauma or death during sea crossings; confinement for weeks or months in crowded reception centers.

Scholars have drawn attention to the moral logics perpetuated by and through state institutions that frequently compel migrants or those laboring on their behalf to perform narratives of suffering and demonstrate migrants' "deservingness" (Fassin 2005; Ticktin 2011). By and large, these narrative scripts render migrants as "victims" who must be made legible to the humanitarian state (Cabot 2013; Fassin and Rechtman 2009; Giordano 2014; Ticktin 2011; Willen 2014). The following words from one small business owner revealed the ways that citizens and noncitizens in Sicily were intimately familiar with and negotiated the logics of deservingness as they applied to migrants.

> I can tell you with certainty that there are ethnic groups that integrate better with respect to other migrants because they have certain characteristics that are considered more favorable or desirable. . . . "Migrant" does not denote a homogenous group; they have very diverse origins, and so we could talk for hours about if they have more or less difficulty being accepted here. Certainly, the little Black baby with his pudgy face and streaming tears is always going to garner more sympathy and receive more help here than the Moroccan man who yells "Allah!"

These examples—the "little Black baby" and the "man who yells 'Allah!'"—attest to how migrant deservingness plots on a spectrum and translates into varying experiences and degrees of assistance, from community-based associations to health and social services. While workers and volunteers within the realm of street-level *accoglienza* attempt to push back against these logics, they are simultaneously constrained in the range of services that they can provide and the forms of care that are allowed to materialize.

Community-Based Associations: "Helping to Build a New Life"

In 2014, outside of Rome's Centro Astalli, I spoke with several migrants as they stood in line waiting for a meal.[9] Simba, nineteen years old and originally from Mali, was particularly eager to share his story. He had said farewell to his parents and siblings more than one year earlier, fleeing civil war and crossing by boat from Libya after paying €1,300 to a smuggler. He had been intercepted at sea, transported to Lampedusa, and transferred to a reception center in Catania, where he remained for eleven months. When I met him, he had been in Rome for about two weeks. He explained that he was staying at a friend's apartment but that he didn't know where he would go next. Since his quest to find work had been thus far unsuccessful, he had been coming to Centro Astalli every day for food. A man toward the end of the line who had been listening in on our conversation shouted, "Italy gives us papers, health insurance cards, but then does nothing more for us."

After speaking with Simba, I walked toward the end of the line to hear more from the man who had called out to us. Daniel introduced himself by showing his health insurance card, which noted his birthplace as Ghana and his age as thirty-five. He and his friends described how they had been camping out at Roma Termini, the central train station, for several weeks, some of them for over a year, despite there being no access to toilets or bathing facilities on site. Daniel vowed that he was "praying every day" that things would change. More migrants stepped into line until the center closed for the day. With nowhere else to go, most of these men would be returning to makeshift encampments at Rome's central train station for a brief rest before returning to Centro Astalli the following day. Until something better came along, their lives were revolving around the limited resources that this center could provide.

Over the course of my fieldwork, I was increasingly disheartened to find that outside of reception centers, migrants struggled to find work or housing, to acquire food; most had yet to realize their ambitions of sending money to family. Moreover, they were disillusioned by the level of hostility toward im/migrants in Italy. Considering that many migrants arriving in Italy through the central Mediterranean had incurred an enormous debt to human smugglers, they were extremely anxious about being able to repay this debt while also scraping together the resources to build a new life for themselves in a foreign setting.

Nova and her husband, Tareq, ages twenty-five and thirty-nine, respectively, had been living in Palermo for merely two months after fleeing their home in Libya. Born to an Italian mother, Nova enjoyed the privileges of dual Italian and Libyan citizenship. She had two older siblings already living in Italy, but her parents had stayed behind. Unlike other migrants arriving from Libya, Nova did not need a human smuggler to transport her across the Mediterranean; she and Tareq simply booked a flight. Although it seemed that Nova had adjusted to life in Palermo rather quickly, having spent time in Italy throughout her childhood and being fluent in the Italian language, Tareq found himself less at ease. Meeting the couple for coffee one morning near Palermo's Teatro Massimo, Tareq explained that he was struggling to learn the language and that this was a barrier to finding work. For the time being, they were surviving on the modest savings they had been able to accumulate in the few years that they had been married.

Nova and I met in May 2017 while she was volunteering at the reception desk at Palermo's Centro Astalli. She had been volunteering at the center four days per week, primarily assisting with the daily breakfast service and offering her skills as an interpreter for Arabic-speaking clients. Her competency as a native speaker of Italian meant that she could socialize easily with staff and volunteers, a trait that distinguished her from most of the migrants frequenting the center. Volunteers working the front desk were usually native to Sicily or had arrived from other EU countries through student exchange programs. Tareq accompanied her to the center most days to attend the highly popular Italian-language group classes offered in one of the center's classrooms. In my few encounters with Nova and Tareq, I sensed they shared a deep, mutual affection and respect for one another. Yet even happily married, they were clearly struggling to navigate the challenges of this new life.

Nova and Tareq were among the many thousands of both recently arrived and more established migrants utilizing services at Palermo's Centro Astalli. Founded in 2003 by a group of local *palermitani* in the neighborhood of Ballarò—"a cultural crossroads for centuries that now constitutes the ideal setting for *accoglienza*" (Centro Astalli's brochure, "Dove Siamo")—the center occupied a multistory building located on the edge of a piazza. It seemed that most migrants learned of the center through word of mouth, possibly because the center itself was rather nondescript from the outside and somewhat difficult to find in Ballarò's serpentine complex of narrow streets.

Bulletin boards advertising housing (shelters or places for rent), jobs,

Figure 7. Donated clothing and a garden art installation in
Centro Astalli's courtyard. Photo by author.

items for sale, upcoming local events, soccer sign-ups for youth, and a
schedule of the center's activities greeted visitors at the entrance. Visitors
could come to do laundry, take showers, or attend language lessons and
computer literacy courses in one of its classrooms. An enclosed courtyard
on the backside of the building invited visitors to engage in art and garden-
ing activities and to donate or collect clothing (figure 7). Every morning,
the reception area bustled with the energy of dozens of men, women, and
young children seeking to use the showers, obtain assistance with their
legal paperwork, or seek advice on a range of housing, healthcare, and

employment issues. A crowd often formed outside the center's entrance as individuals waited for their name or number to be called by volunteers in the reception area. Crowds also formed in the reception area in anticipation of meal services, though visitors were discouraged from lingering in the dining area to allow for feeding as many people as possible.

On each of my visits to Centro Astalli, I marveled at the warmth exhibited by staff and volunteers. Migrants I met in Palermo who had been to the center generally described an overall positive social environment. In a local magazine feature about the center, some migrants who had been interviewed were quoted as lauding Centro Astalli for playing a pivotal role in "finding [their] own autonomy." One woman elaborated, "To still be [in Palermo] after so many years signifies for [us] that [our] positive experiences have outweighed the negative ones [because of places like Centro Astalli]." A staff member added, "[We do this work] because there are still so many, too many people in chronic poverty, who suffer from marginalization and social exclusion, who find themselves in conditions of vulnerability, for whom we should be doing more, not just providing rescue at sea, but making efforts toward integration."

While Palermo's Centro Astalli had initially opened as an Italian-language school, the suite of services available on site had significantly expanded in the fifteen years of its operations. A brochure foregrounded the center's commitment to "the individual with their expectations, needs, crises, and above all, their hopes, helping them to build a new life." During the time of my research, Centro Astalli offered various forms of support corresponding to *prima accoglienza* (primary reception): daily meals prepared on site, bathing facilities, laundry facilities, food assistance, clothing, medicine, medical care, and medical consultations. In addition, Centro Astalli delivered services corresponding to *seconda accoglienza* (secondary reception) that focused on enhancing practical skills and autonomy. Examples of *seconda accoglienza* were vocational training and preparation for the labor market, orientation to the Italian legal system, computer literacy, linguistic literacy, after-school care for children, driver's education, and cooking classes. The center's seventy or so volunteers, many of whom were migrants themselves, were instrumental in helping coordinate *seconda accoglienza* activities. Center staff managed volunteers and specialized in *l'ascolto* (literally, "listening"), which allowed them to respond to the particular circumstances and needs of individuals.

In May 2017, I accompanied a social worker to observe his interactions with visitors over several days at the *centro di ascolto* operated by the Agrigento chapter of Caritas. Nico had been conducting *ascolto* activities for several years, consulting migrants on matters ranging from "bureaucratic, judicial, and legal matters to housing and employment mediation." He visited with about eight to ten clients each day that the *centro* was open, answering questions about applying for residence permits and finding a place to sleep, and helped demystify the process of accessing the health system, among other services. He met privately with clients in the order that they arrived, entering some details in an electronic records system about each individual and the purpose of their visit. A Nigerian woman visited, conveying her frustration that her attorney ostensibly failed to make progress with her application for a residence permit. Nico sympathized with her, saying, "You feel like an object. I understand you.... Maybe your vision for the future is different from their plan for you." She could not recall the name of her attorney, but Nico promised to follow up with this person about her case. A young French-speaking African man visited upon having received a frantic phone call from Nico urging him to come to the center. Nico needed to inform him that he had been kicked out of a shelter because he violated its rules by allowing an unauthorized guest to enter with him. Since the young man spoke very limited Italian, Nico primarily communicated using Google Translate; a French-speaking, computer-generated voice relayed how the situation was beyond Nico's control. Others came in seeking residence at a reception center, or they asked Nico to broker difficult conversations or misunderstandings with landlords, employers, doctors, and lawyers.

From Nico's understanding, Italian authorities consistently failed to share essential information during disembarkation and at centers for initial reception. "Recently arrived migrants are often dropped off and abandoned at train stations or in the middle of nowhere with no money or instructions of what to do next or where to go for help," he said. Among some of the more obvious consequences, he noted, migrants maintained "high levels of distrust toward institutions," even organizations like his own that "existed for the purpose of assisting migrants." This distrust, he surmised, ultimately deterred many migrants from interacting with institutions.

"Convivenza": Living Together in the Context of a Family

Beginning in October 2015, Nico was also serving as the coordinator for Yes We Host, a migrant housing program inspired by the pope's call that same year to host "a refugee in every parish." Families with a spare room or detached unit could elect to engage in a form of *convivenza*, or living together, with migrants who needed housing. As a gesture of its gratitude, Caritas Agrigento provided a very modest reimbursement (about €250 per month but only if a household presented receipts showing an increase in expenses) to offset any costs incurred by families for utilities, water, clothes, and food.

Nico explained that while families were the "fulcrum" of the initiative, churches also served a key function in mediating this "accoglienza famigliare" (familial reception) by acclimating both families and migrants to conviviality and nurturing a sense of familial connection among all who participated. He elaborated: "A fundamental approach in this work is that of the involvement of the local church: families who belong to a church benefit from some education about what comprises familial reception." In recounting the history of the initiative, Nico extolled the more personal and "diffused" form of hospitality that characterized familial *accoglienza* and distinguished it from social relations within reception centers: "[Yes We Host] emerged with the objective of giving hospitality inside a family, in a familial context, and exposing migrants to something different from their experiences in Italy's reception system." Active participation by families and migrants was expected because both groups were considered "target audiences": migrants were provided an alternative to "institutional circuits" of reception, and families and ecclesial communities were primed to welcome individuals from "different backgrounds and cultures" (program website). Moreover, Caritas Agrigento asserted that the family should play a central role in strengthening the autonomy of migrants and reducing their reliance on institutional and charitable forms of support (Caritas Agrigento 2015). In a video that Nico shared about the project and its participants, families fondly recalled exchanges with and learning from migrants about certain customs, music, and foods from their countries of origin.

Yet this family-based form of reception was not devoid of challenges. Aside from overcoming the "hurdle of accepting migrants into one's own home," Nico cited issues among both current and prospective participants concerning objectives of the initiative and the amount of work required.

> Problems have to do with the size of the house, the presence of children in families, young men being placed in a home where the wife was sometimes alone, and the age or maturity of migrants.... We heard from many interested individuals who said they would be willing to offer space for discounted rent in their homes, but this is something different. This isn't *accoglienza* within a family.... We wanted to create a vehicle for integration among participants.

He alluded to families that had imagined a less demanding role: "Our approach is based on constant monitoring by phone, with visits, formal meetings. To participate and find the time is difficult for many families." Nico also related how migrants had verbalized their own struggles with participation in the initiative.

> In the reception center someone probably has a place to sleep, eat; they provide the basics and don't ask for anything in return, but there aren't the benefits of living with a family. But the benefits come with challenges, because living with a family means forming a relationship based on reciprocity: "I'm available to do something for you, so you're then available to help me. I'm here for you to get to know me and my story, who I am."

Yet some participants showed resistance to engaging in relations of reciprocity as articulated by Nico. In its first year, the program arranged housing placements for eight individuals from Ghana, Mali, Gambia, Côte d'Ivoire, and Nigeria with four Sicilian families. Midway through its first year, two families withdrew. Without delving into specifics, Nico alluded to the general discomfort experienced by both families and migrants in acclimating to this type of living arrangement.

Nico assured me that Caritas Agrigento did not exclude anyone from participating in the program. Although unofficially they favored "the inclusion of refugees and persons seeking international protection," all were eligible to apply. Nonetheless, they still adhered to specific procedures for determining placements with families.

> We required interviews with migrants who were interested. As a prerequisite, these individuals must have already been in contact with us, perhaps through an Italian-language course or other services that we offer. Or if we didn't already know them, we tried to find ways to get to know them better prior to an interview for the project. We then evaluated the extent to which they were willing to participate, where they were hoping to migrate or resettle ultimately, how open they were to developing a relationship with a family, health status—if there were health reasons that would complicate their being able to live with a family. This was only for the first interview. We had a second round of interviews, but many could not come due to scheduling conflicts with school, work, and other reasons, so they told us, "I don't think this program is for me." I also noticed there was less interest among people in their mid-twenties and older because they desired more privacy [than what they suspected would be granted through familial reception].

As I came to learn from friends in Sicily, these types of housing initiatives were also becoming popular outside of Agrigento. For instance, a Palermo-based organization was matching households with a spare room that were interested in "an intercultural exchange" with migrants in need of housing. In one local magazine's story, "Doors (and Hearts) Open for Migrants: We Who Receive Them in Our Homes," participants revealed the various reasons that they were motivated to engage in this type of *accoglienza*, described by one volunteer as a form of "active citizenship" (*cittadinanza attiva*). There were parents who had seen their adult children move away from Sicily and found themselves with an empty nest. One host family elaborated, "Politics today are looking to divide people rather than to unite them. Just because this is happening in politics doesn't mean that we have to make the same mistake." Migrants who had benefited from this form of *convivenza* alluded to how families had helped them work, study, or discover a sense of belonging by encouraging them to feel that they were among (adoptive) kin. One young man said that *convivenza* had imparted to him feelings of "serenity and tranquility" that were helping him focus better in school.

Health Providers: Caring for Those in a "Fragile Social Position"

Ale was a "transcultural mediator" based in Palermo whose office I visited in 2014. An immigrant from Mauritius, she had been living in Italy for more than thirty years. She was fluent in Italian, English, and French and had received formal training in Rome at the National Institute of Health, Migration, and Poverty. As a transcultural mediator, Ale primarily assisted migrants with utilizing the Italian health system. Accompanying some fifty patients weekly to medical examinations, she was in exceedingly high demand.

The day that I made my first visit to meet Ale, she was quite busy attending to clients who were seeking mediation and interpretation services. As I waited outside Ale's office for an interview, I observed that many clients arrived for their scheduled appointments while nearly as many arrived without appointments. Noting how inundated she was with requests for her time, I regretted imposing myself on her busy schedule with my request for an interview. During the hour or so that I waited in Ale's reception area, she emerged several times, appearing increasingly weary and irritated with clients. At one point, I overheard her chastising an elderly client for coming in without an appointment and another for failing to complete essential paperwork. When we did finally convene privately in her office, she assured me that this was a normal day. She then proceeded to articulate the multifaceted nature of her job, which included accompanying women to medical appointments, assisting clients with accessing healthcare, finding housing (for clients requiring round-the-clock care), and disputing medical claims. While on first impression, Ale may have seemed insensitive to the circumstances of her clients, she was fulfilling all the responsibilities of medical interpreter, mediator, and social worker, and then some. Despite the high volume of migrants seeking Ale's assistance, funding for her position had been tenuous, and the clinic where she conducted the bulk of her mediation relied primarily on volunteer physicians.

Yet, as I came to learn quickly, people like Ale were indispensable to the success of migrants in accessing the healthcare that many of them so desperately needed. Even some of the migrants I met who had a *permesso di soggiorno* (residence permit) and valid health card faced myriad barriers to accessing the Italian health system, despite technically having full access to it (Carney 2017; for similar examples outside of Italy and in Europe, see also Castañeda 2012; Larchanche 2012; Sargent and Kotobi 2017). These barriers most often consisted of misunderstandings about how to navigate the healthcare system as well as language barriers. Practitioners often relied on interpretation services by phone to navigate language barriers, but as one social worker underscored, this method was "very precarious" for the reasons that the service was very impersonal and health providers could not always connect with an interpreter.

In May 2017, I visited a government-funded health center for migrants in Palermo that specialized in both social and health assistance, including general medicine (*medicina generale*), gynecology, and pediatrics, as well as prevention programs such as diabetes classes. Dozens of patients and clients visited the center daily to consult with its full-time staff of two physicians, two pediatricians, a nurse, and a social worker. The health center also relied on a number of part-time staff and volunteers consisting of diabetes specialists, gynecologists, social workers in training, teachers, and high school students. To accommodate the wide linguistic diversity of patients, staff members were versed in English, Arabic, French, Spanish, and Bangla, as reflected in its brochure (figure 8). The brochure stated that the health center aimed to "Promote the health of all foreigners living in Palermo; Ensure access to health services that aligns with the right to health of immigrants; Work in an integrated network with public entities, volunteers, and nonprofit organizations; Provide support and information to staff and visitors on the themes of health and health services for immigrants; Participate actively in regional, national, and international projects to promote immigrant health."

During one of my visits to the health center, I met with a social worker, Elena, whom I had met a few years earlier. Hundreds of photos and cards from past and current clients adorned the walls of Elena's office; she had no trouble recalling the backstory of each memento while we shared a carafe of coffee and a platter of local pastries that she had ordered, a gesture she proclaimed was an expression of her "ospitalità siciliana" (Sicilian hospitality). Reflecting on the current political and economic circumstances that were making life increasingly difficult for *siciliani*, Elena alluded to the more specific consequences for migrant health and psychosocial well-being in this context. She contended that poverty and

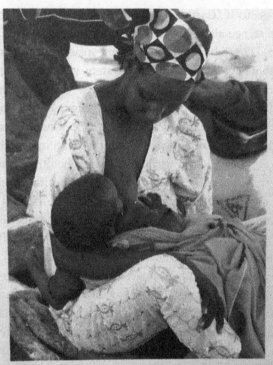

Health centers for foreign citizens
Centres de santé pour les citoyens
étrangers
Centros de salud por los ciudadanos
extranjeros
Centrele de sănătate pentru cetăţenii
străini

المراكز الصحية للمواطنين الأجانب

□ □ □ □ □ □
வெளிநாட்டினருக்கான சுகாதார
மையங்கள்

Figure 8. Informational brochure for a government-funded health center.
Photo by author.

poor health status among migrants in Palermo, and Sicily more broadly, traced to state failures to establish a more streamlined, long-term system of migrant reception and integration.

> I should tell you that we don't have many guarantees because we are in an economic situation that is not good, we are in recession. . . . In reality what has happened is that [migrants] get embroiled in a system for years during which they are without documents. They are then excluded from the system of protection, they are further marginalized. For migrants who have been here for years, we have completely ruined them, because *we* are in decline. We don't have work to offer them, we don't have a house to give them. . . . So they end up in the streets having to ask for charity.

Other migrant health practitioners I interviewed in Sicily concurred with Elena's assessment of health decline as a consequence of the broader marginalization of the foreign-born population, especially *irregolari*, those migrants who had been in Italy "for years without documents."

Although there is ample evidence of how immigration status, whether documented or undocumented, can have a significant impact on the health outcomes of immigrants (Willen 2019; Willen et al. 2011), the particular "illegitimacy" and moral depravity ascribed to those who are undocumented propels the notion that immigrants are "undeserving" and further restricts their access to and use of healthcare services (Larchanche 2012). Lacking a health card, *irregolari* were usually forced to pay some portion out of pocket for health services. As explained to me by a social worker based in Agrigento:

> *Irregolari* are not always recognized in Italy as having a "right to health," and thus their employers will not honor time off for health reasons. These migrants only use health services in the case of emergencies, but then they must pay out of pocket and continue working [or risk losing their jobs and wages]. I recently dealt with the case of a man who hurt his knee on the job, but his employer expected him to continue working, even while injured. Any healthcare expenses he incurred himself.

The National Institute of Health, Migration and Poverty, headquartered in Rome, supports the expansion of clinics for "irregular" and undocumented migrants throughout Italy. In a meeting with one of the institute's directors in 2014, he explained that NIHMP had been managing nine "social medicine" projects focused on delivering free healthcare to "irregular" migrants: "We want to reduce emergency room visits, as these are most common among migrants but also the most expensive both to them and the [welfare] system." NIHMP had developed several ongoing research and training opportunities, including trainings in migrant medicine, annual training manuals, and distance- and e-learning modules. The director emphasized that "migrants and asylum seekers, despite arriving basically healthy, develop health problems after living here for one to three years, because of unemployment, homelessness, stress, lack of healthcare, and violence." He worried that even among migrants who were entitled to fully access the health system because of their legal status, many individuals were misinformed about their rights and often deferred seeking care.

The director of a separate migrant clinic in Palermo discussed how they had to "pioneer a field of migrant medicine in the absence of the state doing anything about migrant health." Responding to the question, "What health problems are most common among immigrants?," he said, "The diseases we see most frequently are attributed to difficult living conditions and thus to a fragile social position." Echoing the concerns that had been shared with me by social workers, migrant health practitioners, and others who were delivering forms of basic assistance to recently arrived migrants, this physician surmised that health decline began in reception centers. His suspicions had been corroborated by several reports, including studies conducted by the International Organization for Migration and Médecins Sans Frontières. For instance, a report by IOM (2013, 10) complained, "Extended duration of the asylum application and the subsequent uncertainty for migrants' future coupled with limited opportunities for education, training, meaningful occupation, [and] overcrowding conditions are considered as major additional factors affecting migrants' wellbeing." In addition, IOM found significant variability in the implementation of health guidelines among reception centers: "The collection of health-related data is left up to the reception facilities, where ... standards and procedures differ greatly from one centre to another" (11). And volunteers with Médecins Sans Frontières underscored that "medical data from [our] projects for migrants in Italy and Greece show that the majority of the medical conditions are due to poor reception conditions" (MSF 2015).

Rather than subscribe to behavioral models of health and disease, this physician articulated an understanding of migrants' structural vulnerability as a core determinant of poor health (see also Metzl and Hansen 2014; Quesada, Hart, and Bourgois 2011). He added, "Simply put, we could say that the most important form of therapy is *accoglienza* in the truest sense of the word: attention to a transcultural approach based on listening and valuing the life of another, whatever history or culture to which they belong." This practitioner, similar to many others immersed in the realm of street-level *accoglienza*, was all too familiar with the symptoms of chronic anxiety, depression, insomnia, and suicidal ideation that afflicted migrants in the process of resettlement. These symptoms were palpable evidence of "what crossing borders does to the psyche and body" (Giordano 2014, 5).

THE COSTS OF DISPLACING RESPONSIBILITY

Scholars have speculated that Italy's entire immigration apparatus—from disorganized reception procedures to restrictive and punitive citizenship and immigration laws governing differential access to resources—is designed to deter migrants from staying in the country (Geddes 2008). As argued by Kersch and Mishtal:

> By-products of the Italian immigration system, such as sluggish healthcare access, extended legal liminality, and delays in entering Italian society at large, seem to encourage migrants to flee Italy to seek out new lives elsewhere. Consequently, temporality functions indirectly as a tool of the State, wherein migrants are discouraged from staying, and after leaving are no longer Italy's "problem." That is, as a result of the way that migration policies are enforced in Italy, many migrants feel their lives would be better in other parts of Europe. (2016, 118)

Continuing with this logic, this chapter has sought to demonstrate the ways that in "abandoning" Sicilian institutions and street-level actors to assume responsibility for *accoglienza*, the "question of migration" is perceived as less of an Italian problem. This may be categorized as another instance of the politics of deterrence as these have shaped migrant trajectories and governed bordering practices elsewhere (see De León 2015). It is via this dynamic that blame for problems with the reception apparatus—from quasi-illegal practices to human rights violations—is conveniently attributed to those outside of government.

With a politics of irresponsibility as the backdrop, street-level *accoglienza* in Sicily emerges as a site of care and contestation. Organizations and groups operating within the realm of street-level *accoglienza* are embedded in the broader political context of the nation-state and increasingly oversee a larger share of the social safety net as governments adopt austerity measures and move toward the privatization of services. These entities have been adversely affected by shrinking welfare states and constrained by an economically precarious environment, leaving them to compete with each other for limited sources of funding (Muehlebach 2012; Snyder 2011). Logics of deservingness permeate and constrain this sphere of assistance available to migrants; sites of street-level *accoglienza* may reproduce exclusion even as they foster inclusion.

Centro Astalli seeks to support migrants' efforts to regain autonomy. While undoubtedly addressing a major gap in the social safety net for migrants, the center struggled to overcome many of the challenges that often hindered similar organizations. With limited staff and funding, the center operated with irregular hours, and certain services such as bathing facilities were only available for short periods each day. Similarly, Caritas Agrigento was limited in its staff, with usually only one or two people working in its *centro di ascolto*, and it was open only at select times. And while those who conducted *l'ascolto* tried to the best of their ability to advocate on behalf of migrants and connect them with resources and services, sometimes listening was all they could offer. Nonetheless, on a weekly basis thousands of migrants residing in Palermo benefited from visiting Centro Astalli—and dozens from visiting Caritas Agrigento—attesting both to the widespread demand for the services provided by these organizations and to their resilience in operating with extremely limited resources.

The experiences of migrant health practitioners highlighted here epitomize the ways that those performing street-level *accoglienza* often find themselves grappling with the demands of unreasonable caseloads and inadequate institutional support. Whereas street-level workers were often instrumental in helping alleviate migrant suffering, they were not impervious to the emotional and psychosocial vulnerabilities that surfaced in the realm of *accoglienza*. In the book, *Tears of Salt*, the Lampedusan physician Pietro Bartolo explains how in receiving migrants—some dead, others alive—at the shores of his island and in his clinic, he increasingly depends on those in his community for moral support: "When despondency threatens to get the better of me, they give me the strength to keep going" (Bartolo and Tilotta 2018, 24). These labor conditions can take an emotional toll on health and social workers, hampering their ability to perform the emotional labors often mandated by their professions. Nonetheless, health practitioners strive to forge relationships through the process of reception and to undo the violence—structural in the form of barriers to healthcare access, epistemic in thwarting migrants' knowledge systems—that relegates many migrants to a chronic state of health decline.

Working against attempts to discipline, isolate, and shape the subjectivity of individuals who are put to social death, those performing street-level *accoglienza* openly reject the disciplinary state apparatus that continues to constrain the life chances of both citizens and noncitizens in Italy (Carney 2013, 2014). Although "island of hope" speaks to the sense of hope embodied by migrants arriving in Sicily, it also corresponds to the aspirations embodied and imparted by street-level actors who persist in administering care in this setting despite certain inevitable "failures," tensions, and risks. Migrants are not simply the passive beneficiaries of these caring practices, as exemplified in housing initiatives centered on *convivenza*. While many of my informants agreed that a more grassroots form of reception was necessary to redress the shortcomings of Italy's reception system, the former should not be a substitute for the latter; rather the two should be operating in tandem.

While this chapter has highlighted the repeated instances of state abandonment punctuating the migrant reception apparatus and characterizing reception practices across Italy, hereafter I focus strictly on Sicily, where the provision of *accoglienza* has often been accompanied by explicit acts of migrant solidarity. Such actions by ordinary citizens and noncitizens constitute an aspirational project that both articulates with and subverts broader political and economic arrangements.

4 Migrant Solidarity Work

> Palermo proves itself to be a solidarian [*solidale*] and
> multicultural city.... Over the last few years the city and its
> inhabitants have seen the extraordinary efforts of citizens
> participating in [migrant] reception at its port.... [These
> citizens] come together with passion and professionalism
> at every disembarkation to receive hundreds of migrants.
> Each disembarkation is a rediscovery of the authentic
> Palermo, wherein associations, public administration, and
> keepers of the peace cooperate to reconstruct, one dowel at
> a time, the deteriorated mosaic that has resulted from an
> economic, political, and social crisis without precedent....
> We are being constructive with others rather than working
> against one another.... [Palermo] is a city of solidarity.
>
> —Agnese Ciulla, Social Citizenship Adviser

RECONSTRUCTION IN THE "CITY OF SOLIDARITY"

In a 2016 guest editorial in a local magazine, Agnese Ciulla, a prominent
palermitana, underscored the urgency of reconstructing "the deteriorated
mosaic" in the "city of solidarity." She invoked recent *sbarchi* events to
speak more broadly to a process of social reconstruction in Sicily that had
been rendered necessary by the effects of austerity—"an economic, political, and social crisis without precedent." As a metaphor for the social body,
the mosaic included citizens and noncitizens. Migrants were depicted as
both catalysts for this process and active participants in "the rediscovery
of Palermo."

This chapter draws from ethnographic observations of and interviews with activists in "the city of solidarity" who, like Agnese, invoked a range of metaphors and discourses in describing the meanings and actions encompassed by their migrant solidarity work. Responding to Annemarie Mol and colleagues' (2010, 9) provocation that "perhaps care practices can be strengthened if we find the right terms for talking about them," I examine migrant solidarity work as both a site of caring labor that directs its therapeutic potential toward the collective, or social body, and an aspirational project to reconfigure the social organization of care amid welfare state rollbacks. Surfacing in the narratives of charismatic individuals, affective ties among ordinary citizens and noncitizens, and physical spaces throughout Sicily, migrant solidarity work indexes material and agentive transformations, an antidote to widespread emotional collapse and alienation, and aspirations to improve collective well-being. For the purposes of this chapter, I focus primarily on these activities in Palermo, for the reason that it represents a "frontline community," as recognized in social movement discourse (Bazurli 2019). While all of Sicily is arguably on the front lines of recent im/migration and broader struggles by *siciliani* for autonomy and dignity within Italy and the EU, Palermo has been distinguished by the city government's pro-migrant policies and support for migrant solidarity activism. Moreover, similar to other pro-migrant cities in Southern Europe, Palermo's urban environment, with its density of people and organizations, has made it conducive to catalyzing relationships among activists and activist organizations that are characterized by "trust, solidarities, and collective identities" (Bazurli 2019, 7).

MATERIAL AND AGENTIVE TRANSFORMATIONS: "THE MIGRATORY PROJECT"

For nearly twenty years, Antonio had been working with migrants in various capacities as a volunteer at disembarkations, as a political activist, and as a member of a small missionary community on the outskirts of Palermo. With his wife and their three children, he shared a large housing complex with a few other missionary families. The complex included two apartments that were reserved specifically for migrants in need of hous-

ing. He enlightened me with the history and philosophy of their missionary community during a conversation in early 2017.

> Our apartment building was acquired by a group of priests. Three of the five
> apartments are occupied by missionary families. We decided as a group to
> live together and to share resources, so expenses are shared. We also ear-
> mark a portion of our pooled money for migrant reception, so in the other
> two apartments we host migrants who are in a difficult situation, especially
> women who arrive pregnant or with children.

Since 2008, Antonio and his family had provided housing to over sixty
migrants. Echoing the concerns of many social workers and activists
regarding the widespread problems in state-sponsored reception, Antonio
asserted that housing alternatives were in especially high demand.

> We host because the CAS [Centri accoglienza straordinaria] are extremely
> inadequate places for reception. [Migrants] need another option. The pre-
> fecture has given us approval, we don't charge a cent, and we pool our money
> to help this person. And thanks to mediators and lawyers, we make a con-
> sultation and say, "You can stay here until you feel ready, you decide when
> to go. If you want to apply for asylum, I will accompany you in this process."

Antonio and his neighbors assisted migrants who resided on the premises with enrolling in language courses, scheduling medical appointments,
and, depending on the level of interest or willingness, acquiring legal
assistance with the documentation process in Italy. As he noted, he and
his family had approval from the local government to provide housing to
migrants. Sometimes they hosted migrants who were not seeking asylum
in Italy but planned to migrate elsewhere in the EU.

> We've had people say that they don't want to apply for asylum, that they're
> headed for other destinations in the EU. Like the Eritrean woman with
> her twins who was here recently, she got off the boat without saying any-
> thing, because her migratory project was clear: to get as far as possible
> without saying anything [to authorities]. We heard from her by phone and
> on Facebook that she is in Germany; she told us about how things were
> going. We're in contact with many [former residents], but there are also
> many who we never hear from again. The important thing, though, is that
> we support them in their decisions. Self-determination is a fundamental
> concept for us.

As with the Eritrean woman, Antonio offered migrants protection from the authorities and extended them support in circumventing EU regulations that threatened to restrict their mobility. It was important to him to uphold their "migratory project" and "self-determination," even when this implied that he would have to engage in illicit activities and assume his own share of risk.

Antonio defined "success" in his work as fundamentally determined by "when [and if] a migrant realizes the ultimate objective of her migratory project." Yet he noted, "Today [fulfilling the migratory project] is very, very complicated." He gave an example.

> It's lovely when [migrants] call you to say, "I've arrived in Germany, I'm with my parents, I'm finally at home." The story of Titti, for instance, an Eritrean woman, one of five survivors of the shipwreck in 2012 that killed seventy-five people; she was saved. She became an actress, starred in the film *Terraferma*, and stayed with us for nine months. Today she is a mother and living with her fiancé in the Netherlands. Together they have two children.

Titti's story was an exceptional one. Not only had she been successful in migrating to the Netherlands, but she had discovered a career in the cinema, starring in the award-winning Italian feature film *Terraferma*, which tells the story of a young asylum seeker arriving pregnant at the island of Lampedusa.

Antonio alluded to myriad barriers in the form of systematic injustices—often connected to private financial interests—that hindered migrants from fulfilling their migratory projects: "The [institutional] system [of reception] is very awful, oppressive, and most migrants suffer immensely. Psychological problems are daily, problems inside the reception centers are daily. The state, the system, wants to use these people for a profit." He related these systematic injustices to the way that migrants were viewed by society at large: "Migrants provide a source of economic activity without which *we* would be in need. Migrants have no rights. They are thrown to the streets by traffickers and work as caregivers in our homes for our parents at a price that we decide, and if they don't have a residence permit, we can do whatever we want with them." Exploited at the discretion of Italians, particularly if they were lacking legal status, migrants, in turn, had strong feelings of distrust for individuals or institutions that could potentially help them. Referring to the "psychological problems" produced by these structural conditions, Antonio explained how migrants often internalized their subordinated status, subsequently eroding their hopes and ambitions and foreclosing possibilities for them to realize their migratory projects.[1]

For many migrants, the prospect of staying in Sicily is counterintuitive to their migratory projects. As a result, they do not recognize the practical purpose of participating in economic and social life, such as making an effort to learn Italian. A young woman who volunteered with a Palermo-based migrant-serving organization explained, "Some organizations struggle to identify prospective students because many migrants think of themselves as being here for a short time, and thus are only in Italy for a brief transit."

Nonetheless, Palermo's reputation as a pro-migrant city and fears of encountering politically hostile or otherwise difficult circumstances elsewhere persuaded some migrants to stay. In doing so, they made efforts to learn the Italian language, often through organizations such as Centro Astalli that offered courses free of charge. It also happened that many of those volunteering as instructors in such settings considered themselves engaged in migrant solidarity activism. Michele, one of the instructors at Centro Astalli, explained his reasons for volunteering.

> Ever since I started teaching Italian as a foreign language, I've always been motivated by the reason that most people arrive here, who have escaped war, hunger, famine, violence, etc. They hope to find fertile ground on which to stabilize themselves. I observed this firsthand many years ago when I was in the military and helping refugees arriving from Yugoslavia. The moment in which they stop here and their stay becomes semipermanent—in the sense that they stop here for a time that is not brief—to be able to stay healthy, to be able to relate with others, above all with *siciliani* because we are extremely solidarian in our DNA [*nei cromosomi*], the best thing would be to learn the language and open oneself up to the group. I feel that I serve as a first hoop in this process, and when migrants pass through me and my Italian lessons, they have a chance at a better life.

In discussing migrants who decided to remain in Palermo, Michele highlighted the practical purposes of learning Italian: it helped "stabilize" migrants, facilitate their social inclusion, and improve their material possibilities. His two years of service in the Italian military during which he helped with receiving refugees from the Balkans had been a formative experience, one that endowed him with a particular sensibility in relating to his students. His Italian lessons served as one means through which Michele was able to assist students with a host of daily challenges, from enrolling children in school to problems with one's job or bureaucratic matters within the Italian legal system.

In addition to his volunteer work, Michele was a strong advocate for broader investment by all levels of government in migrant integration, especially in education and Italian-language programs. In particular, he regretted the lack of government-sponsored programs devoted to supporting language instruction for migrants: "I'm of the thinking that if you teach Italian to a migrant and the migrant can then aspire to find a good job, why not do it? Why wouldn't the government, the commune, not sponsor courses for migrants?" Similar to more progressive activists in Sicily and elsewhere in the EU who argue that receiving countries should "provide not only the legal and economic means for immigrant integration but also a welcoming attitude" (Feldman-Savelsberg 2016, 178), Michele believed that responsibility for migrant integration resided with the receiving country. Another Palermo-based activist and director of a small nonprofit in the field of media production who was equally critical of the lack of government investment in migrant integration explicitly linked the notion of migrant solidarity to improving the material and agentive capacities of migrants.

> It is always a double-edged sword, because there are interventions that do more harm than good. Are they going to resolve someone's problems, or will they offer a temporary solution? For instance, "You're cold? I'll give you a jacket." This is really charity, not solidarity. Solidarity would be, "You're cold? Let's make sure you have housing, that you're able to find a job, and that you can pay your rent."

Migrants I interviewed who had lived in Sicily for several years often shared these sentiments about solidarity as catalyzed through material and agentive transformations. As one Senegalese woman who had been residing in Palermo articulated, "For me solidarity is helping me to do things. To read. To work. To do that which I had never imagined being able to do."

ANTIDOTE TO EMOTIONAL COLLAPSE: "ALL OF US ARE AFFECTED"

On a Thursday evening in May 2017, I attended a language class for migrants being taught by Michele. Of the dozen or so students in attendance that evening, most were in their teens or twenties. Over the next hour, Michele playfully invoked a range of practical scenarios, from returning a malfunctioning mobile phone to a vendor to inquiring with an employer about a job opportunity. His students responded favorably, most of them eager to practice their burgeoning Italian-language skills with Michele and one another. Over coffee after class, we began discussing recent displays of migrant solidarity in Palermo and how these contrasted with appeals by Italian and European leaders for "solidarity" in responding to its "migration crisis." He mulled over their differences.

> Solidarity starts with [migrant] *accoglienza.* I'm someone who does and would do everything to recognize the rights of people on the move. When a boat arrives, reception should be a true and sincere reception and not a military reception. You should give [migrants] a possibility of feeling at home.... Unfortunately, however, solidarity is [often] turned into pity. And this is a mistake, because to be aligned with someone who comes from much worse conditions than you means that you have to support putting that person in conditions that support a better life.... Solidarity is not just made through the provision of housing, food, or medicine, but requires empathetic assistance. To show empathy toward others. I do this in my work: from the first day of class, I put myself in the shoes of another, of migrants, of people I've had the fortune of getting to know. And if they realize and recognize this empathy, and if you recognize them as people who have escaped a country at war or in poverty, they find solidarity.

In his framing, Michele interpreted migrant solidarity as beginning with a "true and sincere" reception animated by empathy (an emotional, caring labor) rather than humanitarian intervention, charity (pity), or a militarized response. It also required investment in the "conditions that support a better life." He added that there was a relational aspect to migrant solidarity: "To me, the foreigner is a source of enrichment, of cultural enrichment. I'm not talking about that which is economic but rather the exchange of experiences and of life." By his logic, the "foreigner" should not be viewed as a passive agent but rather as someone who actively enriches the host society. Activists frequently regaled me with similar sentiments in their assertions that migrants were a "resource" and stressed their contributions to society that extended far beyond their roles as wage laborers.

Michele alluded to extant hostilities toward migrants, even in Palermo, to highlight the political significance of his work.

> You should know that Palermo, for as much as it seems open to migrants, it is actually not 100 percent open, because people have certain prejudices. The people often don't recognize that the migrant is here because he escaped his country as a refugee, from war or from misery. They think he comes here to steal jobs from others. Obviously, this is completely false. As you know, migrants arrive here because they had [no other option but] to abandon their countries.

Similar to Antonio, Michele emphasized the importance of trust in relating to his students.

> If migrants trust you, if they understand that you are not going to judge them for their past, for their background, if they understand that you are aware of their hardship, of their suffering, of their pain, of their poverty, and you put yourself on the same level as them, in you they find a healer, of their soul, of their mind. Also, if there is a serious problem, because many do indeed tell you something in secret, you have to decide what to do, whether or not to intervene or speak with someone about the problem they are experiencing.

Recognizing the vulnerable position of many migrants, volunteers like Michele performed the emotional labor required for gaining trust and facilitating a more balanced exchange. Yet this emotional labor at times both enriched the experience of being an activist through yielding affective attachment and complicated it with ethical considerations. Many of the people I interviewed attributed their activism to being overcome by a sense of obligation, feeling as if their fates were henceforth irrevocably intertwined with those they sought to help and mobilize with for justice.

Establishing trust in order to facilitate support to migrants was also identified by Antonio as one of the most challenging aspects of his work: "But the people who arrive by sea, after all they have endured, they don't trust me. Why should they trust me after they've been treated so poorly by everyone else they've met? After they've had a relative killed or witnessed a close relative or friend die at sea?" To work through these challenges,

Antonio relied on his family for emotional and moral support: "Gaining one's trust is very difficult for me, and we need the support of others in our lives to make sure that we are keeping ourselves fed and healthy to continue this work; otherwise many more would be much worse off without us."

Interpersonally and through his social media presence, Antonio was very outspoken about the unrelenting tragedy of migrant deaths at sea and emphasized grieving as one of the most radical acts of migrant solidarity. In the summer of 2017, Antonio invited me to attend the funeral services in a small town located in the province of Trapani for two young migrant children who drowned off the coast of Palermo several months before. They were five and eight years old at the time of their deaths, having fled Côte d'Ivoire to join their older sister (age fifteen), who was also in attendance at the funeral services. She was the one who identified their remains, Antonio informed me. Accompanied by the psychologist from her center of residence for migrant youth, she held a bouquet of flowers while dressed completely in white as a large excavator and the cemetery's groundskeeper spread heaps of dirt over the two grave sites. Some thirty others were also in attendance at the funeral, including a group of migrants from West Africa who resided in the nearby town, other missionaries, and a cultural mediator. We stood together for the next hour, silently watching as dirt filled the graves. Before the burial, they held a brief ceremony according to Muslim tradition and recited in Arabic. The local *commune* had provided bouquets to be placed atop the burial mounds, which were surrounded by the tombs of Italian families (figure 9).[2] Directly adjacent to the new burial mounds was the headstone of an unidentified migrant who drowned in 2015; inscribed at the top were the words, "my name is written in the sea" (il mio nome è scritto nel mare). Shortly after the funeral services, a strong Saharan wind blanketed the entire north coast of the island, kicking up a thick cloud of dust that had traveled from the African continent and across the central Mediterranean, settling over the province of Palermo and suffocating pedestrians with poor air quality. That the wind intensified as we departed the cemetery and did not dissipate for the next two days seemed tragically poetic.

Recognizing a need to bring disparate groups together in a process of social healing, groups such as Arte Migrante had formed to encourage citizens and noncitizens to engage in alternative forms of communication as

Figure 9. Burial mounds for two migrant children who drowned in early 2017. Tombstone in foreground commemorates an unidentified migrant who drowned in 2015. Photo by author.

a means to forge community and feelings of belonging. In February 2017, I convened with the organizers of Palermo's chapter of Arte Migrante for the first time via Skype after I had sought a preliminary interview. The five organizers appeared on my computer screen as slow-moving, pixelated bodies—the result of a poor internet connection—huddled closely together so that they would each appear on camera: Gemma (age 26), Emmanuela (age 26), Laura (social worker, age 26), and Giuseppe (university professor, age 41), all originally from Palermo, and then Sa'id (student, age 19), from Cameroon. They had gathered to tell me more about the philosophy and origins of Arte Migrante and to provide some context for the event that I would be attending very soon for the first time, namely, their bimonthly evening gathering at the Oratorio Santa Chiara (a large community complex overseen by the Catholic church)—"a point of reference in the neighborhood, somewhere that many go in search of refuge," an Arte Migrante organizer said—in Palermo's Ballarò. They insisted it would be a festive event, one that brought together ordinary citizens and noncitizens around food, music, and performance art.

Over the course of our hourlong video chat, these grassroots activists outlined a typical Arte Migrante evening, which consisted of three phases.

> The first phase starts with introductions, so we play icebreaker-type games to have everyone get familiar with each other. The second phase is the social dinner in which everyone shares something to eat or drink—but no alcohol out of respect for those who may abstain because of their religious beliefs or other reasons. We eat together, and continue to socialize, in a spirit of conviviality. The third phase is that of artistic expression during which each person presents their own art.

They added that there were "many forms of artistic expression, of imparting to others a beautiful moment, of sharing a journey," and that this "journey" sometimes translated literally into theatrical reenactments of migratory journeys to Italy.

When I attended one of these bimonthly gatherings some months later, organizers commenced the evening by inviting attendees to go around in a circle and personalize the statement, "To be free for me, would mean..." Some participants completed the statement by expressing their desires for emancipation and liberation from financial debts, material needs, racism and prejudice, and self-conscious or self-denigrating thoughts. The organizers then invited us to go into the adjacent courtyard for the second phase of the evening: the social dinner. Potluck-style, the smorgasbord included small trays of *pizzette*, pastas, roasted potatoes, pastries, and cheese and crackers, as well as bottled water and soda. While some participants snacked and mingled, others prepared for the third phase of the evening by adding their names to the list of performances jotted down on a whiteboard. By the time the performances commenced, more than fifty people had gathered inside, taking a seat on one of the floor rugs or in chairs (figure 10). Over the next couple of hours, performers captivated our attention and evoked a range of emotional responses, from laughter to tears, with their one (wo)man shows, storytelling, folk music, poetry, and comic sketches. During musical performances, others joined in by clapping their hands or playing one of the percussive instruments that were dispersed around the room.

Figure 10. Participants gather during the "third phase" of the evening with Arte Migrante. Photo by author.

While organizers clearly desired to bolster confidence within the group and to encourage everyone to perform, they also emphasized an openness to and acceptance of all levels of engagement. This was also made necessary by the linguistic diversity of participants and the fact that most group interactions were in Italian, and occasionally English. When I asked if attendees ever experienced performance anxiety, the organizers explained that feelings of social pressure yielded a productive tension in disrupting the "comfort zones" of individual attendees and bridging the social distance that characterized most other aspects of their everyday lives. The organizers had intentionally chosen to precede the performance segment of each bimonthly gathering with the social meal in order to alleviate feelings of intimidation and anxiety within the group and to allow the third phase to be as transformative as possible. One of the activists engaged with Arte Migrante's events suggested that the performance segment served as a form of social healing not only for participants who had experienced extreme shyness but also within the collective. She said, "When they express themselves in this space, they overcome this fear, gain self-esteem and confidence, and all of us are affected by these transformations in our relationships."

Arte Migrante launched in Italy in 2012 with the aim of creating "meeting spaces to share experiences and to facilitate social interaction through the arts" (Facebook page, Arte Migrante Palermo). The organizers of Palermo's Arte Migrante, predominantly students in their late teens and twenties, emphasized its grassroots and participatory character. They conveyed the project as one of social inclusion that involved "not only migrants but also students, homeless, workers, everyone in general," noting how none of these groups had been spared the effects of recent political and economic crises in the region. Gemma, for instance, explained that even though as a social worker she spent her days interacting with migrants in the "immigration field," opportunities for building friendships seldomly arose in this context. In contrast, Arte Migrante afforded an "opportunity to open ourselves and share an evening together that otherwise wouldn't happen; to be with migrants, to be with the homeless, because in reality we don't often realize these modes of interacting [across the social spectrum]."

From our first interaction over Skype to convening at the bimonthly event, members of Arte Migrante reiterated how they sought to create "uno spazio" (space) and "uno strumento" (instrument) for participants to "find their own humanity" and "open [up about themselves]." According to one of the youth organizers, the "art" in Arte Migrante denoted an expression rather than an aesthetic, wherein art was a medium of communication and a vehicle for social inclusion: "Our everyday lived realities are not very simple. But art is a simple thing and above all succeeds in fighting against barriers to diversity, because art is simply the expression of oneself in diverse forms. And I think this is key in the project of Arte Migrante: putting people of diverse backgrounds in communication."

Aside from the bimonthly gathering, social media platforms were the principal means of communication within the broader Arte Migrante network. In posts on its Facebook page, Arte Migrante referred to bringing "your curiosity to meet new people and the desire to share your experience" and to sharing "an artistic performance: music, songs, dances, poems, tales." "Feel free to express yourself as you wish" and "Do not miss the opportunity to know new people and new cultures from all over the world," were additional posts. Besides messaging through social media, Arte Migrante members I spoke with conveyed aspirations of diversifying its strategies and specifically engaging in more "face-to-face outreach: on the street, in schools, in centers of migrant reception and in the community." As they asserted, "Young, outgoing people with diverse backgrounds and language competencies" were instrumental to advancing their mission and disseminating their message.

ASPIRING TO COLLECTIVE WELL-BEING: "A UTOPIC VISION FOR THE WORLD"

In addition to providing housing among other forms of material support to migrants, as well as his activism in preventing migrant deaths at sea, Antonio volunteered with a small association that monitored Sicily's migrant reception centers, giving "special attention to the rights of migrants and how they are being recognized or not at these centers." Antonio extolled the association's mission and how it aligned with his own political values.

> [The monitoring association] is a form of resistance to injustice, against an unjust system. So it also represents a political act: what inspires me today is the fight against a system that makes death; it kills people. I want a more just world for my children, so politically I seek to deploy a utopic vision for the world. Doing my small part, through my decisions, I want something different. Migrants [in general] today are seen as worth less than business, worth less than money. They are outside of the economic system; they are seen to have no worth. Animals have more rights than migrants today.

Noting that migrants were considered by society at large to exist "outside the economic system" and "to have no worth," Antonio expressed his aspirations for alternatives to the logic of the free market economy. This was one of many instances in which activists highlighted how their work in the realm of migrant solidarity coalesced with broader concerns for collective well-being, justice, and an alternative to hegemonic racial capitalism.

On one occasion, I implored Antonio to delineate the changes he viewed as necessary to undermine what had become such an unjust system of migrant reception and integration in Italy. He immediately named the government's complicity with corporate and private interests as the primary problem: "I'm compelled to repair the injustices created by Western governments, by governments that concentrate their power and take advantage of the rest of the world for their own enrichment. I do not condone the widespread impoverishing of territories, people, cities, and entire nations, so I try to combat and denounce this system." He added:

> Above all else, we need to return the system to the people and away from private interests. Private interests control everything today; today you have the example of Trump in America. If we allow money to rule everything, we can sacrifice people: we can kill them at sea, in Libya, in the desert, so we don't see; or we can kill them in our fields, in our centers [of reception]. So we can sacrifice them for money and power. The "Dio Denaro" [money god] opens these mega-centers [of reception] that generate immense profits [for private interests] at the cost of migrant suffering. The change must be putting people at the center. This is utopian, I know, but to be specific: if every Italian town took in migrants, there would be two in every city. Two. There wouldn't be a need for reception centers, police ... so it's not true that there is an invasion. There are concrete examples of towns that have welcomed migrants, that have given them vacant houses, trained them in the Italian language and in work, and these towns have been revitalized thanks to the migrants living there.

For Antonio, the underlying cause of an unjust system of migrant reception related to corrupt interests and an obsession with profits, exacerbating extant structural inequalities and the always already uneven life chances of migrants. He aspired to a "utopic" vision of society with "people at the center," to the project of migrant reception more equitably distributed across society, an end to racial profiling and policing, and a "revitalized" collective. But for now, these remained aspirations: "The hope is that if there is social cohesion, everyone will be better. But it's not this way today. Instead, death is constant. It is a weight that we carry."

In mid-February 2017, I received an invitation from Antonio on Facebook to attend a demonstration that he was helping organize with his missionary community in Palermo. They had titled the event "Abbatiamo i muri" (Let's Break Down Walls) and had received endorsements from over a dozen other local organizations. In the event description, the organizers outlined a number of demands, broadly categorized as "saying no ... to the war on the poor" and asking that "the rights of all" be recognized, summarized as follows:

1. avoiding bilateral agreements with insecure "third party" countries to block migrants from entering the EU;

2. ending ethnic and racial targeting of migrants for expulsion, unfair asylum procedures for minors, egregious delays in processing of asylum applications, and heightened criminalization of migrants; and

3. demanding human rights for all citizens and noncitizens.

Organizers also called for investing more resources in humane reception, expanding the criteria for asylum eligibility, guaranteeing the protection of human rights, and adopting measures to protect migrants of precarious legal status.

A few months later, more than six hundred leftist activists from across Sicily gathered in the coastal enclave of Taormina to bring forward similar demands to leaders at the end of the G7 summit. The "No G7" protest had been organized and publicized across the island weeks in advance (figure 11). Demonstrators led with signs declaring, "Sicily marches against the powers of the world" and "Stop with imperialism, war, racism, the police state, fascism—revolution is the only solution!" Interviewed by the newspaper *Giornale di Sicilia*, several activists asserted that this was "a protest for and by Sicily" and denounced the militarization and exploitation of their island for security purposes. They derided the hypocrisy of costly security measures during the summit, including military patrols along the coast, while government-led migrant search and rescue operations had been virtually abandoned. In Palermo, UNICEF along with a handful of local government officials and organizations orchestrated a "mock" rescue at sea along the city's waterfront as another form of protest during the G7 summit (see chapter 6). Participants in this event implored policy makers at the G7 to respond swiftly and meaningfully to the ceaseless tally of migrant deaths at sea, especially of many children and adolescents. Like demonstrators at the "No G7" protest, organizers of the mock rescue condemned the costly security presence on both land and sea for being considerably more organized and robust than any of the EU's search and

Figure 11. Printed announcement posted on a Palermo building for the "No G7" protest. Photo by author.

rescue operations in the Mediterranean. From the perspectives of migrant solidarity activists, there was no mistaking whose lives were regarded as worthy of protection and whose were to be policed or left to die.

While President Trump was vilified on "No G7" posters as one of the many "evils" of the world, alongside other national leaders, media coverage of the Taormina protest precisely underscored him as "the preferred target" of scrutiny.[3] Prior to arriving at the summit, President Trump visited the pope at the Vatican, an event that had been highly anticipated by both American and Italian news networks. While Trump had been condemned for his draconian appeal to strengthen and "shut down" borders, the pope had been hailed as a saint and spokesperson for the open borders movement and for compassion for displaced persons, regardless of creed or origin.[4]

In their work on immigrant rights activism in the United States, Pallares and Gomberg-Muñoz (2016, 9) allude to "tangling" as a discursive strategy in which activists "emphasize the complex interconnectedness of undocumented people and the US citizens, showing how the well being of US citizens often depend on undocumented members of society." The protests leading up to and surrounding the G7 summit seem to represent one such instance of tangling, as the logic that animates this strategy also underpins many of the meanings of solidarity offered to me by activists, most of whom reside in Palermo. These activists emphasized mutuality and collective well-being. As a thirty-something *palermitano* told me, "Migrants should have equal status with Italians. They are the new citizens. So any measures to improve their situation should also support the expansion of welfare to improve the lives of everyone else." And a fifty-something *agrigentino* said, "Solidarity is sharing one's destiny. This sharing is more important than anything else." Yet, almost always, they underscored these sentiments as aspirations, particularly amid the hostilities that separated not only citizens from noncitizens, but citizens from one another. For instance, a forty-something *agrigentina* explained:

> Solidarity is regarding the other as your equal, affording them equal dignity and possibilities. Unfortunately, this [ideal] is very far from us in this particular moment, because there are many divisions even among Italians. But still, solidarity is ensuring that others are living in circumstances equal to your own. It can be any gesture that uplifts someone to experience life as you do. It is really a form of sharing: bringing the other to where you are, giving them the same chances that you have.

SOLIDARITY WORK: A RISKY, RADICAL, AND ASPIRATIONAL ENTERPRISE

> To be in solidarity with migrants right now in Europe is
> regarded almost as a form of collusion. We won't stop,
> though, because the humanity and life of every single person
> is inviolable and sacred.
>
> —Palermo-based human rights activist, June 2018

Solidarity is not a new concept; its origins can be traced to the inception of the welfare state (Muehlebach 2012). More than half a century ago, Hannah Arendt ([1963] 2006, 79) discussed solidarity in terms of "a community of interest with the oppressed and exploited . . . aroused by suffering but not guided by it." Nonetheless, over time its popularity has oscillated with different political regimes and across geopolitical contexts, as underscored by the Palermo-based human rights activist quoted above. The politics dictating its expression reveal how solidarity is both familiar and suspect, galvanizing devoted supporters while also provoking criminalization by the state.

As an "emotionally resonant" category, solidarity has been invoked across the political spectrum as "part of a master narrative perpetuated by a range of actors in the welfare community, including neoliberal reformers" (Muehlebach 2012, 9, 171). Its co-optation and appropriation in political discourses, "drawing together . . . disparate projects and agents while seemingly eradicating historical and ideological difference"—a problem Muehlebach identifies as ventriloquation (171)—arguably makes it much too elusive as a potential object of ethnographic inquiry.

Instead of uncovering the myriad and shifting discursive applications and registers of solidarity per se, in this chapter I have sought to illuminate the particular set of practices and economy of affects that comprise *migrant solidarity work* (Ahmed 2004; Caldwell 2017; Oliveri 2015). In continuing to analyze permutations of solidarity work, it is the task of the ethnographer to investigate "how diverse groups build connections and a sense of common purpose, how people who have chosen to struggle together deal with unequal relationships of power, and how they remain open to new adherents and project a broad appeal" (Gill 2009, 668). The activist narratives highlighted in this chapter provide a glimpse into the meanings and actions that these social actors associate with migrant solidarity as well as the role of solidarity work in their lives.

As conveyed by activists like Antonio and Michele, the "migratory project" is at the heart of solidarity work and necessitates material and agentive transformations. Migrant solidarity activists seek to uphold the self-determination of migrants even as this may require that they assume certain risks. As Michele argued, orientation to language opens the door to material and agentive transformations. These activists hold host societies and their governments accountable for constraining migrants' mobility and their integration. They do not view their own actions as activists as motivated by charity or humanitarianism. As the sociologist Craig Calhoun (2010, 35) explains, "Charity is typically seen as a moral way to relate to people who suffer, but not necessarily as a way to end suffering." And Muehlebach (2012) holds that charity is the virtue that also wounds by means of reproducing power relations that sustain the subordinated status of recipients or beneficiaries. Similarly, humanitarianism, described by Calhoun (2010, 39) as part of "the 'civilization' that colonial powers sought to bring to the peoples they conquered," does not demand changes to the social or political structures that render violence and human suffering. Humanitarianism is often deeply imbricated with these violent structures (Ticktin 2011).[5]

These activists further distinguished solidarity work from humanitarianism, charity, and "hospitality" (accoglienza), in that they sought to redistribute risk among the collective, or what my informants sometimes framed in terms of "sharing one's destiny." Solidarity work is risky, as state institutions have adopted increasingly punitive measures against "crimes of solidarity." Yet concerns about chronic threats to collective well-being (e.g., alienation, material insecurity, economic precarity) supersede concerns about more proximate risks, including the threat of one's solidarity actions being criminalized (remember the case of Captain Carola Rackete presented at the start of this book). In hypothesizing the impetus for people assuming "solidarity actions," and specifically in the Italian context, the political scientist Nicola Maggini (2018, 130–31) surmises that "having a good frequency of social connections fosters higher levels of life satisfaction and happiness but can also give people access to a wider range of possible support in times of need, producing positive outcomes at a community level." Similarly, in her study of social solidarity clinics in Greece, Cabot (2016, 161) demonstrates how solidarity initiatives facilitate healing of the social body: "Through solidarity, society—reconceived as an active and living force—is framed as both the repository and recipient of care and healing." Across these settings, migrant solidarity work may serve the very practical purpose of transforming the affective possibilities of citizens and noncitizens.[6]

Activists reflect on how solidarity work in practice also entails affective aspects, experienced, for instance, in efforts to cultivate trust and mutual understanding with those they seek to align with. Arte Migrante, for instance, attempts to level the social distance between citizens and noncitizens by creating space for participants to engage with one another through artistic expression. As addressed by Antonio, the affective aspects of solidarity work sometimes implied that one also address certain embodied and affective needs to ensure the social reproduction of solidarity.

The anthropologist Theodoros Rakopoulos (2015, 144) observes that in Greece, "solidarity cannot be conceived outside the backdrop that austerity has carved, as it arises as an alternative horizon for people's lifeworlds, while dictating immediate action." I extend his arguments to the Sicilian context to suggest that migrant solidarity emerges as an "alternative horizon" where ordinary citizens and noncitizens form new alliances and undertake collective action for material, affective, and political ends. As exhibited by the "No G7" protest and other public demonstrations, migrant solidarity is often deemed inseparable from collective well-being as migrant solidarity activism coalesces with broader struggles for autonomy and dignity of *siciliani* positioned as they are in Europe's southern periphery.

My interlocutors assert that, in contrast to charity and humanitarianism, solidarity work explicitly calls for radical structural shifts. Seeking to reposition migrants as active rather than passive agents in collective care and well-being, those performing solidarity work refute claims that migrants are "a drain on the state" (Andretta and della Porta 2015) while also pushing back against attempts by the state to exploit this population. As a radically politicized caring labor, solidarity work rejects the very logics that have relied on regimes of stratified reproduction (Boris and Parreñas 2010; Colen 1995; Mullings 1995).

In challenging hegemonic structures and institutions that constrain their material, affective, and political possibilities, citizens and noncitizens engaged in this form of activism must frequently negotiate and reconcile with the ambiguities, tensions, and frictions pervading solidarity work (Rozakou 2012). As observed by Athina Arampatzi (2017) in her ethnographic work in Greece, distinct subjectivities emerge within spaces of solidarity; these are spaces of becoming and thus index a politics of becoming as actors negotiate differences and aspire to alternatives. Solidarity work may "give rise to new visions of belonging" (Rakopoulos 2015, 144), but as an aspirational project it does not necessarily yield transformations in the structures and logics that dictate the terms of formal belonging and political citizenship. Subsequently, the benefits and costs of migrant solidarity work are often distributed differentially among ordinary citizens and noncitizens.

As highlighted in the case of Arte Migrante, activists struggle to consistently align migrant solidarity work in practice with its proposed ideals. Most interactions at its bimonthly gatherings were first and foremost in Italian and in English second. Recently arrived migrants with limited proficiency in either of these languages, and possibly limited literacy, were likely to be both unaware of Arte Migrante events and unable to meaningfully participate in the social gatherings, a reality not lost on organizers within their network. The fact that they operated through the support of volunteers to promote and organize events and relied on local donations may also have inhibited their ability to broaden participation. Moreover, despite the laudable intentions of Arte Migrante's organizers, they were not as effective in recruiting more diversity in its leadership. At the time of this research, the majority of its core organizers identified as *palermitani*. Considering the extent to which Arte Migrante relied on social media platforms and word of mouth, the relative lack of diversity among its leadership may have weakened its potential for facilitating the types of interactions to which organizers were aspiring. To some extent, migrants were disproportionately burdened with the project of belonging; they were expected to insert themselves and become active participants even though they were at a considerable disadvantage. However, organizers were also cognizant of such flaws in translating solidarity work from theory to practice and were actively seeking ways to strengthen their efforts.

Recent scholarship on contemporary sanctuary activities and the New Sanctuary Movement serves as a crucial reminder of how any movement for migrant solidarity must reconcile with power inequalities between citizens and noncitizens (Czajka 2012).[7] Considering that government officials and activists have worked together at "the edge of legality" (Barzurli 2019, 356) in the Sicilian context also renders solidarity work particularly ripe for comparison with sanctuary practices. This body of literature has alluded to ways that in their willingness to defy the law by protecting asylum seekers and refugees, sanctuary activists have begun to disrupt the "protected and protector" binary (Squire and Bagelman 2012, 150; see also Mitchell 2017). Proposing that "sanctuary is enacted in much more diffuse terms across the urban environment" and because "those taking sanctuary enact themselves as political subjects in their own right," Squire and Bagelman call for rejecting depictions of those seeking sanctuary as "victims" (147). Instead, by shifting our "attention from practices of *seeking* sanctuary to practices of *taking* sanctuary," we may disrupt "the distinction between 'recipient' and 'provider'" (160; original emphasis). Evidence of squatter settlements (see, e.g., Mitchell and Sparke 2017; Mudu and Chattopadhyay 2016) and migrants refusing to leave reception centers (a theme that I revisit in chapter 6), especially in the absence of suitable alternatives for housing, further underscores how enabling migrants to define the parameters of solidarity work is increasingly necessary for advancing migratory projects in the European context.

This chapter has examined the various meanings and iterations of migrant solidarity work as it has been mobilized by activists in the city of Palermo. The actions of these solidarity workers augment existing networks of direct support as well as help advance movements in support of immigration, human rights, democracy, and societal welfare. The next chapter shifts focus to another thread of migrant solidarity work in Sicily: the forging of fusion foodways.

5 Edible Solidarities

> It's not only foreigners who work here but Italians as well.
> While we all prepare the food, there is something more
> than just the food: we share a certain solidarity, a will to do
> better. We work together. We integrate together. We share
> about our cultures and origins with one another.
>
> —Chef Mareme, cofounder of Ginger restaurant in Agrigento

Dusk descends on the medieval town of Agrigento. Stealing views of the Valley of the Temples, I walk briskly along Via Empedocle—a street bearing the name of the nearby Porto Empedocle, recent site of several migrant disembarkations—to arrive in time for my reservation at Ginger. For months I have been corresponding with the restaurant's owners, Carmelo and Mareme, but tonight marks our first in-person meeting. It is high season in Agrigento; the town's bustling gastronomic scene and some of Sicily's most pristine beaches located a short distance away near the famous Scala dei Turchi (Turkish Steps) draw in throngs of tourists. Arriving at the restaurant perspiring, short of breath, and with my toddler clinging to me at the waist, I am greeted by Carmelo and Mareme, who appear quite relaxed despite the full house they are anticipating tonight. Over the next two hours, we savor *antipasti, primi,* and *secondi,* each dish featuring ingredients whose provenance is either Sicilian or Senegalese. Once the evening rush is over, Mareme leads me into the kitchen to meet her staff and then dines with three of her children at the table adjacent to ours. Carmelo joins some friends at another nearby table.

Even before she competed on *Cuochi di Italia* (Cooks of Italy) in 2020 and dazzled a national television audience with her culinary genius, Chef

Mareme was a quasi-celebrity in Sicily. Originally from Senegal, Mareme arrived in Sicily in 2003. She followed her husband who had arrived some years earlier in search of better economic opportunities. In the years that Mareme and her husband were together in the province of Agrigento, she stayed at home to care for their four children, three of whom were born in Italy, while he struggled to find work. Mareme's husband eventually returned to Senegal, and she remained in Italy. Suddenly faced with the pressure to provide for her family, Mareme immersed herself among other culinary professionals in Agrigento and put her long-standing passion for cooking to work. Soon enough she was competing (and winning) in the Cous Cous Fest World Championships in San Vito Lo Capo in western Sicily and preparing catered meals through Al Kharub Cooperative. In late 2016, Mareme assumed the role of head chef upon the opening of Ginger.

This chapter examines forms of migrant solidarity work enacted through and around the unique foodways being forged in Sicily's "multi-cultural" restaurants. Drawing on ethnographic observations and interviews, I analyze the social relations, notions of power and identity, and forms of political mobilization surrounding the forging of fusion cuisines that combine culinary practices from throughout Africa, the Middle East, and Sicily. I compare and contrast Agrigento's Ginger with Moltivolti, a "multiethnic kitchen" in Palermo's Ballarò neighborhood that opened in 2014. Similar to the forms of migrant solidarity work I discussed in the previous chapter, these food establishments, I argue, seek to transform the material, affective, and political possibilities of both citizens and noncitizens. However, they differ from volunteer-based forms of solidarity work in that, operating as businesses, they seek to dissociate from and imagine alternatives to debt and recession, austerity regimes, and the volatility of global markets. In focusing on these businesses and the broader web of social and economic relationships in which they are embedded, this chapter engages with the emergent body of scholarship that "associates debt and recession with new livelihood practices in the European context" (Rakopoulos 2014, 192). Beyond seeking to cultivate new livelihood practices, these businesses explicitly marshal a participatory vision of migrant integration and subsequently assume a prominent role in combating antimigrant and racist sentiments and in demanding structural change.

FUSION FOODWAYS: A RECIPE FOR SOLIDARITY?

Scholars of critical food studies have extensively documented how food-based social movements, such as the movements for food justice and food sovereignty, contest neoliberal and racial capitalist logics inherent to the global-industrial food system while also working to enact alternatives to this paradigm (Alkon and Guthman 2017). The diverse forms of activism highlighted by these scholars reaffirm that food is one of the most important social and cultural domains for inciting political mobilization against systems of inequality and oppression. Immigrants, importantly, including many Black and Indigenous people as well as other communities of color, have often been at the forefront of movements to confront injustices within the global-industrial food system, deploying food as a site of political resistance in the context of diaspora (Abranches 2014; Carney 2015, 2016; Garth and Reese 2020; Mankekar 2002; Mares 2019; Minkoff-Zern 2019; Murphy 2018; Pérez and Abarca 2007).

As the birthplace of the slow food movement, Italy boasts a rich history of political mobilization centered on the food system (Petrini 2004). Italian citizens and noncitizens have fought against the deregulation of markets, the industrialization of agriculture, and trade liberalization by creating opportunities to de-link from these globalizing processes and to cultivate alternatives (see also Wekerle 2004). For instance, Italy's solidarity purchasing groups—Gruppi di acquisto solidali (GAS)—consist of "households that establish mutual coordination for the purpose of purchasing food and other products (shoes, clothes, detergents, etc.) directly from producers, who are selected in accordance with ethical and solidarity principles, the most important of which are respect for the environment and for people" (Fonte 2013, 232). There are some sixteen hundred GAS in Italy today whose annual collective purchasing power represents more than €80 million (Grasseni 2013). These groups "reinvent value by reweaving [social] relations" and "shift economic practices away from the sole consideration of profit maximization" (Grasseni 2013, 60, 29). As the anthropologist Giovanni Orlando (2015, 347–48) explains, in establishing "direct relations with farmers and distributors, [these] ethical consumers not only express, but also practice, solidarity.... [T]his practice points to a desire by some groups of people for a more active kind of citizenship."

While the fusion food establishments that I present as case studies in the pages that follow indeed share some characteristics with Italy's solidarity purchasing groups, such as assessing value based on social relations and alleviating an emphasis on monetary profits, they are also distinguished by their more radical approaches to migrant integration.

As forms of intercultural communication and exchange, fusion food-ways may also act as sites of resistance that destabilize problematic representations of and discourses about migration (Rorato 2020). In merging systems of food-specific knowledge and practices, fusion foodways may yield the "construction of collective identities and identifications," thereby allowing participants to "'cook, taste, and feel' their collective affiliations" (Grosglik and Lerner 2020). While the forging and elevation of fusion cuisines often precedes their widespread appropriation and consumption by an elite class of consumers, an exclusive focus on the market-based dimensions of fusion foods tends to obscure the sincere intentions of culinary professionals and their supporters to forge alliances around the intersections of diverse and complementary culinary practices.[1] As a site of socially reproductive foodwork, the resources and labor that intersect through the forging of fusion cuisines represent another instance of recon-figuring the social organization of care (Beagan 2008). In the context of my research, migrants are reimagined as active agents and collaborators in this process of social reproduction, one that articulates with the aspira-tional project of migrant solidarity while also critiquing austerity regimes and restrictive immigration policies.

SOLIDARITY AT THE "GASTRONOMIC BORDERS": FOODWORK AS A SITE OF CARE

> As Italy swings right, the layers of cuisine [in Sicily] reflect
> the traditions of an island that has adapted to centuries of
> immigration.
> —Wendell Steavenson, "'Our Island Is Like a Mosaic':
> How Migrants Are Reshaping Sicily's Food Culture"

In 2018, Mayor Leoluca Orlando of Palermo presented Moltivolti—the self-proclaimed "multiethnic kitchen"—with a prestigious civil award.

He was recognizing the restaurant for its model of migrant integration, which was explained to me by Giovanni, one of Moltivolti's cofounders, in early 2016: "Moltivolti has as a mission to be a model of integration that grows with the surrounding region because we are convinced that the only engine of growth within society is through social relations: if these relations are absent from a project as it develops, the project dies." He added, "The objective of the restaurant is to transmit cuisines of various cultures." His sentiments were echoed by Shapoor, one of the head chefs at Moltivolti who had arrived in Palermo several years earlier, after fleeing war in Afghanistan: "When all are seated together at the table and eating things that come from various parts of the world, there is space for respect and integration" (Sagona 2018).

On any given day, the five chefs from five different countries collaborating in Moltivolti's kitchen "mix their cuisines together" to offer patrons a smorgasbord of "siculo-etnico" (Sicilian-ethnic) fusion recipes from *caponata* and *bruschetta del giorno* to *brik tuninese*, couscous, moussaka, *doppiaza afghana*, and *mafé senegalese*. Moltivolti, whose name means "many faces," changes its lunch and dinner menus daily, attracting a wide range of clientele. Among its regulars are human rights and social advocates who work in the adjacent co-working space, university students, young professionals, families with young children, tourists, and migrants in pursuit of food from back home. Moltivolti provides patrons with intricate details and transparent descriptions of the origins—sometimes indefinite or disputed—and contents of each menu item to enhance intercultural food literacy as well as its broader social project of "constructing a solidarian reality, where no one is 'host' or being 'hosted.'" "Our menu, mixing languages and flavors, is a symbol of our 'many faces,'" staff members of Moltivolti explained (Buondonno 2020). For instance, the *doppiaza afghana* is described as "our veal stew with oil, water, and onions, served with rice. It includes onion prepared two ways to achieve a different consistency for each: one set of onions are softer and caramelized; the other set is cooked to be crunchy." The *mafé senegalese* is "a light and simple white rice served with a seductive and delicious stew of meat in a peanut butter base." They privilege the culinary knowledge of their mostly foreign-born kitchen staff in designing the menu: "Every chef on our staff has brought with them a small piece of their story, of their journey, recipes and modes of preparing ingredients that have enriched our menu, giving homage to the freedom of movement. Sergio, the *lasagna carasau*. Balde's *mafé*. Aliou's *thiudijen*. Anna's *polpette di pane*, Shapoor's *doppiaza*. To eat with us is to travel, discover, to engage" (Moltivolti Instagram post, August 7, 2019). Chef Shapoor liked to combine "recipes from the Mediterranean and the Middle East." In an interview with the Rome-based newspaper *Corriere della Sera*, Shapoor explained, "I adapt my own recipes with the palates of *palermitani* in mind, as a gesture of thanking them for all they have given me." Among the nearly thirty staff members who attend to activities in the kitchen as well as the dining space of the restaurant are individuals who claim origins in Afghanistan, Zambia, Côte d'Ivoire, Senegal, Gambia, Bangladesh, Spain, and France. Those who help design the menu each day learned to cook from their mothers or other important caregiving figures in their lives back home or arrived in Italy with previous restaurant experience.

Ginger opened in 2016, distinguishing itself in Agrigento's food scene by serving a variety of dishes combining influences especially from Senegal and Sicily guided by the slogan, "eat ethically, eat ethnically" (*mangia etico, mangia etnico*). The restaurant was a member of Al Kharub Cooperative, an umbrella organization that supported organic agriculture in the surrounding region of Agrigento. The directors of the cooperative (and proprietors of the restaurant), Carmelo (Sicilian, originally from Agrigento) and Mareme (Senegalese, arrived in Agrigento in 2003) explained, "Since we live in a border region with many migrant communities, one of the objectives of Al Kharub—whose name we'll mention is an Arabic word—is to create opportunities for inclusion and integration with communities of migrants in our surrounding territory." Ginger's kitchen doubled as a space for Project Norah, a culinary and vocational training program for migrants.

By invoking terms such as "intercultural" and "multiethnic" in describing their fare, both Moltivolti and Ginger sought to challenge stereotypes and mainstream, pejorative discourses about migration. For instance, a prominent theme across both settings was the notion of food as a political and cultural instrument that permeates borders and reduces social distance. An advertisement announcing the opening of Ginger played on the notion of culinary traditions as "borders" to be traversed: "Ginger is food from Africa but also the stories and lives of women and men. It is our belief that it is possible to live in an inclusive community, more 'colorful,' solidarian, and open to the future. And now Ginger evolves. It is not only an African kitchen but also the infusion of [African] traditions into the food of [the Sicilian] territory that uses surprising aromas and flavors to break through gastronomic borders." Carmelo and Mareme reclaimed the language of a migrant "invasion" as a means to instead exalt the culinary contributions of migrants. They challenged perceptions of migrants as victims, criminals, or "drains" and represented them as resourceful, knowledgeable agents. These ideas were reiterated during an interview with Carmelo for the Palermo newspaper *La Repubblica* in which he described the table as a site of "union" where food could help to shift attitudes toward migrants: "Our dream is to open our own restaurant in which we can bring two traditions into union at the table, looking to negate the idea of the migrant seen only as a 'worker,' but also as an entrepreneur and resource for the region. We want to eliminate the misperceptions that render social distance. And at the table, you can."[2] By Carmelo's calculus, the table was a space for the materialization of solidarity work and for the fruits of solidarity work to be savored. In contrast to the feminization, exploitation, and subordination of migrant labor that commonly characterize the food service industry, Moltivolti and Ginger explicitly privileged migrants as they asserted autonomy and mobility in their culinary settings and informed the creative aspects of forging a cuisine with their culinary knowledge. "Intercultural" and "multiethnic" served as critical ideological and discursive frameworks surrounding the creation of fusion foods, indexing the social relations through which citizens and noncitizens actively co-labored within each establishment to negotiate identity, knowledge, and collective belonging.

With Ginger's Project Norah, Mareme sought to transform the material and agentive prospects for migrant women. In this culinary training program, Mareme gave participants the necessary practical skills for working in commercial kitchens while also familiarizing them with foods from Sicily and particularly the surrounding province of Agrigento. Mareme articulated the impetus for the program in terms of solidarity.

For me, solidarity doesn't only mean helping someone, bringing them food one day so that they can eat. For me, solidarity means making sure that I have access to a livelihood and that I feel at home. It's not just giving me food or clothing, no. It's helping me to fit into and belong to this place where I live, and to know this culture.

She explicitly connected solidarity to material and agentive transformations as well as to belonging. Responding to Mareme, Carmelo elaborated on the implications of solidarity work for collective well-being.

I think solidarity has a very strong tie to the concept of sharing, of sharing one's destiny. I don't say this to be cute. Sharing means accompanying someone on their path in life, seeking a way together to overcome a difficult or problematic situation. As Mareme said, it is not only giving someone food or clothes. Solidarity is being close to someone, to a group of people, sharing destiny, in whatever way, and to find and contribute to one's life, rendering it better.

Carmelo and Mareme underscored how for them the project of migrant integration and the ethical principles of solidarity superseded economic interests within their cooperative. They emphasized that an unwavering commitment to migrant solidarity was especially needed at a time of great political turmoil. As Carmelo put it, "Unfortunately, the world, Europe, and Italy are starting to feel the force of the far right, of intolerance, of walls.... [F]or us, in this moment, we have a major responsibility to do what we are doing. Because in this moment, it is necessary to work against the augmentation of hate and violence. We feel this responsibility even more, and we are even more determined to plow ahead in this direction."

In describing her involvement with Project Norah, the vocational training program she established for migrant women, Mareme related that she was "living her dream."

I'm helping people who are in a situation similar to my own: they live alone with their children, they haven't found work, and they live in a country that is not their own. This cooperative has given me the possibility of realizing my dreams, to help others realize their own as well. As a woman, as a mother, I can now tell you that I'm very satisfied because I'm doing what I always loved, including seeing that other women here get to study and work and not only stay at home.

For Mareme, it was important that she not only contribute to improving work prospects for migrants but also challenge ideas about women's work being confined to the home: "Part of my work in the cooperative is helping others find work. We have [Project Norah] so that refugees and women can integrate, develop professional skills, and find work." Whereas women's foodwork is often devalued and uncompensated, Mareme championed the opposite through becoming an award-winning, nationally renowned professional chef. She emphasized the right of migrants to exercise their own agency and to pursue their hopes and ambitions: "Even if we don't live in our own countries, we should continue to have our dreams and to pursue them. This is the path we walk at Al Kharub."

Mareme may have realized her ultimate dream by outperforming nineteen other chefs on the television program *Cuochi di Italia* and winning the title "campionato del mondo" (world champion). Upon returning from her victory, Agrigento's mayor held an evening affair in Mareme's honor and thanked her for bringing immense pride to the region. Mareme's ascension to the rank of professional chef has been especially remarkable amid heightened antimigrant sentiment stoked by Italy's far-right politicians and widespread, entrenched discrimination based on race, gender, and citizenship, aspects of social difference that articulate with and restrict access to various occupations for migrants, especially migrant women. In Italy, as in much of Western Europe, migrant women's labor opportunities have been mostly confined to caregiving, domestic work, and sex work (Agustín 2003; Cole and Booth 2007; Degiuli 2016). Mareme's prominent role at Ginger contested the racialization and exploitation of migrant women's bodies and also the devaluing of women's foodwork and their systematic exclusion from the prestigious title of "chef" (Hendley 2016). Moreover, Mareme made herself and her culinary inventions highly visible on social media (figure 12). Her role in pioneering and visually depicting a certain type of fusion cuisine further challenged the hegemony of "white Italian culture" (Frisina and Hawthorne 2018, 720) as she staked claims on culinary practices deemed "Italian" and blended them with her own. These included pastas and risotto (with shrimp, salted peas, lemon or lime zest, and African herbs), lamb and other meats marinated in African spices, and seafood stews. Similar to the struggles for recognition and representation by Black women in Italy discussed by Annalisa Frisina and

Figure 12. Portrait of Mareme from Ginger's Facebook page.
Photo by Elis Gjorretaj.

Camilla Hawthorne (2018) as the work of "everyday anti-racism," Mareme emerged as an agent of her own representation through her aesthetic performance. Mareme's online engagement was not an isolated exception but rather connected to the ever-growing digital universe through which "young black Italians have been able to connect, achieve new levels of visibility, and create relatively autonomous spaces for discussion, political organizing, and cultural production" (Hawthorne 2017, 158). And as Pamela Kea (2016, 91) writes in her essay, "Photography and Technologies of Care: Migrants in Britain and Their Children in the Gambia," such "displays of 'self-fashioning'... are crucial in garnering recognition of migrants' achievements and success to family and friends back home."

DISMANTLING ANTIMIGRANT AND RACIST SENTIMENT, FEEDING POLITICAL MOBILIZATION

Revenue from Moltivolti helped support the adjacent co-working space that served as headquarters for several human rights and social justice-oriented organizations. As of early 2020, there were twelve organizations operating in the co-working space, and included among them was a clinic for undocumented migrants, an antiracism activist organization, and a group of Nigerian women mobilizing against human trafficking. The restaurant was also one of the entities actively engaged in fund-raising and outreach efforts for the search and rescue NGO Mediterranea Saving Humans. In an interview with the communist journal *Il Manifesto*, the owners explained, "The organizations use the space for free, or contribute what they can, such as public writing, or facilitating a connection; they share an identity and a struggle for solidarity. And either during work or after work, they come into the restaurant to have a beer or eat something, because they know they're supporting an organization with limited resources but that is playing an important role."[3]

The restaurant's location in the bustling neighborhood of Ballarò was also strategic in making it a hub for solidarity work. They regularly collaborated with like-minded organizations in the neighborhood for political ends, such as in staging the SOS Ballarò sit-in in early February 2020. Protesting Matteo Salvini and the effects of his policies, particularly the security decree, the sit-in was described on social media as an effort "to defend the idea of an open community that does not operate on fear." The post continued:

We are proudly defending a neighborhood against depictions of it being dominated by criminals. Instead, many who live here grow up without the opportunities that should be guaranteed to them. Salvini does not dare come here because he knows the dear price that we have paid because of him. The security decree worsened the conditions of many of our co-citizens [*concittadini*], augmenting their social marginalization and profoundly altering the quality of life in our community.... We will continue to defend our beautiful neighborhood and protect the security of everyone that comes here, including having rights and work.

Giovanni explained the decision to position the restaurant and co-working space in Palermo's historic center in the following terms: "We established [Moltivolti] in Ballarò, a particularly [interesting] area because of both its degradation and perceptions of it as occupying the margins between legality and illegality." Consistent with Giovanni's description, many of my Palermo-based informants alluded to Ballarò as a space of liminality, between legality and illegality, where the Mafia and clientelistic social relations still influenced commerce and development but not exclusively. He elaborated, "Ballarò is also special because it offers one of few examples of migrants living in the center of the city and not at the periphery. Migrants are often confined to the periphery of big cities, but in Palermo they live in the historic center. So you see them here. Here they are inevitably visible." Giovanni's observation that Ballarò is "one of few examples" where migrants were highly visible and centrally located underscored how migrants' spatial isolation and exclusion from Italian city centers impeded their efforts to gain autonomy and fulfill their migratory projects.[4]

Giovanni emphasized how Moltivolti strived to distinguish itself as a place of community gathering and belonging. He noted, "Many migrants come to Moltivolti because they see it as a place where they can celebrate birthdays and weddings, or other major life events. And this is a wonderful thing. It means that they don't come [to Moltivolti] as guests. Instead, they feel at home." In addition to serving fusion food and providing co-working space, Moltivolti hosted a variety of community and private events such as weddings, lectures, film screenings, dance parties, birthdays, concerts, and fund-raisers. For its fourth anniversary celebration, Moltivolti hung a large map of the world in the center of its dining space on which it invited its staff and patrons to plot their "dreams and needs, desires and origins" (figure 13). A small text box to the left of the map bore the statement, "The liberty to move is a fundamental human right." Using the hashtag #noborders, Moltivolti added many photos of the

La mia terra è dove poggio i miei piedi

Figure 13. Moltivolti's "map with no borders." Photo by author.

string-adorned map to its Facebook page with the provocation, "Where do you come from? And where would you like to go? In our world without borders, the only lines are those of your desires."

Similarly, Ginger sought to cultivate feelings of community and to deliberately incentivize patrons to become active political agents in matters of im/migration. In addition to serving lunch and dinner five days a week, Ginger hosted a bimonthly concert series known as "Ginger Unplugged" to highlight social justice issues of local relevance. Despite the logistical headache that often accompanied the planning and execution of these events, Carmelo felt that the music, like their food, was "a vehicle for conveying our message" of migrant integration and solidarity. He added, "I always say that food and music are among the most powerful instruments for surmounting barriers. They also provide the opportunity for work, disproving the false belief that migrants come to our country to take jobs from Italians: this is not true. In fact, we are demonstrating the opposite, and we are creating with migrants a work opportunity for both migrants and Italians, improving their know-how."

Contrary to the belief that migrants "steal jobs" from Italians, Carmelo argued, migrants were a catalyst for generating new livelihood opportunities for both citizens and noncitizens. He explained how the combination of music and food helped diversify Ginger's clientele: "[With the music events] we're reaching people who perhaps don't know the restaurant yet and come only for the event. They come inside and then become enthusiastic about what they find and eat, and they become our clients." Carmelo and Mareme together acknowledged that regular clientele and repeat customers had a vital role in sustaining Ginger and the cooperative: "The beautiful thing we see is that the same people always come back, bringing their friends, and this indicates to us the fact that they are pleased with their experiences here."

Ginger engaged in other strategies for transmitting its political message to broader audiences. Although some of these efforts could be seen as marketing strategies, these were not easily discernible from its political advocacy and pro-migrant politics. Its Facebook page, for instance, aside from hundreds of photos of food, videos of dance performances, and event announcements, shared by both site administrators and past clientele, was particularly useful, as Carmelo claimed, for "transmitting important information and our message." Part of this message was conveyed through the principles of the cooperative. According to the restaurant's Facebook page, the name of the cooperative, Al Kharub, symbolizes the "carob tree...an evergreen tree. It belongs to a long-lived species even though it is slow-growing. It is characteristic of the Mediterranean terrain." The statement continued, "It is a symbol of our cooperative that unites different cultures, those local and those of migrants, who comprise its membership. It is inspired by the basic principles of the cooperative movement: mutuality, solidarity, association among cooperatives, and respect for others. The cooperative strives for social-multiethnic integration of *extracomunitari*, migrants, asylum seekers, and refugees." In alluding to the history (and future) of the Mediterranean region as a nexus for cultural exchange via the botanical legacy of the carob tree, Ginger rejected Eurocentric configurations of belonging—dictated by geopolitical borders and controlled by nation-states—and instead emphasized its aspirations for cultivating a community that fostered a sense of belonging on its own terms. Shortly after the national elections of March 2018, Ginger was very active on its Facebook page, offering "posts of solidarity" in response to recent race-based violence against Black Italians and migrants. And in one of its advertisements, the restaurant proclaimed that "racists don't dine here."

Giovanni also underscored the role of social media in promoting Moltivolti's message of migrant solidarity, constructing belonging, and fostering a community of like-minded supporters: "Without a doubt Facebook is the medium used to make all of our activities public, from the commercial to the noncommercial." Many of the posts on Moltivolti's Facebook page reflected the efficacy of its messaging. As an example, one patron posted, "I've never given the highest rating to a restaurant, but in this place, there is something more than just the food. Here lives the dream of a society made of friends who share with and respect one another." Its social media presence suggested a number of possible migrant solidarity-inspired slogans for the restaurant, including "La mia terra è dove poggio i miei piedi" (My land is where I rest my feet), "No borders," and "Sharing experience." At the time of my research, staff members were distinguished by their black shirts with "Moltivolti—No Borders" printed in white text. Moltivolti also utilized social media to vehemently condemn antimigrant sentiment and to incite political activism and mobilization. For instance, one of the page's administrators shared an exchange with a Facebook user who had accidentally asked to join the group. She had asked, "Wait, your pub is for a mixed clientele of Italians and *extracomunitari*?," to which he replied, "Yes, absolutely," prompting her to respond with language that supporters of Moltivolti readily recognized as xenophobic and racist. Within hours, throngs of Moltivolti supporters posted comments conveying their general opprobrium and reproach of antimigrant sentiment. One follower of the page quipped, "What is meant by a 'mixed clientele'? Since when have there been spaces for locals that prohibit migrants?" Another declared, "All of my solidarity! I love your place." Occasionally, Moltivolti used its Facebook page to solicit support from its base in crowdfunding campaigns such as one that raised several thousand dollars for a young migrant who had been diagnosed with leukemia while residing in Palermo and was trying to reunite with his family.

Yet social media only represented one small facet of both Ginger's and Moltivolti's missions to promote migrant solidarity. Giovanni of Moltivolti shared his view that the success of local efforts to promote migrant integration hinged on their level of engagement with broader politics.

> If our restaurant was just a happy island [*un'isola felice*], where everything functions but at the same time there wasn't parallel progress in the entire region that surrounds us, I think that we would have a difficult time, because we would be separate from the region, or we would remain only a happy island, where things continue to function but only when there is money. Instead, our hope is to grow with the region. To achieve these ends, we've partnered with different associations, businesses, and migrant groups in various efforts, so that through this exchange, they can also grow together with us.

In invoking the image of a hypothetical "happy island," Giovanni voiced his disapproval of enterprises focused on migrant integration that did not also seek to shift practices within the wider web of institutions, organizations, and citizens of a "surrounding region," referring to Palermo but also the rest of Sicily and even to some extent Italy. In an online episode of the show *Local Heroes* called "A Recipe for Integration," one of Moltivolti's cofounders was quoted as saying that some of their peers have warned them against being so forthcoming in their political opinions, but they challenged this idea and sought to be unapologetically political. To these ends, in the summer of 2018, Moltivolti published a manifesto as part of a social awareness campaign to rally against racist, antimigrant sentiment and to debunk myths of "a migrant invasion" in Sicily. They collected signatures from dozens of local organizations in support of the manifesto that Palermo's daily newspaper later published online.[5] They had also partnered with Mediterranea Saving Humans to host several fund-raising and volunteer recruitment events that same year. The NGO was described on Moltivolti's Facebook page as "an Italian action of moral disobedience against the dictate of nationalism and racism. Mediterranea navigates at sea but has need also on land: to construct a space of solidarity and resistance, to save all of us from a present and future of hate and intolerance." Similarly, Ginger organized the "Sea of Love" concert in July 2018 in response to the "climate of hate" that allowed for the rising death toll of migrants at sea, stating it had done so "because we are a culture of life, not death."

SOLIDARITY ECONOMIES AND FUSION FOODWAYS
AS SPACES OF BELONGING

Moltivolti and Ginger are examples of how citizens and noncitizens have been collaborating in the production of alternatives to restrictive modes of belonging that have been imposed by modern nation-states through violent bordering practices. Solidarities forged around the edible provide a means through which citizens and noncitizens may circumvent the boundaries of political citizenship and engage in social, cultural, and economic citizenship (Ceuppens and Geschiere 2005; Del Castillo 2007; Flores and Benmayor 1997; Kessler-Harris 2003). Alternatives to political citizenship deserve special attention in view of the ways that austerity regimes and far-right populist politics have excluded or severely marginalized both citizens and noncitizens (Muehlebach 2018). Migrants tap into "transnational configurations of belonging" at Moltivolti and Ginger by imbuing fusion cuisines with their own culinary knowledge and practices (Mankekar 2002; see also Mares 2012). Migrants have a prominent role as partners in these enterprises as well as in the broader social projects around which they were founded. These establishments reimagine fusion foodways as part of an intentional effort to build a more equitable society and diverge from the perspective of state institutions in advancing a project of migrant integration that regards noncitizens not simply as economic assets, but as valued members of a community.

Migrants are heralded as primary agents in the transmission of culinary knowledge and practices of fusion foodways that, in turn, allow them to preserve this knowledge and a connection to their homeland(s). The application of migrant knowledge in the forging of fusion foodways in this context should not be conflated with the ways that capitalism has repeatedly and violently extracted and appropriated knowledge and resources in ensuring its own reproduction.[6] Rather, preparation and consumption of familiar foods in the context of migration and displacement is particularly significant for sustaining connections to homeland and within social networks, preserving systems of knowledge and memory, reconstituting the self in foreign settings, and enacting relations of care (Carney 2015; Dossa 2014; Gasparetti 2012; Hayes-Conroy and Sweet 2015; Himmelgreen et al. 2007; Janowski 2012; Johnson 2016; Mares 2012; Mintz 2008; Sen

2016). Maria Abranches (2014, 266) notes that "homeland food is... an important basis for counteracting migrants' adverse experiences in terms of both unfamiliar tastes and the discomfort brought on by exogenous foodstuffs, which... weaken the migrant's body." Preparing, exchanging, and consuming familiar foods represent important sites of care and survival as they hold the potential to enhance "feelings of stability, order, and continuity" (Abranches 2014, 263) in what otherwise might register as hostile and inhospitable environments. In her study of food practices among Senegalese migrants in Italy, Fedora Gasparetti (2012, 264) suggests that "[food] strengthens the internal cohesion of the group while contributing at the same time to narrowing internal differences among migrants themselves." Homeland foods thus afford possibilities to reaffirm group and individual identity for people in diaspora and act as a buffer against social isolation and marginalization in the context of resettlement.

It may be suggested that an emphasis on the "intercultural" or "multiethnic"—akin to discourses of "multiculturalism"—as it permeates both establishments obscures the ways that broader structures of inequality remain ever present and translate to uneven social relations and possibilities within the project of migrant integration (Chin 2017; Hale 2002; Hall 2000; Pratt 2002; Riccio 2002; Speed 2005). For instance, the map on the wall at Moltivolti suggested a "flat" world where "dreams, needs, wishes, and origins" of humanity surfaced on a single dimension. Yet no one at either Moltivolti or Ginger would deny the disparities between staff and patrons relating to differential experiences of race, nationality, gender, and legal status. Since I was unable to access spaces of interaction among workers for any prolonged period, I am left wondering how these workers negotiate inequalities in the kitchen and also in the broader institutional context of the restaurant. It should also be noted that domestic workers in the privacy of Italian households are likely forging fusion foodways as well, but they enjoy less privilege and visibility in this work. How might we conceptualize their role in the project(s) of migrant integration and edible solidarities? Future research might explore this question.

While the promotion of fusion cuisines could be argued to serve profit-making motives by appealing to the tastes of elite consumers, this is not a readily evident practice at either Moltivolti or Ginger. Although the teams behind both establishments could not necessarily anticipate and prevent fetishization or commodification of "exotic" foods, they do not subscribe to "multiethnic" and "intercultural" discourses for the purposes of tapping into a specific market niche. Moreover, as Roberta Sassatelli (2019, 2) observes in her discussion of Italian foodways, "Creolization and hybridization are indeed a feature of any cuisine." By calling explicit attention to this hybridization, Moltivolti and Ginger are catering to much "more than just the food," as noted by Chef Mareme and patrons who frequent both establishments. Similar to the effects of migration in other parts of Southern Europe, where food has mediated "new spaces of communication and coexistence" and at times has resulted in "social transformation" (Bou 2020, 2), these migrant-centered enterprises intentionally tap into food for its political potential.

By providing a buffer against economic risks through strengthening social relations and improving local livelihoods while also facilitating migrant integration and political mobilization, Moltivolti and Ginger coalesce around food as a site for transforming the material and agentive possibilities of citizens and noncitizens, enacting (affective) resistance, and caring for collective belonging and well-being (Caldwell 2004; Mares 2012). These enterprises resemble solidarity economies, defined as livelihood strategies that seek to "replace disembedded market relations of exchange with obligations of reciprocity within a general call for political mobilization" (Rakopoulos 2015, 165). In contrast to the market-based logics of neoliberal capitalism, Giovanni and Carmelo both underscored the value of social relations rather than economic capital as constituting "the engine of progress." Although neither would dispute the practical function of money in supporting their operations, they still viewed the success of any business as nearly impossible without the social bonds that would sustain it over time. In foregrounding social relations and migrant integration and giving comparatively less attention to their bottom line, businesses like Moltivolti and Ginger closely articulate with the set of shared principles guiding solidarity economies. Posited by Penn Loh and Julian Agyeman (2017, 262) as the "cornerstone ideas" of solidarity economies, these include "a view of humans as interdependent social beings," the balancing of "individual and collective interests," "collective ownership and cooperative management," and integration of noncapitalist "forms of exchange, production, and ownership." Yet as scholars and advocates have observed, paradoxically solidarity economies also develop within the broader web of hegemonic market-based arrangements, the very arrangements that they seek to usurp and transform.

Anthropologists have recently suggested that the emergence of social solidarity initiatives in the European context represents the "flipside" of crisis (Cabot 2016). In regard to solidarity economies more specifically, Rakopoulos (2014, 196, 164), for example, proposes a "dialectical relationship between crises and solidarity" wherein solidarity economy indexes "a democratic challenge to austerity politics—or . . . a movement, in other words, aiming to democratize the economy and thereby promote an alternative vision of democracy." Democratizing the economy in this setting entails in part demanding representation and recognition within a system that has obscured the conditions of labor and exploited a hierarchy organized around race, gender, and citizenship while surrendering power to private interests. As another means of eliciting and broadening participation, hybrid for-profit and nonprofit entities like Moltivolti and Ginger have been engaging in grassroots reclaiming and revitalization of urban space both in Palermo and in Agrigento where structural deterioration and underdevelopment have historically been the norm. These revitalization efforts tread against the historically unethical, exclusionary, and ostensibly corrupt decision making by political elites in Sicily who have routinely appealed to class relations of patronage and clientelism (Chubb 1982; Cole 1997; Orlando 2015).

The fusion food establishments that I examine in this chapter explicitly reject antimigrant and austerity politics that they have come to associate with the marginalization of ordinary citizens and noncitizens. As possible emergent expressions of a solidarity economy in Sicily, Moltivolti and Ginger exhibit the desire and aspiration to stave off or prevent future crises by transforming material, affective, and political possibilities for collective well-being. Although the emergence of solidarity economy is intrinsically intertwined with the political and economic marginalization of both citizens and noncitizens in Southern Europe, Moltivolti and Ginger as quasi-expressions of solidarity economy represent more than the "flipside of crisis." In contemplating the meanings of solidarity, Carmelo and Mareme reaffirmed a commitment to sharing one another's destiny, redistributing risk, and working toward something better (see also Carney 2017a).

Despite the overall optimism expressed by staff at both Moltivolti and Ginger, these businesses inevitably faced certain challenges in staying afloat. Proponents of a solidarity economy argue that entities must connect with others to scale up and achieve broader structural changes. This corresponds to one of the main critiques of a solidarity economy: "There is danger that the entities making up the solidarity economy will remain fragmented as islands within the dominant economy. This fragmentation may be further fueled by competition for funding and resources between entities" (Loy and Agyeman 2017, 277). Giovanni of Moltivolti was grimly aware of this risk when he spoke of the hypothetical *isola felice*. Another concern is that solidarity economies risk being perceived as yet more "market solutions" to a set of problems associated with free market capitalism. Reliance on commercial social media platforms such as Facebook does not help mitigate this concern, even though the use of social media proves effective for many solidarity economy projects in disseminating their philosophy and broader messaging. Yet the proprietors and staff of both Moltivolti and Ginger recognized the imperative to identify other strategies for disseminating their message and mobilizing a broader public to take political action.

UPHOLDING THE SANCTITY OF FOOD IN SOCIAL LIFE

In September 2018, the small Italian town of Lodi made headlines around the world when its right-wing, anti-immigrant mayor implemented a policy that led to segregation of Italian-born children from children of foreign-born parents at school lunches. The policy demanded that foreign-born parents obtain documentation to demonstrate a lack of assets in their countries of origin—which is nearly impossible for most of them to do—as a means to prove financial need that would qualify their children for lunch subsidies. Within weeks of the announcement, several thousand citizens and noncitizens across Italy donated to a crowdfunding campaign to cover the cost of lunch for these schoolchildren, protesting the segregation of children at mealtimes and citing Italian values of commensality and the sanctity of food in social life.[7]

Fusion foodways and the enterprises that center on them represent one thread of migrant solidarity work being enacted by citizens and noncitizens in Sicily. Moltivolti and Ginger/Al Kharub align in employing fusion foods, investing in and caring for relationships, and engaging in different forms of political mobilization and advocacy to counter and resist populist anti-immigrant as well as austerity politics. It is by means of these strategies that both establishments seek not only to ensure their own social reproduction and long-term viability but also to actively facilitate more radical approaches to migrant integration.

The next and final chapter examines the experiences of migrant youth in Sicily and the various ways that they organize or that others organize on their behalf to protect their rights, improve their prospects for the future, and forge alliances of solidarity.

6 Caring for the Future

The migrants arriving here are getting younger
and younger.

—Member of the Italian Parliamentary Commission on
Childhood and Adolescence

"BAMBINI SENZA CONFINI"

In Sicily during the summer of 2017, everyone everywhere seemed to be
fretting about the "migration crisis." Within humanitarian circles, there
was particular anxiety about the increasing numbers of *minori stranieri
non accompagnati* (unaccompanied minor arrivals). They cited numbers
from UNICEF: more than 25,800 unaccompanied minors arrived in Italy
by sea in 2016, almost twice as many from 2015, and accounting for 15
percent of all arrivals. By June 2017, the number of unaccompanied minor
arrivals had increased by another 22 percent and accounted for 92 percent
of all children arriving through the central Mediterranean route (UNICEF
2017). The Italian Ministry of Labor and Social Affairs (2016) reported
that most of the unaccompanied minor arrivals were male (94 percent)
and between the ages of sixteen and seventeen (82.2 percent).[1] Noting
these trends, the Italian Association of Lawyers for Families and Minors
(Associazione italiana degli avvocati per la famiglia e i minori) organized
a daylong emergency conference, "Bambini senza Confini: Protezione,
tutela e cura dei minori stranieri non accompagnati" (Children without
Borders: Protection, Guardianship and Care of Unaccompanied Minors).

"Bambini senza Confini" was held in the ornate quarters of Palermo's Palazzo Chiaramonte and brought together attorneys, government officials, health and social workers, and representatives of humanitarian organizations. Attendees photographed the meeting hall's cathedral windows, engraved wooden ceilings, and marble floors and listened to panels on the topics "Without Mother or Father in a Foreign Land" and "Who and How Many Are the Unaccompanied Foreign Children and Youth in Italy?" In his opening remarks, the chancellor of the University of Palermo underscored the importance of "coinvolgimento pubblico" (public engagement) in responding to migrant youth. He was followed by a member of Italy's Parliamentary Commission on Childhood and Adolescence (Commissione parlamentare per l'infanzia e l'adolescenza), who emphasized the "younger and younger" ages of migrants who were arriving on the shores of Italy, seeing it as "un ingresso a Europa" (an entry point to Europe). Noting the ways that migrant youth lacking a legal guardian were easily targeted by traffickers and criminal organizations and faced uncertain futures (*incertezza di futuro*), participants called for "ensuring that every minor knows his or her rights from the moment they arrive" and widespread action characterized by "looking to migrant youth as a resource instead of a problem."

Both governmental and nongovernmental actors commonly frame migrant youth as "victims" who have been denied an authentic experience of childhood. It is impossible to dismiss concerns about the vulnerability of migrant youth considering the myriad instances throughout history in which state institutions have denied a child's age, circumvented asylum procedures, and deported children and young adults without due process or incarcerated children and youth as adults. Nonetheless, the imposition of Eurocentric social, cultural, and legal norms in human rights law and the approaches of host societies to managing migrant children and adolescents tend to eclipse other ideas and beliefs about childhood, the human life course, and the onset of adulthood as these vary across societies. For instance, the EU Action Plan on Unaccompanied Arrivals states, "The [EU] Commission places the standards established by the United Nations Convention on the Rights of the Child (UNCRC) at the heart of any action concerning unaccompanied minors" (EU 2010, 2). Without adequate interventions and surveillance by institutions, migrant youth are perceived as being at risk of developing delinquent or criminal behaviors. For instance, the anthropologist Lauren Heidbrink (2014) observes that governments often attempt to "rehabilitate" migrant youth by socializing them to childhood norms that characterize the host society.

These perceptions of migrant youth as both "at risk" and "risky" subjects operate in tandem to discipline migrant youth and social or institutional actors working on their behalf into particular affective states that ultimately restrict the mobility and autonomy of this population. Enacting solidarity with migrant youth, as many of my research participants have explained, often requires pushing back against these perceptions, as well as the restrictions placed on young people's possibilities for citizenship and belonging. But such a mandate is often easier said than done. In her study of unaccompanied migrant youth in the United States, for instance, Heidbrink (2014, 30) underscores efforts by advocates to acknowledge "children as important social actors" while also navigating the seemingly intractable "disparity in power between children and adults."

In this chapter, I bring attention to the specific experiences of migrant youth in Italy's reception apparatus and the ways in which they have been (un)accounted for in the aspirational project of migrant solidarity. I draw on my own interviews and ethnographic observations pertaining to migrant youth's experiences of arriving in Italy and street-level *accoglienza*, as well as their struggles for recognition by state institutions and for representation within society at large. I discuss the complicated ways that solidarity is mobilized both *for* and *with* migrant youth. To what extent do those providing support to or aligning with migrant youth care to actively include and enlist migrant youth and account for the future(s) of solidarity work? What possibilities exist for migrant youth to assert themselves across these settings and to shape their own migratory projects? While exploring these lines of inquiry, I seek to remain cognizant of how the information provided in this chapter may be exploited by different individuals and institutions *against* the "best interests" of this population. Rather than reinforce perceptions of migrant youth that ultimately constrain their material and affective possibilities, this chapter is informed by social actors who are attempting to imagine alternatives to restrictive modes of citizenship and belonging for migrant youth in Italy. Moreover, I argue that the case of migrant youth offers a unique vantage point from which to examine solidarity work as it transcends social boundaries between citizens and noncitizens as well as temporal boundaries between present-day and future generations.

YOUTH IN THE RECEPTION APPARATUS

During a *sbarco* in Palermo in the summer of 2017, the year of peak arrivals by unaccompanied migrant youth in Sicily, I observed an orientation with migrant youth being facilitated by representatives of the organization Save the Children. Prior to commencing the orientation, humanitarian workers had distributed brochures to these youth that displayed the official insignia of the EU, the Italian Ministry of Interior, the United Nations High Commissioner for Refugees (UNHCR), and the International Organization for Migration (IOM). The brochure read:

> Welcome! You are safe now! We would like to give you some information! If you are under 18 and you have arrived in Italy without your parents, spouse, brothers, and sisters above 18 or other relatives, according to Italian law, you are considered an unaccompanied minor and cannot be expelled and you can have a stay permit until the age of 18. If you are an unaccompanied minor, you cannot be held in reception facilities with adults and you have the right to be housed and receive assistance in Italy in residential houses for minors. In case of serious doubts in relation to the age you declared, and in case you do not have documents to show to the authorities (such as passports or ID cards), the Italian authorities can ask you to collaborate to assess your age, through interviews or medical tests.

Over the course of an hour or more, the Save the Children representatives proceeded to explain the steps involved in the identification process and the nuances of declaring minor versus adult status. They noted that these migrant youth would soon declare minor (or adult) status while providing other details to authorities about their nationality, age, and reasons for migrating. One of the representatives urged the young people to be honest with authorities because failing to do so could jeopardize their chances of acquiring the documents necessary for accessing work or health and social services. Paradoxically, this representative then suggested some minutes later that prevaricating about one's age could be advantageous, as claiming adult status would improve one's eligibility for employment. Some of the youth in attendance nodded their heads to show their understanding. As I helped distribute supplies from a nearby tent, I noted the extreme fatigue among the youth who had disembarked merely minutes before. They had been famished for days, perhaps weeks, and were recovering from prolonged exposure to the hot Mediterranean sun. And now they were being told that they were "safe." Despite the best intentions of the Save the Children representatives, it was unclear how much these young people were able to focus or even able to understand, given that the entire orientation was in English.

As I learned from a physician who explained the nature of his work using X-rays during a talk at the "Bambini senza Confini" conference in Palermo in May 2017, authorities not only assessed age through the "verbale," or intake interview, at *sbarco* events. They sometimes also conducted forensic evaluations such as measuring growth of cartilage in and around limbs and teeth, as well as sexual organs, to approximate a person's age. However, I found that most social workers detested these practices and the use of biometrics in asylum cases. Consistent with other forms of subject making that heighten one's "legibility" to the state (Fassin and Rechtman 2009), such physical assessments, combined with psychological assessments to determine an individual's credibility and deservingness of asylum, were viewed by many involved in migrant reception as invasive, unnecessary forms of retraumatization.

While Italian law dictates that the social services of host municipalities provide adequate resources and facilities for the care and housing of unaccompanied minors, harrowing accounts from NGOs and humanitarian organizations as well as from migrant youth themselves suggest otherwise. In 2016, Médecins Sans Frontières reported that most centers for initial reception failed to separate unaccompanied minors from adults and supplied only minimal provisions: one set of clothes, a pair of flip-flops, and a €5 telephone card (often an inadequate amount for contacting relatives in a foreign country or altogether useless if there was no functioning phone from which to place a call). An investigation by the NGO Human Rights Watch (2016) revealed that children at a reception facility in Sicily's southern port of Pozzallo "had not been able to contact their parents or other relatives to tell them that they had survived the journey." Social workers

I interviewed regretted that stays of unaccompanied minors at centers for initial reception, or hotspots, frequently surpassed the maximum 48- to 72-hour limit, extending sometimes up to five weeks. A report from Oxfam (2016, 3) underscored the implications of extended stays: "This means never changing their clothes, even their underwear, and not being able to call their family." Many of these humanitarian organizations had withdrawn from collaborating in center operations, explicitly citing inadequate conditions for the reception of minors.

Several of my informants underscored how Italian authorities abandoned migrant youth once they were released from reception facilities, consistent with the experiences of the migrant adults I discussed in chapter 3. The director of a Palermo-based nonprofit explained, "It's not a pretty situation for unaccompanied youth because they receive very limited support. They may receive a little help at first, for instance, with obtaining a residence permit and maybe some training in fostering their autonomy, but then nothing. Many end up being delinquents or working in the black market." As described by this director, the lack of measures to protect this population may have heightened the risk of delinquency and criminality, including escapes by youth from reception facilities to reunite with relatives in other regions of the EU, most often in Northern Europe. The coordinator of a job training program for migrant youth told me:

> We know that in the last few years, there has been a notable increase in the number of migrant youth arrivals and unaccompanied minors in Italy. It is a very worrisome situation in Sicily because being a territory that receives many arrivals, and also the place where migrants are first identified, very often, after minors have been identified and held at initial centers, they escape, looking to get to northern Italy or Northern Europe. We don't always know if they reunite with their relatives or if they end up working on the black market or in some form of child exploitation. By now this is public knowledge. The press talks about it ceaselessly, but no one is really doing anything about it.

In 2017, Oxfam reported that due to mismanagement of Italy's migrant reception system, some twenty-eight unaccompanied migrant youth simply "disappeared" each day (cited in ANSAmed 2016). The report further elaborated on the squalid conditions faced by youth outside of centers.

In the summer, the parks and gardens around the train station in Catania are full of children who spend the whole day waiting to get on a bus for Rome or Milan, from where they hope to continue their journey farther on into mainland Europe. After a couple of days in hotspots, or initial reception centers, they run away, sleeping in the open at night or in an abandoned car park—a flat cemented area full of garbage on which they spread cartons and blankets to sleep. They wash in the basin of the public fountains and eat at the Caritas Help Center.

Many of my informants—both citizens and noncitizens—bemoaned the quasi-homeless status of these youth, who frequently lacked food, access to potable water, changes of clothing, or a place to sleep and survived on the charity of select NGOs that occasionally supplied them with snacks, sandwiches, toilet paper, and soap, among other provisions. The circumstances preceding the departure of migrant youth from reception centers in Italy were also of grave concern to humanitarian organizations such as Save the Children that lamented the systematic frequency with which these "escapes" occurred. Save the Children issued a statement in 2014 calling for the immediate closure of centers that could not prevent minors from escaping (World Bulletin 2014).

While the specter of "disappearing" minors triggered an array of practical questions and concerns regarding the well-being of migrant youth, comments on the elusiveness of migrant youth rarely touched on the broader question of from *what* (or from *whom*) these youth had "disappeared." As emphasized by many of my research participants who worked in some aspect of migrant *accoglienza*, often what were described as inexplicable "disappearances" were actually instances of minors asserting their migratory projects and deciding that better (and safer) opportunities awaited them elsewhere. Migrant youth I implored to share more with me about their decisions to leave reception centers often related feelings of distrust toward or misunderstandings with staff. Sometimes centers closed entirely or kicked them out without advance notice. A reception center employee who provided "cultural mediation" to unaccompanied minors, alluded to some of the circumstances that generated distrust by youth toward center staff, ultimately leading them to vacate these spaces: "I think one aspect of the problem has to do with the fact that the money that the Italian government allocates as per diem to arriving migrants goes to the associations providing reception rather than directly to the migrant, who ends up receiving only a small fraction." She added, "There's of course a lot of alarm around potential pedophiles intercepting them," echoing concerns shared with me by other reception center staff who believed that migrant youth were particularly vulnerable to traffickers or those with malicious intent. Some suggested that minors were intercepted by criminal organizations before they even arrived in Italy, recalling instances in which youth were recruited by human smugglers to transport boats of migrants across the Mediterranean and then faced trial and imprisonment by the Italian government.

In some ways, the care administered by these centers intersected with state interests in surveilling and monitoring this "unauthorized" population. Heidbrink (2014, 2) has suggested, "Independent, or unattached, migrant children...threaten the notion of how children can and should act. Their unauthorized presence and exercise of 'independent' agency threaten the state's reliance on the nuclear family as the site for producing future citizens." This may help explain why directors and staff often prioritized the forging of emotional bonds, as I discuss further below: to ensure some level of attachment that would prevent youth from leaving prematurely. Outside of centers, migrant youth were no longer visible, manageable, and docile from a governmentality perspective. Thus, in some cases, describing migrant youth as "missing," "escaped," "runaways," or "disappeared" registered less as concern for youth well-being and more as shorthand for conveying the crisis of young people having slipped from the grips of state institutions. Rather than adhere to procedures delineated and prescribed by state institutions, these young people had ventured on their own, taking matters into their own hands to "put stress on the reception system and show its inconsistencies. Many escape and react against the attempt to confine or disperse them" (Campesi 2018, 502). Ironically, such "disappearances" helped these youth come out of the shadows of state institutions.

Programs such as Accoglierete Onlus in the southeastern port of Syracuse demonstrated how addressing the needs of unaccompanied minors and educating them on their rights could be helpful in preventing harm to this population and possible "disappearances." This organization had been active in promoting the role of voluntary legal guardians—someone to act in the "best interest" of youth and protect the rights to which they were all legally entitled. Oxfam (2016, 9) argues, "Guardianship plays a vital role in determining the extent and quality with which the institutions fulfil their responsibilities in taking care of children who are unaccompanied. Shockingly, it can take up to eight months until a guardian is appointed. This is especially true in Sicily, due to the vast number of arrivals." In the absence of resources to appoint guardians, some organizations developed less formal but nonetheless helpful mentoring programs. UNICEF, for instance, had organized a mentoring program in Palermo through which migrant youth were connected with adult mentors who were citizens and had undergone appropriate screening and training prior to mentoring.

Humanitarian and nongovernmental organizations were continuously advocating for significant overhaul of Italy's—and the EU's—reception procedures for unaccompanied minors. Proposed changes to EU policy issued in 2016 included securing protections from exploitation and violence, replacing detention of migrant youth with housing alternatives, reuniting families, giving all unaccompanied minors legal status, and ensuring access to education and health care. Oxfam noted that Italy, in particular, should "set up a national reception system that can support all arriving unaccompanied children, increasing the number of places available both in initial and in secondary reception (SPRAR), ensuring standardized services are provided, and guaranteeing the monitoring of the standards of the facilities and adequate selection and training of the staff." Moreover, the organization called for "dignified and safe temporary reception for children moving across Italy," "the rapid appointment of legal guardians for all unaccompanied children," standardization of "identification and age assessment processes so that they are always carried out in a child's best interests and in agreement with the International Convention on the Rights of the Child," and integration through education and vocational training (Oxfam 2016, 9).

In March 2017, the Italian parliament responded to widespread scrutiny of its mishandling of minors by approving a law that outlined comprehensive standards of care for unaccompanied minors. Measures introduced in the law included a reduction in the amount of time that unaccompanied minors could spend in primary reception centers, the creation of a ten-day window during which authorities were obligated to confirm the identities of unaccompanied youth, and guaranteed access to healthcare. The humanitarian community responded with praise, deeming the law "the first of its kind in Europe" (AP 2017). Since then, however, Italy has implemented sweeping changes to its reception procedures that corresponded to changes in the national government, and reception centers were facing impending closure or significant rollbacks in government funding.

STREET-LEVEL (YOUTH) *ACCOGLIENZA*

Asante reminded me of a boarding school but not the sort of boarding school loathed by those who lived there. Inside, the hallways were always bustling with young people as they came and went to classes, meals, and other events. Staff and residents socialized in the outside courtyard or set up board games on one of the tables in the cafeteria (figure 14). Contrary to the reports of dreadful living conditions in reception centers throughout Italy, I usually found people here smiling and seeming to genuinely enjoy one another's company.

Formerly a hotel for students and tourists, Asante was founded in late 2015 as a reception center for unaccompanied minors in Palermo. As of mid-2017, Asante housed close to 140 youth residents, with twenty full-time employees. While individual stays at Asante were not to exceed sixty days according to Italian law, most Asante residents lacked alternatives because of age restrictions or lack of vacancies elsewhere. The majority of residents thus typically stayed at Asante anywhere from one to two years. The facility included a front reception area, cafeteria, classrooms, and about fifty bedrooms that each accommodated two to three residents.

Asante offered many activities, classes, and services for its residents in its efforts to create a familial atmosphere and to promote integration of migrant youth in Sicily. Daily activities varied, but every week there were classes in music, art, Italian, and pizza making (*pizzaiolo*), which was also intended for vocational purposes. Many residents played in a local soccer league, hosted and produced the center's youth-directed radio station (Radio Asante, to which I was invited and spoke as a guest), or accom-

Figure 14. Asante's cafeteria. Photo by author.

panied staff on sight-seeing tours of Palermo. Staff members remained on site the entire day and assisted residents with a variety of needs and requests such as completing paperwork for residence permits or obtaining a health card. As recounted by Vicenza, one of Asante's cultural mediators:

> We take care of our residents. We're there from morning until night. Sometimes we even forget our own homes. The center depends on the level of rapport among us: these youth arrive, with the baggage of their past, they are not trusting. So the first thing we aim to do with them is to find a way to build rapport and trust and to understand their needs and help them as

much as possible. And then they grow up, and to see them grow up brings me such joy because they represent the fruit of our labor. The unfortunate part of this work is when they leave us, but many keep in touch.

Other Asante staff echoed Vicenza's sentiments, underscoring how they aspired to (re-)create the conditions of home and family for migrant youth. These workers often assumed a guardian role by "taking care" of youth residents, building "rapport and trust" with them, and lending support as they matured and eventually moved out. They sought to help youth residents feel "a casa loro" (at one's own home) and to accommodate their particular needs as much as possible. Upon arrival and registering as residents, youth worked with Asante staff to complete a "Map of Skills" questionnaire that collected biographical details such as educational background, previous work experience, and level(s) of interest in vocations and careers spanning the arts, sports, healthcare and education, public service, science, retail, and professional trades. They also conducted introductory psychosocial evaluations of residents, asking about the composition of their family, their migratory projects (reasons for migration and expectations, desires, and future plans), and health conditions. In ongoing psychosocial evaluations, Asante residents were asked questions such as "Can you rest well and relax?," "Do you have problems falling asleep?," "Do you feel protected here?," and "Have you built bonds and new friendships?"

Many of the Asante residents with whom I interacted shared that they experienced feelings of kinship with staff and one another. They expressed physical affection to staff members upon returning home from classes, work, or soccer practice; compared certain staff members to being like an older sibling; and regularly confided in staff about their everyday frustrations and struggles as well as successes.

Located only a few kilometers from Asante, Blossom House was a "family-style" communal housing facility for unaccompanied minors between the ages of fourteen and eighteen. Palermo's *InComune* magazine described the center as "a place of protection and exchange of different cultures and traditions, where youth recount their troubling experiences and find the space for listening and expression that they have yet to have." The housing facility shared its grounds with a school for young children, many of whom were of refugee status and had foreign-born parents. While the origins of Blossom House extended back to 1998, I learned from its directors during a visit in May 2017 that they had reopened the center in 2011 as a response to the recent influx of asylum seekers and refugees coming across the central Mediterranean.

Although much smaller than Asante, housing up to only ten residents at a time, Blossom House intended to increase its capacity to fifteen, as the two women who managed operations there told me. They contrasted the advantages of the relatively low capacity of the communal housing facility with the disadvantages of larger reception centers: "A structure for ten or fifteen youth guarantees the possibility of care and attention superior to that of a SPRAR, where there are sixty or more residents. Hence, the individual is given the utmost attention. This model helps guarantee the rights of these youth as outlined by the UN."

Controlling for a smaller number of residents at Blossom House, according to these directors, allowed them to uphold a human rights agenda that attended to the individual needs of residents. One means by which they enacted this agenda was developing individualized education plans (*progetto educativo individualizzato*) that identified the necessary training and educational path for youth to "insert themselves into the realm of work and social life." Staff and volunteers revisited and refined these plans with youth over time while considering their reflections and shifting interests. The directors at Blossom House viewed insertion in the realm of work as a necessary first step to entering Italian society.

At the time of my initial visit to Blossom House, it was housing youth from Mali, Nigeria, Eritrea, and Gambia. There were five staff members and two volunteers overseeing operations of the facility and providing support to residents. The facility had been renovated in recent years and offered spacious, clean quarters to its residents, who were assigned in pairs to each room. In addition to a large communal kitchen, the facility had a recreation room, meeting rooms, and multiple bathrooms. During my tour, I met the center's housekeepers—two women, from Gambia and Mali—as well as one of the lead educators (a native Italian) who lived on site. One of the center directors described a typical day as follows:

> It is the classic day of a family. We progress in the manner of a family. Wake up around 7:30 or 8:00 in the morning, get ready for school, have breakfast,

and head out. Later residents return home for lunch, which is prepared in the meantime by one of our staff. However, if one of the residents is at home, they'll help with any preparation of the meal. After lunch there are various activities, principally school, but others participate in sports or volunteer work such as at one of the local parks where they can go to cultivate gardens, or they get involved in some other local service work.

Centers for migrant youth such as Asante and Blossom House stipulated that residents attend public schools, earning a diploma or certificate from primary and secondary institutions along the way, and study Italian either on site or at a nearby language school. From the perspective of many social workers and Italian-language instructors working with both migrant minors and adults, access to educational resources supported youth's attempts to integrate socially. One language instructor, Michele, told me, "She who arrives here and goes to school fares much better. But youth are also more open-minded; they're ready to make new friends, including with locals, and thus readier to integrate."

Both Asante and Blossom House steered youth residents toward various forms of civic engagement such as team sports, volunteering, and public service. In this regard, centers mimicked the role of a family in mediating state interests through the conditioning of its future citizens (Boehm 2012). This practice of nurturing a family environment also extended to how Blossom House dealt with conflict or transgression among residents. The directors underscored expectations of emotional, reproductive labor in sustaining this "family." As explained by one of its directors, they worked with residents to resolve conflicts within a group setting, which also required input of emotional labor: "They work in groups.... We discuss every single episode from the perspective of the group, observing the growth of the individual with the entire community." They encouraged their residents to engage in the "collective labor" of thinking critically and objectively about the underlying causes of migration while also inflecting this labor with their "subjective experiences and emotions" (Blossom House newsletter, July 2015). The directors of Blossom House spoke passionately about how they were invested in the future well-being of residents: "We encourage them to recount their stories but with a look to the future.... The objective of this project is to prepare these youth to have everything necessary to be able to think of and hope for a better future." In turn, the directors claimed, former residents were also invested in maintaining relationships with center staff: "They find us and keep in touch as soon as they leave, via phone, email, social media, Facebook."

Despite differences in the size of operations at each site, Asante and Blossom House adopted similar approaches to housing migrant youth. Both organizations sought to cultivate feelings of collective ownership (and responsibility), belonging, and family—of being at one's home ("a casa loro")—by involving residents in the maintenance and operations of facilities and enlisting them in the emotional, reproductive aspects of conviviality. In addition, they sought to promote youth autonomy and the individual interests of residents by offering multiple educational, vocational, and recreational opportunities. Yet these centers were also determined to prevent residents from leaving before they reached the age of eighteen, when they would be considered legal adults according to Italian law.

ORGANIZING FOR AND WITH MIGRANT YOUTH

> It's important to help people understand, to give them a first-hand account of the everyday life of a migrant.... The people who can best explain this kind of situation are the ones who had to leave their countries to come here to Italy.
>
> —Eighteen-year-old codirector of a migrant-led media project, quoted in Claudio Accheri, "By Migrants for Migrants"

Migrant youth were instrumental during the time of my fieldwork to advancing policy debates and shifting public attitudes more favorably toward migration. There were several instances in which I observed migrant youth being enlisted in both public awareness campaigns and more radical forms of activism. Some of these efforts were initiated by humanitarian organizations like UNICEF, while others were less platform-specific and more decentralized, allowing migrant youth to assert roles in telling their own stories and calling for specific forms of action.

On a warm Sunday evening in the eastern Sicilian port of Catania, I attended the "Bambini/giovani in pericolo" (Children/Youth in Danger) benefit organized by UNICEF at Palazzo Manganelli. As the sun gradually disappeared behind the city's Baroque architecture, an Ottocento dance troupe distinguished by their traditional attire arrived at the entrance of the palazzo. They ascended the red-carpeted marble staircase into the reception area for the evening's benefit, followed by me and other attendees. Several exhibitions dotted the ornate quarters of this seventeenth-century building, including an African art installation and a photo exhibition depicting rescues of migrant children in the central Mediterranean. With my toddler in tow, I passed a grand salon where many elegantly dressed *catanesi* had begun to assume seats for tonight's main program. An official-looking gray-haired gentleman initially turned us away, explaining that the seats were reserved for people "whose direct participation is necessary for this event." His assistant retrieved us shortly thereafter to escort us to chairs in the back row of the salon. A sound track of classical music played for the next several minutes as attendees anticipated the start of the program.

A young Italian woman turned on her microphone to welcome attendees, her nervousness quite palpable as she related her *emozione* (excitement) for this evening's program. The man who had dismissed my daughter and me some minutes earlier accompanied her onstage as they introduced themselves as the emcees. Following some formalities such as opening remarks by UNICEF representatives, the emcees restated the purpose of the benefit: to raise awareness about the dangers inflicted on migrant children and youth in coming to Italy. They introduced the young migrants who had been invited to give "testimonianze" (testimonies) to the audience, beginning with a Gambian woman. Closing her eyes as though to recall her lines, she described her boat voyage across the Mediterranean. Within minutes, her toddler, who had been sitting in the front row, began dancing around at her feet demanding attention. The male emcee interrupted the woman mid-testimony to request that she quickly finish and return to her seat because her child was proving a distraction. She was followed by two young men from the Gambia and Egypt to share about their harrowing sea voyage across the Mediterranean. Speaking last was a twelve-year-old Syrian girl who appeared uncomfortable onstage, standing next to an interpreter who spoke on her behalf. Altogether, these testimonies accounted for about twenty-five minutes of the evening's three-hour program.

Over the next two hours, the emcees entertained attendees with appearances by public servants, dance performances, and food. UNICEF staff orchestrated an awards ceremony during which they recognized the cara- binieri, or military police, the coast guard, the *guardia di finanza* (more military police), the Catania mayor's office, and the *vigili del fuoco* (fire brigade) for being "ambasciatori" (ambassadors) of UNICEF's mission. Speakers repeatedly referred to the "spirit of solidarity" (*spirito di solidar- ietà*) exhibited by *catanesi* whose support was deemed essential to migrant rescue, reception, and staving off the dangers posed by the migratory journey. Each received a trophy and was photographed with the emcees. UNICEF staff distributed certificates one at a time to each of the event sponsors, who were also then photographed. The emcees then announced the most anticipated phase of the evening: the Ottocento dancers' perfor- mance. Attendees flooded the salon while holding up their phones to cap- ture photos and video of the troupe enacting ballroom dances typical of the nineteenth century in Italy. Finally, the emcees invited us to exit into the adjacent courtyard for samples of "multiethnic" cuisines. Attendees flocked to one of several tables to sample bite-size servings of couscous, egg rolls, quesadillas, and falafel that had been elegantly presented on white tablecloths. Some moments later, the catering staff entered the scene in dramatic procession offering attendees *arancini* (Sicilian rice balls) from silver platters (figure 15). Surveying the large crowd that had gathered out- side, I noticed that the migrant youth who had given their testimonies earlier were now huddling together in one corner of the courtyard. Aside from some limited interaction with the UNICEF staff and volunteers, the youth seemed rather forgotten by attendees.

As the evening drew to a close, it was increasingly evident that the ben- efit was intended to entertain donors and flatter law enforcement while thanking them for their exceptional "humanity," whereas the difficult realities faced by migrant youth remained hidden. Carefully monitoring migrant youth as they offered *testimonianze*, the organizers presented an image of unaccompanied minors as "victims" who warranted rescue and care by Italian citizens. As observed with the Gambian mother, digres- sions from this script registered as reasons for escorting the youth off stage. Curiously, the event did not address the ways that state institutions and law enforcement often thwarted young people's migratory projects and policed them in public spaces. Such interventions and forms of sur-

Figure 15. Catering staff line up to present *arancini* to guests at "Bambini/giovani in pericolo." Photo by author.

veillance in Italian society constituted formidable threats from the perspectives of the youth themselves.

The day before the start of the G7 summit in Taormina in May 2017, UNICEF hosted a ceremony along the Palermo waterfront in which local schoolchildren participated "in a symbolic rescue of paper boats to commemorate the thousands of children who have risked their lives crossing the Central Mediterranean" (UNICEF 2017). With this event, UNICEF sought to "send a message to the G7 to take action to safeguard children on the move" (UNICEF 2017).

I arrived at the site of the ceremony to find upbeat music blaring and schoolchildren cheering and playing while waving UNICEF flags. Several cameramen dotted the edge of the small harbor to conduct interviews, attesting to UNICEF's efficacy in garnering media coverage of the event. With the sun shining over calm waters, the majestic mountainside clearly visible in the distance, and attendees dancing to the music, the organizers

Figure 16. Local schoolchildren anticipate "rescuing" of paper boats. Photo by author.

had succeeded in creating a festive atmosphere despite the morose nature of the subject at hand: migrant deaths, specifically of minors, at sea.

The emcee welcomed attendees and thanked the UNICEF volunteers (distinguished by their blue vests), Palermo's mayor, Leoluca Orlando, the global vice president of UNICEF, and an admiral from the Italian coast guard for helping make the event possible. Shortly thereafter, schoolchildren were invited to the beach in anticipation of the "rescuing" of paper boats (figure 16). From small boats anchored a short distance offshore, UNICEF volunteers began to release the paper boats into the water. The emcee then encouraged the children to begin "rescue" operations (figure 17). They plowed into the water excitedly, giggling and splashing as they approached the paper boats set adrift. The emcee promptly interjected:

> I see boats that are sinking. Unfortunately, this happens also in reality. We're waiting for these youngsters to rescue the boats and bring them ashore....

Figure 17. "Rescuing" of paper boats commences. Photo by author.

There are some rescued boats! ... Bring them here, bring them here! ... The first boats have just arrived. ... We would ideally like to rescue a boat that is still in good shape. Can we do it? There's one, there's one in good shape! Maybe we've been able to save some people on it as well. ... Obviously, to the parents here, the coast guard is supervising so that our little "rescuers" are not at risk of anything; they're completely safe.

The ceremony was a form of theatrical reenactment in which these school-children were summoned to perform rescue activities and "'save' the small boats as a way to remember the children whose lives had been lost on unseaworthy boats while seeking refuge in Europe" (La Repubblica 2017). Of course, the stakes were much lower in this setting than in any real search and rescue operation; as the emcee reassured parents at the event, they were closely monitoring the safety of their children.

As the schoolchildren continued their rescue efforts, Palermo's mayor informed the crowd of how their city had always been welcoming to outsiders and that immigrants were central to its history. The emcee then passed the microphone to a few young migrants who were there representing youth reception centers, to relate their own experiences of being rescued at sea. Although these youth were able to speak for several minutes, most of their comments were muffled by clamoring schoolchildren who seemed distracted by the music, balloons, and paper boats, yet whose presence nonetheless was essential to executing the event.

I do not highlight the Catania fund-raiser and Palermo "boat rescue" events here to disparage the different actors and institutions involved in their production. Undoubtedly, many of them had been compelled by profound concerns for the well-being of migrant youth. However, the overall framing of youth as helpless victims in these contexts did not accomplish much in shifting constraints on the material, affective, and political possibilities for this population.

Later that afternoon, I rode in the car with a few young men and staff from Asante to attend a public screening of the documentary film *Io sono qui* (I Am Here) in a renovated industrial zone of Palermo. The film told the story of the three young men with whom I had shared a ride, Omar, Dina, and Magassouba, who arrived in Sicily as *minori stranieri non accompagnati* after their arduous journeys through the Sahara and across the central Mediterranean. I had met the film's protagonists at Asante some hours before the screening; they came looking for Asante's director, who had promised them a ride. They appeared before us freshly showered, dressed in white linen shirts and slacks, and grinning from ear to ear in anticipation of the screening and the question-and-answer session that would follow, with them front and center. While visibly excited, they showed no signs of nervousness. This would be their second public appearance; the film had already screened to a sold-out audience at Palermo's majestic Teatro Politeama the month before.

Some two hundred residents of Palermo packed the theater for that day's screening. From onstage, an attractive young woman formally welcomed guests and prefaced the start of the film by briefly recounting the history of events in the Mediterranean since "the Arab Spring of 2011 to 2012" and stating how it "was our imperative to give dignity to these people." The film began with the testimonies of Magassouba, Dina, and Omar, in which they explained how the problems they fled were so severe that it was worth risking their lives. There were scenes from past *sbarchi* at the port of Palermo as cultural mediators from Asante provided some descriptions of the initial reception. The film showed migrant youth playing soccer, taking art classes, speaking with a resident psychologist at Asante, on a walking tour of Palermo, in music class, and in Asante's pizza-making class. Later, there was a scene in the forest during which the three migrant youth expressed nostalgia for their homelands; one said that he had abandoned his mother, a fact that he would rather not be reminded of. Another explained that he had been arrested and tortured and then lost his parents to violence in his village. The film concluded by highlighting two stories: the friendship that had blossomed between Magassouba and Dina and the unofficial adoption of Omar by a Sicilian family.

Following the screening of the film, the emcee invited Magassouba, Dina, and Omar, as well as the entire staff of Asante and the director of the film, to join her onstage for a brief question-and-answer session (figure 18). She turned first to the three youth.

EMCEE: I asked Magassouba earlier, "How did you ever decide to tell your story?," to which he answered, "I decided to tell it because you all saved my life, and so I want to share this story with you." So, Magassouba, do you think that your story, all that you have recounted, can change the thinking of many people?

MAGASSOUBA: Greetings everyone. I'm very pleased to see so many of you here today. I'm very excited, and I thank you for being here. Yes, I can change many things. People who don't know about this immigration, I can change how they think, impart my experience to them, to everyone who wants to know about immigration.

EMCEE: Dina, how difficult was it for you to tell your story to so many people, given the strong and sensitive content?

DINA: First off, hello everyone, thanks for coming to see this documentary today. To answer your question, it's difficult to tell of what happened because it is painful. When you think of this experience, you prefer not to talk about

Figure 18. Film cast and center staff from Asante gather onstage at a screening of *Io sono qui*. Photo by author.

it. But it's important to share because some people don't know about it, they are indifferent to immigration. It's not just something in books or on television, but something that happens in real life.

OMAR: I want to salute everyone who came here to understand how we came to Italy. I think you have understood something.

In reflecting on his adoptive family, Omar added, "I enrolled in school, something that I would have never been able to do in Africa. I finished high school thanks to them [his Sicilian adoptive kin]. Who knows? Tomorrow I might become a great doctor in Europe!" The comments shared by these three young men elicited vigorous applause. After posing some questions to particular staff members from Asante, the emcee turned to the film's director, Gabriele Cravagna, to elaborate on his motives for making the film. He stated:

> Thinking of the coverage on television, in the news, and most everything, I realized that it was doing injustice to this population. I thought we should make something else, to help show what happens after migrant youth arrive. I chose this subject because I thought we should focus on what happens after a *sbarco*. Migration is natural. I migrated to Rome, others have migrated to Sicily, others to elsewhere in Europe or in the world. So it is something very natural but mistakenly perceived as an invasion or emergency. The story I wanted to show here is very different—that many organizations are intervening in ways that are intelligent and consistent with the values of solidarity.... This is the second screening of *Io sono qui* in Palermo, and it's beautiful to see how much interest there is from our own citizens around this theme. At the first screening there were a thousand attendees, way more than I expected. Palermo has responded so positively.

Both the title and the marketing of the film reflected the director's commitment to subverting some of the mainstream coverage of recent migration through the central Mediterranean. The title *Io sono qui* suggested that the voices of the three migrant youth were being foregrounded in the film's narrative and gestured to a broader refusal by these youth to be made invisible. One trailer for the film began with a young migrant narrating in Italian, "You cannot begin to imagine the significance . . . of me beginning to recount this experience."

Following the screening, I learned from others involved with the film's production that they hoped these eyewitness accounts from migrant youth themselves would help shape public opinion and inspire political mobilization among audiences. They expressed interest not just in connecting with audiences in Italy; they inquired about bringing the film to the United States for a public screening. Since its 2017 debut in Palermo, *Io sono qui* has screened at several national and international film festivals and garnered an award for Best Documentary Short in 2018 at the Los Angeles Film Awards. In addition, schools across Italy have screened the film for students as a means to examine prejudices and stereotypes surrounding im/migration and to humanize the experiences of young people seeking better futures in Italy.

Launched in 2017, the Palermo-based project Funkino: Cinema for Inclusion was a participatory film laboratory that offered vocational skills to migrants between the ages of fifteen and twenty-four and mentored youth in film as a medium of storytelling. The intensive vocational training program provided participants with both theoretical and hands-on knowledge of the different aspects of filmmaking, such as directing, cinematography, sound effects, and operating equipment, while also engaging them in all phases of film production and postproduction. As narrated by participants in a promotional video for the project, film served as a medium for them to "express themselves, their ideals and their ideas," by "creating a story, a story that has a public impact." Migrant youth participants thus recounted their experiences in the communal setting of the participatory laboratory and wove them together into the format of short films.

Alessio Genovese, founder of Funkino and an acclaimed Italian filmmaker, envisioned participants collaborating in the production of short films that would contribute to a larger project focused on foregrounding migrants' voices in educating a broader public about contemporary im/ migration to the EU through Sicily and in facilitating the insertion of migrants in an industry that had systematically excluded them. He was not alone in his critiques: others have argued that "a persistent lack of critical thinking among Italian film-makers on the matters of representation and authorship continues to drive migrants from opportunities in the [film] industry" (Horsti 2019, 237; see also Grassilli 2008).[2] With the support of donations from a crowdfunding campaign and grants from UNHCR, Funkino hosted four iterations of the film laboratory training in 2018 and 2019 during which participants convened for several hours each day over the span of several weeks to develop the content for a short film. While we shared coffee and brioche in one of Palermo's hip cafés, Alessio and Daniele, the primary coordinators of the participatory film laboratory, articulated the various ways in which they strived to uphold each person's migration narrative in piecing together content for the short film. In video footage of one iteration of the lab, participants proposed themes on age, neglect, the "teenage crisis," and redemption to possibly inform their script. In reflecting on the process of storyboarding with her peers, one female participant noted, "There are fifteen of us, and each of us has contributed an idea. We can put them together to make something important. This will make people understand that we can think for ourselves, that we have ideas of our own." A young man added, "We shared many stories that we wove into one." One young woman asserted, "It's important to tell these stories because with them we are actually saving lives and encouraging others."[3] In another video documenting the project, participants were shown playing music together as they recorded the sound track for their film.

Transforming public dialogue about migration, and the role of migrants in the labor market, for instance, is a core objective of the participatory film laboratory. In short, Funkino seeks to promote the social inclusion of migrants while using film as a medium for inciting political mobilization and catalyzing social change. Toward such ends, Daniele proposed that they "look to find a way into public schools in Palermo, to create some form of exchange between migrant youth and their peers to develop audiovisual, mini-documentary projects together." They were also interested in entering film festival circuits and pursuing other opportunities to screen the short films with audiences throughout Italy as well as abroad as a means to cultivate more awareness and shift policies on migration. Importantly, they hoped to secure the funds to travel to these screenings for all participants in the project.

Funkino: Cinema for Inclusion also reflected recent entrepreneurial engagements by younger generations of *siciliani* who were facing limited opportunities to earn a living wage. These youth, debating the decision to migrate north or stay close to their families and extended social networks, often pursued unconventional career paths that coalesced around concerns for social justice and collective well-being. The core of Funkino's team represented this younger demographic. Reflecting on how the economic situation in Sicily helped explain the project's genesis, one of the team members, a twenty-something *siciliano* who had returned to Palermo after graduating from a university in northern Italy quipped, "There are glimpses of a change in the collective psychology [in Sicily]: there's a sentiment of willing change that's probably an indicator of the future or some coming rebirth. [This desire and will for change] define the present sentiment; it's a sentiment that's also optimistic in general."

SOLIDARITY WORK BETWEEN CITIZENS AND NONCITIZENS, PRESENT AND FUTURE GENERATIONS

The approaches to foregrounding migrant youth in solidarity efforts such as those convened by Funkino and documentary films helped contest dominant perceptions of and preoccupations with migrant youth that have historically constrained this group's agency. Similar to the work of *testimonios* shared by undocumented youth in the United States, as argued by Genevieve Negrón-Gonzales (2014, 274), the voices of migrant youth in film and other forms of Italian-based media in this context helped generate a counternarrative in which youth "negotiate the tension between the dominant societal discourse about immigration and their own lived experiences." This counternarrative pushes back against representations of the Mediterranean as a "white Italian-European" space and exposes how "present-day migration is related to the circulation of financial assets and the exploitation of resources" (Proglio 2018, 410). Rather than being reduced to the category of victim through an objectification of their stories (see Giordano 2014, 165) or being further invisibilized, migrant youth, through *Io sono qui* and similar projects, are provided with an opportunity to negotiate the terms of their own belonging. The potential of migrant youth participation in these endeavors articulates with the enabling of youth of color in Italy "to connect, achieve new levels of visibility, and create relatively autonomous spaces for discussion, political organizing, and cultural production" (Hawthorne 2017, 158).[4]

In analyzing the Rome-based Migrant Memory Archive (Archivio delle memorie migranti), "a collaboration between scholars, activists and migrants who recognized the need to provide a 'sympathetic' listening context for migrant narratives and to ethically disseminate these narratives in the public sphere in Italy and beyond," the media studies scholar Karina Horsti (2019, 233) advances a theory of cosmopolitan solidarity. Connecting to the concept of cosmopolitan cinema as a genre of film that "generates politically significant public dialogue and engagment," cosmopolitan solidarity "crosses not only group and spatial boundaries but also temporality" (Horsti 2019, 233, 242; see also Rovisco 2013). Horsti (2019, 242) argues that it is precisely "sensitivity to the temporal dimension" detected in the forms of archival activism exemplified through participatory film projects in the European context that attends to "solidarity between past, present and future generations." As material forms, these cinematic media provide "evidence for future generations that will look back at the present time" (242). Mobilizing a participatory aesthetic, the Migrant Memory Archive centers "currently marginalized memories that might one day be acknowledged as part of the cultural heritage of Europe and of the countries of origin and transit" (241). The "mediated memory work" required for the production of participatory documentary films enables the subsequent witnessing by an engaged audience (Horsti 2019; also see Dossa 2014 on memory work). Horsti (2019, 234) notes that "bearing witness is a future-oriented practice. It carries the notion that the present day is the future past." Through witnessing, present-day generations may begin to wonder about how they will be judged by future generations for their complicity with a militarized European border regime.

Efforts to politically mobilize with migrant youth, particularly projects like Funkino and the documentary film *Io sono qui* that engage "participatory aesthetics" and "archival activism" (Horsti 2019), not only advance struggles for youth agency but also hold important insights for understanding broader struggle(s) for migrant solidarity in the Mediterranean. These projects demonstrate the role of memory work in strengthening alliances between citizens and noncitizens through the act of witnessing, as well as in creating solidarities across generations both in the present and in the future. Thus, the aspirational project of migrant solidarity as it is being enacted with migrant youth reveals another important aspect of solidarity work: the transcending of temporal boundaries to forge alliances that will span generations and give rise to new forms of belonging and more inclusive interpretations of collective heritage.

Unlike arrangements of stratified reproduction, migrants in the context of solidarity work, and migrant youth especially, are constructed as co-citizens in reproducing relations of solidarity that aspire to a future population that is distinguished from the past by its racial and ethnic diversity and desires for equality. Solidarity work is thus radical in rejecting social relations that sustain the status quo through extractive, exploitative socially reproductive labor that only ensures the welfare of privileged segments of the population in terms of race, class, and citizenship. Solidarity work engages a form of socially reproductive labor that aims to strengthen collective well-being.

ALTERNATIVE LOGICS

The organizations and media projects featured in this chapter—Asante, Blossom House, UNICEF, Funkino, *Io sono qui*—attest to the various ways that representations of migrant youth and the dimensions of their belonging were being (re)conceptualized in Sicily. UNICEF campaign activities seemed to remain consistent with the dominant logic that guides humanitarian organizations in approaching the question of unaccompanied minors as "victims" who warranted rescue and were unable to advocate on their own behalf. These youth were summoned to provide testimony that would bolster or give further credibility to campaign efforts.

In contrast, organizations and projects like Asante, Blossom House, Funkino: Cinema for Inclusion, and *Io sono qui* suggested that an alternative logic was at work. By promoting social and economic integration (Asante, Blossom House), feelings of autonomy and belonging (Asante, Blossom House, Funkino), and participatory aesthetics and archival activism with youth to incite political mobilization (Funkino, *Io sono qui*), these youth-centered initiatives strived to recognize the rights and agency of migrant youth while also subverting the ideological frameworks of governmental and nongovernmental institutions that had historically viewed this population as a "problem." Rather than reproduce the tropes of migrant youth as "victims" or delinquents and potential criminals, many of these organizations promoted youth as active agents and sought myriad opportunities to cultivate alternative forms of citizenship and belonging.

Epilogue

Every day I try to do my small part to uphold the rights of
all migrants. I'm fighting for a world that no longer exists,
but I do not give up.

—Palermo-based social worker, June 2018

This island is magnetic, and it has always agitated every
propensity, both good and bad. In this respect, I think that
we can forge a different way forward. To me, it is still possible to work toward a different narrative, one that we all
desperately need right now and will continue to need.

—Palermo-based filmmaker, June 2018

As I was putting the final touches on this book, the spread of coronavirus
(COVID-19) had severely restricted travel to and from Italy. For the first
time in their lives, many Italians were experiencing extreme restrictions
on their mobility and responding with fear and panic. During the last
week of February 2020, more than fifteen thousand people were quaran-
tined in northern Italian towns; nobody was allowed in or out. Schools,
markets, churches, theaters, and museums in the northern Italian regions
of Lombardy, Veneto, and Emilia-Romagna were closed. Even soccer
leagues—representing the holy grail of Italian sports—postponed their
seasons. The list of countries that had closed their borders to travelers
from Italy was getting longer each day. Local commerce and global and
domestic tourism were brought to a complete standstill. Commercial air-
line carriers from the United States, for instance, announced indefinite

moratoriums on their flights to major Italian cities. Palermo's mayor, Leo-luca Orlando, raised some eyebrows when he suggested that those travel-ing to Sicily from the north reconsider their travel plans. Ironically, his suggestion provoked accusations by northern Italians that his island was failing to show solidarity with the rest of Italy.

By March 10, 2020, exactly one day before the World Health Organiza-tion declared a global pandemic, all of Italy entered a nationally mandated period of containment that lasted nearly two full months. People were permitted to leave their homes only for groceries or medications. At the peak of the first wave, Italy confirmed more than 6,000 new daily cases of COVID-19. As of early December 2020 (the time of this writing), the country has reported over 58,000 deaths from the virus, one of the high-est counts in Europe, second only to the United Kingdom; meanwhile, Europe is in the midst of a deadly second wave. No doubt, austerity mea-sures of the late aughts played an instrumental role in crippling Italy's capacity to respond, especially within the realm of healthcare (Carney and Ostrach 2020). Relatedly, there has been widespread concern that the COVID-19 pandemic will lead Italy into another recession and initiate a phase of additional austerity measures.

The pandemic has given new life to Europe's far-right populist politi-cians, who continue to disseminate antimigrant propaganda. Yet this will not be the first or last time that migrants are scapegoated for a public health crisis. In the *New York Times,* near the beginning of the pandemic, the journalist Beppe Severgnini commented on its social, political, and economic effects in Italy: "The impulsive mood of recent politics seems to have found fertile terrain, putting Italy in the grip of some sort of health populism."[1] Italy's former interior minister, Matteo Salvini, has been lead-ing the charge stoking fears about migrants as vectors of disease who are infecting citizens with the coronavirus, despite facing criminal charges for actions that he took during his time in office. In February 2020, the Italian senate voted to prosecute Salvini for kidnapping, referring to a partic-ularly high-profile standoff in the summer of 2018 when he refused to allow a ship carrying 131 migrants to disembark in Catania. *The Guardian* reported, "This is only the most recent legal trouble for Italy's most pow-erful populist. [He] has been placed under investigation five times in less than two years, is the subject of one ongoing trial and has been named in dozens of lawsuits for defamation and instigation of hatred" (Tondo 2020).

Emerging in the context of anti-austerity and "Italians first!" political discourses that fallaciously linked the imposition of austerity measures to public expenditure on migrants, Salvini's security decree had been argued as necessary to take resources away from migrants and rightfully return them to Italian citizens, primarily by amplifying security measures. Resources siphoned from migrant reception were thus reinvested in Italian police and military forces to "protect" citizens, ostensibly from some dangerous Other. Yet from the perspective of those having to assume greater personal responsibility in migrant reception and integration activities amid cuts to public spending, the decree meant that they were to absorb greater risk. In October 2020, Salvini's successor at the Ministry of Interior, Luciana Lamorgese, a renowned migration expert and advocate for migrant integration policies, led the Italian government in approving a new security decree that removed the draconian measures introduced by her predecessor.

Recognizing the widespread negative effects of the security decree for social welfare, groups like the Sardines were particularly active in demanding its repeal. The Sardines gained significant media attention both in Italy and internationally in the months preceding the pandemic.[2] What started as a single public demonstration attended by thousands in Bologna in November 2019 quickly advanced into a formidable grassroots movement. Protesting populist and anti-immigrant rhetoric as well as the onslaught of mis- and disinformation promulgated on social media, the Sardines continue to galvanize supporters across Italy as well as abroad, drawing thousands to stage nonviolent demonstrations in cities such as Palermo, Rome, Barcelona, Munich, New York, and San Francisco, to name a few. As with any large-scale grassroots movement, internal disagreements and splitting off by different factions have posed challenges to controlling the movement's messaging. Still, the primary objective of the Sardines has been to end populist politics specifically in Italy but also throughout Europe. More recently, they have been calling for legal action against polarizing figures like Salvini who have broken the law, as well as broader support for nongovernmental and humanitarian search and rescue operations in the Mediterranean like those commandeered by

Captain Carola Rackete. In early March 2020, the Sardines launched a pro-migration social media campaign in which they invited people in support of their movement to publish a photo of themselves with one hand raised, using the hashtag #RestiamoUmani (Let's stay human), because, they said, "we are saying enough to hate, hostility, violence and intolerance; we are saying enough to fear." This campaign, in underscoring the "importance of joining our forces and our bodies," provides some evidence of how forms of affective resistance are being mobilized to promote migrant solidarity in the Mediterranean (ANSAmed 2020).

With Salvini gone from office, Italian ports are technically open once again to migrant disembarkations. While the number of migrants arriving is significantly smaller than it was between 2011 and 2017, few *siciliani* deny that the number will surge again, requiring considerable resources from their island, a place that they believe is one of the world's oldest human crossroads. Recent trends do not necessarily reflect a decrease in the number of migrants and asylum seekers *trying* to reach Europe (Sanchez and Achilli 2020). Rather, they speak to the large sums of money from the EU being directed toward programs aimed at preventing migration—though with highly mixed results—and the impact of Italy's bilateral accord with Libya through which the Libyan coast guard intercepts boats of migrants en route to Europe.[3] Since 2017, when Italy's accord with Libya went into effect, over 40,000 asylum seekers and migrants have been intercepted by the Libyan coast guard and imprisoned in unsafe detention facilities, where they are regularly subjected to exploitation and violence (Human Rights Watch 2020). Despite vehement disapproval by human rights organizations, Italy recently renewed the accord for another three years.

It is hard to say whether populist politics are becoming less or more entrenched in Europe, considering that on January 31, 2020, the United Kingdom made its official exit from the EU. Many policy experts rightly predicted that the Brexit vote in June 2016 could be a tipping point for the resurgence of populist and fascist ideas in Europe and beyond (Virdee and McGeever 2016). Less than six months later, Trump, who had been a vocal proponent of Brexit, was named the victor in the 2016 US presidential election. Another year or so later, in 2018, populist parties were named the victors in Italy's national elections.

The day after the Brexit referendum remains one of the most chilling and unforgettable moments of my fieldwork. This historic vote coincided with my research trip to Sicily in 2016. Sicilian news outlets responded to the outcome of the vote with deep disappointment and bitterness. On the one hand, many of my Sicilian informants could identify with this other set of "islanders" and their desires for autonomy. On the other hand, they viewed the Brexit vote as one of geographic privilege and a complete lack of solidarity with Europe's southern periphery, that is, frontline communities who were responding to record migrant arrivals.

While Brexit provoked negative sentiments among many *siciliani*, it arguably had the opposite effect as well in galvanizing and emboldening supporters of migrant solidarity. Following my delivery of a keynote address at the annual summer school, "Migration, Human Rights, and Democracy," at the University of Palermo on the morning after the Brexit vote, students, scholars, local activists, and NGO and humanitarian workers reaffirmed their commitments to broader struggles for social justice. They challenged me and others in the room to contemplate some of the most pressing questions of our time: "What do we do about current shortcomings by states to recognize and uphold human rights?" "What policy changes, interventions, and shifts in thinking are most urgent, and which institutions and social actors need to be involved?" In short, these participants—most of them students and early career young people—reassured me that an undercurrent of hope was alive and well in the Mediterranean, despite any corruptive efforts to make it otherwise.

The final chapter of this book is currently being orchestrated through the relentless efforts of thousands of ordinary citizens and noncitizens who firmly believe in the aspirational project of migrant solidarity. Search and rescue operations have resumed after a hiatus due to COVID-19. The activists featured throughout this book have been continuing their organizing efforts, advocacy, and mutual aid practices, some adapting to virtual platforms amid the restrictions of nationwide containment, while increasingly framing their work through Black Lives Matter, the movement that originated in the United States but has since swept the globe in the wake of unchecked police brutality, state-sanctioned violence, and the disproportionate toll of COVID-19 on Black communities in the United States. Many groups and organizations have relied on crowdfunding campaigns to restart their activities after enduring months of pandemic-related measures. Meanwhile, anti-Mafia campaigns have been doubling their efforts amid fears that the economic toll of COVID-19 in Sicily is exposing many small businesses to a resurgence of Mafia-related activity.

Solidarity with migrants both in the Mediterranean and beyond will be enhanced through the collective actions of an engaged, radical readership.[4] Readers may circulate stories of solidarity, ideally relayed through the voices of migrants themselves as well as their allies. Perhaps readers will contribute to the digital archive #IOHmedandbeyond by sharing articles, photography, video, art, poetry, and creative writing about migrant solidarity projects happening around the world. Yet it is equally if not more important to bring these exchanges into our everyday lives. We need to make migration—its underlying causes, problematic government and local responses, lived experiences of those who have been displaced and the myriad exclusions they encounter in many "host" societies—a topic of discussion in our families, workplaces, classrooms, and communities.[5] An engaged, radical readership may also show strength in numbers by going to marches, protests, and local events in support of migrants and by contacting elected officials and others in positions of power to influence changes to policy. While policy change is not a panacea for the host of problems we seek to redress, it is indispensable to abolishing structures that perpetuate inequality. Finally, as underscored by Black Lives Matter, we must continue to (un)learn about systemic racism and injustice and strive to understand the plight of migrants around the world as their experiences articulate with legacies of colonialism and slavery, as well as with dispossession, displacement, and other forms of everyday violence brought about by neoliberal capitalism. The onus is on all of us to reject the dominant narrative of migration as an individual "choice" and to demand proactive responses that are more humane, just, and compassionate.

Notes

INTRODUCTION

1. See, e.g., www.thelocal.de/20190703/a-big-win-for-solidarity-with-refugees
-german-migrant-rescue-captain-freed.

2. Much of Sicily's role in responding to Europe's "migration crisis" can be explained by its geographic proximity to migrant-sending ports from which human smugglers conduct their trade. Lampedusa, one of Sicily's many islands, is located less than 70 miles from the northern coast of the African continent.

3. For five consecutive years, from 2014 to 2018, the International Organization for Migration named the Mediterranean the "world's deadliest border" (IOM 2017).

4. Note here that I intentionally avoid reproducing classification schemes that engage the binary of "economic" versus "political" migration. Aside from how such categorizations serve the interests of government institutions in helping to streamline bureaucratic procedures by simplifying decision making, the binary itself is unproductive in that it is a social construction that disregards how the political and the economic are always intimately intertwined.

5. This saying echoes critiques within Chicana feminist theory, i.e., "We did not cross the border; the border crossed us" (see Anzaldúa 1987).

6. These disparaging comparisons of Sicily to Greece in this instance index the nation's sovereign debt crisis and bailout by the European Commission, the European Central Bank, and the IMF in 2010.

7. In explicit reference to the idea of Sicily as separate from Italy, the renowned Sicilian author Leonardo Sciascia coined the concept of *sicilitudine*.

8. Although this book is based primarily on data that I collected in Italy between 2014 and 2019, I have been traveling to the country for research since 2005.

9. All translations of research interactions and interview excerpts from Italian to English that appear throughout this text are mine.

10. This book has made considerable use of social media in the application of digital ethnography. While imperfect for reasons such as being a source of mis- and disinformation, breaching data privacy, and using personal information for commercial ends, widespread adoption of communication technologies—namely, social media tools—by both citizens and noncitizens is one means through which the philosophy and broader messaging of migrant solidarity efforts have been dis- seminated to incentivize political mobilization (Benton and Bonilla 2017). Studies of migration have only begun to examine what is recognized as an "extensive use of information and communication technologies (ICTs)" within "digital diasporas" (Oiarazabal and Reips 2012). In alluding to how "the impact of technology on migration is undeniable," for instance, Pedro Oiarazabal and Ulf-Dietrich Reips (2012, 1334) assert that "the personal computer, the cell phone and access to the Internet have become quotidian resources among migrants who use them to develop, maintain and recreate informal and formal transnational networks in both the physical and digital worlds." These developments precipitate a demand for research that delves into the role of new media, technological networks, and digital storytelling platforms in fortifying not only "transnational and diasporic communities" (Oiarazabal and Reips 2012, 1333) but also relationships among ordinary citizens and noncitizens. See also McEwan and Sobre-Denton (2011).

11. In other words, these unspoken biases within academia for particular types of anthropology (i.e., the heroic ethnography) can portend real material conse- quences in one's career trajectory (Nelson et al. 2017).

CHAPTER 1. AUSTERITY AND MIGRATION
AS MEDITERRANEAN "QUESTIONS"

1. One of his predecessors, Matteo Renzi, the youngest prime minister ever elected, had also been openly critical of austerity politics (Mackenzie 2014). His electoral victory happened midway through my research trip in 2014; Renzi's vow to improve the economic situation of unemployed youth was especially timely as I had met recent college graduates in Sicily who were planning to leave for the United Kingdom, Germany, and Belgium in search of work. However, Renzi resigned just two years later, following the rejection of a nationwide referendum. Many of my Italian informants reiterated claims made by the media leading up to his resignation: in the eyes of his party's opponents and despite accusations by

the EU that his country was falling short of expectations for border enforcement and management of the asylum petition process (New Keywords Collective 2016), Renzi had perhaps been too supportive of asylum seekers.

2. Race-based xenophobia has paralleled the fortification of austerity regimes as well as increasing Euro-skepticism and anti-immigrant sentiment elsewhere in the EU. The referendum in the United Kingdom on June 23, 2016, for instance, that resulted in British citizens voting to exit the European Union had followed months of anti-immigrant campaign propaganda and years of austerity measures that impoverished much of the nation's population (De Genova 2017; Garthwaite et al. 2017).

3. Such political propaganda should not be confused with promotional videos produced by the United Nations High Commissioner for Refugees (UNHCR) and IOM, as the former is not genuinely concerned with the well-being of migrants.

4. *Daily Telegraph*, www.telegraph.co.uk/finance/financialcrisis/9410275 /Monti-plans-Greek-style-takeover-of-Sicily-to-avert-default.html.

5. Ibid.

6. "Italy Worries Sicily's Woes Could Have Ripple Effect," NPR, July 31, 2012.

7. Schneider and Schneider (2003, 233) cite a financial report from the Italian newspaper *La Repubblica* that "correlates rising unemployment in the south and Sicily with the consequent declining level of public investment, which fell from 4.3 percent of GNP in 1980 to 1.3 percent in 1998."

8. "Italy Worries Sicily's Woes Could Have Ripple Effect," NPR, July 31, 2012.

9. *Giornale di Sicilia*, April 26, 2014, https://gds.it/articoli/analisi-e-com menti/2014/04/26/purche-ridurre-le-spese-sia-un-impegno-di-tutti-339852-d39 65ce4-b2fc-4674-8bbd-79886854c183/.

10. *Giornale di Sicilia*, November 22, 2103, https://palermo.gds.it/articoli/so cieta/2013/11/22/-scuole-sicure-e-occupazione-per-i-giovani-studenti-in-piazza -a-palermo-traffico-in-tilt-303900-8cccfccc-572b-4a8a-aba6-ce87dbcac85d/.

11. See, e.g., "Austerity: Suicide, a Modern-Day Greek Tragedy," *Daily Telegraph*, 2012.

12. Andronos International, "Italy: Plumber with No Work Immolates Himself in Sicily," May 11, 2012.

13. With her ethnography of immigrant eldercare workers in the context of Italy's welfare state restructuring, Degiuli (2016, 136–37) critiques how "the growing demand for care and the cost associated with it are better addressed through market-oriented mechanisms and ideologies." Relatives and immigrants are increasingly burdened with the provision and costs of this care (see also Muehlebach 2012). Despite Italy's persistent reliance on its foreign-born population to administer this care, many of my informants commented on the absurdity of the state's failure to reciprocate it. The anthropologist Miriam Ticktin (2011) offers the concept "armed love" as a way of discussing the constraints surrounding care and compassion extended to noncitizens in the context of France. More specifically, she

argues that state actors are discerning in their provision of care to migrants, prioritizing groups that have been deemed morally legitimate (i.e., children, women, trafficked persons), thereby "reproducing inequalities and racial, gendered, and geopolitical hierarchies" (2011, 5).

14. www.tp24.it/2017/04/22/cronaca/il-rapporto-sugli-immigrati-in-sicilia -quanti-sono-cosa-fanno-come-stanno/108981.

15. Until recently, there were an estimated half-million *irregolari* in Italy (Hermanin 2017). This number is suspected to have doubled as an effect of the security decree that eliminated humanitarian protection and pushed thousands of would-be regular migrants into irregular status.

16. Circulation of the Italian term "extracomunitario" in media, politics, and everyday conversations serves as further evidence of such logics at work. Technically describing a person whose citizenship traces to outside the EU community, the term is primarily affixed to migrants from the global South and characterizes them as "low-level workers, criminals, or objects of charity" (Tuckett 2018, 6).

17. Activist groups such as Primo Marzo have been demanding that the parameters of citizenship be reformed to extend voting rights to the individuals who can claim *jus soli* or *jus culturae*. During my research trip to Sicily in 2017, national headlines were flooded with reports of a demonstration held in Milan that garnered over ten thousand attendees and called for comprehensive granting of citizenship to youth who despite having foreign-born parents had spent most of their lives living and studying in Italy. As of late 2017, Italian parliament members were anticipating a proposal for citizenship reform known as "Ius soli," but plans for further discussion were soon derailed by sweeping changes to Italy's central government.

CHAPTER 2. "THERE IS A LOT OF CREATIVITY ON THIS ISLAND"

1. In addition to viewing themselves as separate from Italian or European ancestry, *siciliani* like to further distinguish themselves by province of origin and tend to identify accordingly, such as *palermitani* (of Palermo), *trapanesi* (of Trapani), and *catanesi* (of Catania).

2. In the book *Seeking Sicily: A Cultural Journey through Myth and Reality in the Heart of the Mediterranean* (2011), John Keahey elaborates on the lasting imprint of Arab colonization in the memory and cultural identity of Sicilians: "The Arabs may have controlled Sicily and parts of southern Italy for a mere two and a half centuries out of three thousand years of the island's known human history, but the impact of this relatively brief encounter is shown in the formation of the Mediterranean islanders' attitudes. It is reflected in the origins of many city, village, and family names and in the cuisine. Sicilians followed Muslim methods in the ways they cultivate their land and what they grow. And their closer, innate

sense of connection, DNA-wise and emotionally, with North Africa rather than mainland Europe or even mainland Italy undergirds their sense of self" (120–21).

3. Rarely do industries expand southward to employ workers locally. Moreover, these enterprises occupy a rather vulnerable position within Italy's economy. Following the financial crisis in 2008, for instance, Fiat targeted its Palermo facility for shutdown.

4. www.nytimes.com/2017/11/14/opinion/from-sicily-a-voice-of-discontent-to-scare-all-italy.html.

5. www.unicef.org/eca/stories/how-young-people-sicily-are-changing-migration-narrative.

According to recent estimates, immigrants account for about 3.7 percent (189,169) of the regional population (Osservatorio migrazioni 2018). However, it is unclear what groups are accounted for and excluded from these estimates. Thus, the total foreign-born population could be much higher. Five groups represent almost 60 percent of those who are foreign born: Roma (30 percent), Tunisians (10.6 percent), Moroccans (7.9 percent), Sri Lankans (7.2 percent), and Albanians (4.4 percent) (Osservatorio migrazioni 2018).

6. www.bbc.com/news/world-europe-29534427.

7. www.borderline-europe.de/sites/default/files/readingtips/Sizilienbericht%202019%20final.pdf.

8. www.nytimes.com/2019/05/22/world/europe/italy-palermo-immigrants-salvino.html.

9. Indeed, many of the organizations and businesses I focused on for this research were engaged in activities and mobilizing ideologies that aligned migrant solidarity with anti-Mafia efforts.

CHAPTER 3. THE RECEPTION APPARATUS

1. Mare Nostrum incited moral outrage among Italy's far-right political leaders, who heavily scrutinized the program for its cost (€9 million per month) (MOI 2015). Upon termination of Operation Mare Nostrum in late 2014, the odds of migrants dying at sea significantly worsened, from one in 60 to one in 23 (Edwards and Savary 2016). In late 2014 and early 2015, the EU amplified its own efforts to apprehend human smugglers at sea through EUNAVFOR-Med (European Union Naval Force Mediterranean) predicated on the assumption that doing so would deter future illicit boat crossings. Italy's Operation Sophia, for instance, sponsored the Libyan coast guard to intercept boats of migrants and transport them back to detention centers in Libya. EU governments have routinely solicited the participation of many migrant-sending countries in stemming migrant flows into Europe and "strengthening borders" but with ethically questionable or even reprehensible results (New Keywords Collective 2016). A series of investigative reports found that migrants returned to Libyan detention centers were being inserted in human traf-

ficking rings and auctioned as slave labor. Heightened surveillance in the central Mediterranean prompted human smugglers to employ rubber dinghies instead of safer but more easily detected metal fishing boats, or they abandoned entire boats of migrants prior to possible detection. A report from the British parliamentary committee concluded that anti-smuggling operations overseen by EUNAVFOR-Med ultimately put more migrant lives at risk (European Union Committee 2016). In 2016, Human Rights Watch estimated that there were about 500,000 migrants waiting on the coasts of Libya and Egypt for transport by a human smuggler each summer, when weather conditions are optimal. Some of these migrants never made it farther than a few miles from shore, being intercepted by the Libyan coast guard or drowning. From 2014 to 2018, the peak years of sea migration across the central Mediterranean as identified by my interlocutors, the majority of migrants and asylum seekers who eventually disembarked at one of Italy's ports had been intercepted at sea by the Italian coast guard, Frontex (the EU border enforcement agency), NATO, a passing cargo or military ship, or NGOs such as Mediterranea Saving Humans and Sea-Watch.

2. The Catholic Church provides one such example of how migrants are enlisted in particular social projects. As Cristiana Giordano (2014) has observed, initiatives and programs sponsored by the Catholic Church in Italy seek to rehabilitate migrants, indoctrinating them in the values of the church while denouncing forms of work (i.e., prostitution, drug dealing) and social ties (i.e., with traffickers) that the church deems immoral. Giordano (2008, 2014) demonstrates that in order to be considered eligible for residency, migrant women must file criminal charges (vis-à-vis the *denuncia*) against their traffickers and comply in other ways as they navigate the "diverse social projects" (Giordano 2014, 21) of state, healthcare, and faith-based institutions. Also see ethnographic work by Gray (2013) and Heyer (2012).

3. In the summer of 2018, with changes to elected seats in Italy's national government, the Italian coast guard received orders to deny requests for entry to Italian ports made by vessels transporting migrants.

4. In addition, applying for asylum often makes a person ineligible to work in the EU, and payments through welfare assistance to asylum seekers are notoriously inadequate or slow to materialize if they ever do (Rabben 2016).

5. As discussed in this book's introduction, Italy's government banned migrant disembarkations beginning in mid-2018, after the appointment of its far-right populist coalition led in part by Matteo Salvini.

6. During my fieldwork, I sought and ultimately obtained access only to CDAs and SPRARs. In the descriptions that follow, I compare findings from other studies to the accounts I collected from migrants about all types of centers.

7. The Reception Conditions Directive, for instance, adopted by the European Commission calls for EU member-states to "guarantee a standard of living that can ensure subsistence of asylum applicants, including vouchers or financial

allowances, as well as provide a means for communicating with their families, NGO advocates, and UNHCR" (Kersch and Mishtal 2016, 108).

8. Interior Minister Salvini forced the closure of the CARA in 2019, not out of concern for inhumane conditions, but rather as a gesture of his draconian anti-immigration stance.

9. Centro Astalli belongs to the Jesuit Refugee Service network that has been active for over thirty years in some sixty countries.

CHAPTER 4. MIGRANT SOLIDARITY WORK

1. This is similar to Tuckett's (2018) discussion of migratory "failures."

2. I share this image of the burial sites—taken after the funeral services—not to render migrant deaths at sea a spectacle but rather to convey their immediacy and to bear witness.

3. Although Trump had been unabashedly vocal about his anti-immigration stance, both at the podium and in his policies, his actions were not all that unprecedented given the long history of nationalist exclusion in the United States. As one example, the record number of deportations during Barack Obama's administration prompted his nickname among immigrant rights activists, "Deporter in Chief."

4. In the end, media outlets reported that the actual meeting between the two leaders proved rather unremarkable and devoid of conflict.

5. In studying humanitarian initiatives as these are applied to migrants in France, the anthropologist Miriam Ticktin (2011, 5) introduces the concept "armed love" in reference to how the "moral imperative to act . . . was accompanied by violence and containment."

6. Researchers working at the intersections of im/migration and health have documented the high prevalence of mental distress associated with policing and surveillance of immigrant communities (Gonzales and Chavez 2012; Menjívar 2013; Talavera, Núñez-Mchiri, and Heyman 2010). The fear linked to this distress prevents many individuals from seeking care for physical and mental health problems (Chavez 2012; Hacker et al. 2011). In addition to the heightened fears, anxieties, and poor health outcomes associated with policing, surveillance, detention, and deportation of im/migrants (see, e.g., Carney 2017b), recent research suggests that oppressive or negative attitudes toward im/migrants may actually translate to an overall decline in the subjective well-being—or happiness—of both citizen and noncitizen populations in immigrant-receiving contexts (Chavez et al. 2019).

Conversely, there is strong evidence that im/migrants can have a positive effect on the overall subjective well-being of im/migrant-receiving societies. Recent studies from Europe have indicated "positive effects of ethnic diversity and migrant inflows" on the happiness of native-born populations (Hendriks 2018). In addition, these studies show significant happiness gains among migrants, especially those migrating to Europe from sub-Saharan Africa, the Middle East, and North Africa. Relating the findings of this emergent research on migration and subjective well-being, the Migration Policy Institute concluded that "policies that contribute to migrant happiness are likely to create a win-win situation for both immigrants and natives" (Hendriks 2018).

7. This scholarship is informed in part by work on the Central American Sanctuary Movement. See Chinchilla et al. (2009), Permoser et al. (2010), and Smith (1996).

CHAPTER 5. EDIBLE SOLIDARITIES

1. For instance, see the discussion of the creolization of Cajun cooking in Gutierrez 1992.

2. *La Repubblica,* October 29, 2015.

3. *Il Manifesto,* February 12, 2020. https://ilmanifesto.it/molti-volti-a-ballaro/.

4. Giuseppe Campesi (2018, 497) underscores that "first reception centers are in fact not designed to facilitate contacts between the asylum seekers and local communities, as they are located in remote places (such as military premises, open countryside, and areas not otherwise accessible to the general public) and are organized as essentially 'self-sufficient' islands. In addition to producing a marked form of spatial segregation, this increases the dependence of asylum seekers on humanitarian agencies which in fact further discourages their interaction with local communities, thus hampering their potential integration into Italian society."

5. For the full manifesto in Italian, see http://palermo.repubblica.it/crona ca/2018/08/14/news/il_testo_del_manifesto_antirazzista_piu_liberta_e_diritti _per_tutti_-204051186/?refresh_ce.

6. An apt example here is the violent erasure of enslaved Africans and the knowledge they brought with them during the Middle Passage in enabling white European settlement and establishing the agricultural traditions and foodways in the American South, as described by Judith Carney and Richard Rosomoff (2009).

7. www.nytimes.com/2018/10/22/world/europe/italy-schools-league.html.

CHAPTER 6. CARING FOR THE FUTURE

1. Ten percent were near 15 years old, and 7.8 percent were under 14 years old. In 2016, unaccompanied minors arriving in Italy by sea originated from Egypt (21 percent), Gambia (12.3 percent), Albania (11.4 percent), Eritrea (7.1 percent), Nigeria (6.2 percent), and Somalia (5.2 percent). UNICEF estimated that about 40 percent of unaccompanied minors arriving in Sicily ultimately remain there rather than continue north to other parts of Italy or the EU.

2. Funkino strives to secure paid apprenticeships for as many participants as possible by the end of the training.

3. At the time of this writing, more than fifty migrant youth had participated in the training and the coordinators were applying for grants to fund additional iterations of the lab.

4. In her research with Black Italian youth activists, Camilla Hawthorne (2017, 155) found, "Many young black Italians earnestly followed these global struggles against anti-black violence from the international window afforded to them by Facebook, noting to me the ways in which their struggles against everyday and institutional forms of racism in Italy seemed to be so clearly intertwined with the mobilizations of their sisters and brothers in other countries." I observed a similar strategy among migrant youth in Sicily, as they used particular hashtags (e.g., #gambia, #gambian, #gambianboy, #mali, #malian) on social media to connect with and situate their experiences within a broader diaspora. Youth utilized these platforms both to represent their experiences and to reconcile with the favorable and adverse circumstances they encountered on a daily basis. Such grassroots formations and representations are particularly important for enacting a form of migrant solidarity that subverts the moral impurity assigned to "risky" migrant youth in Italy.

EPILOGUE

1. www.nytimes.com/2020/03/02/opinion/italy-europe-coronavirus-.html ?referringSource=articleShare.

2. The organizers chose this name to suggest that if they stick together tightly, like a school of sardines, they are safer and better able to protect themselves from larger fish.

3. Through the Neighbourhood, Development, and International Cooperation Instrument (NDICI), the EU has been allocating millions of dollars to efforts that claim to be addressing the "root causes" of migration.

4. Readers may contribute directly to the work of the organizations mentioned in this book. Most of these organizations and groups may be found through social media sites—often with English translation—and many are continuing to do fundraising through crowdfunding efforts. They would welcome financial contributions, interest in volunteering or collaborating, and efforts to share about their work.

5. See more examples and read about calls for a Global Sanctuary Collective in Carney et al. 2017.

Bibliography

Abranches, Maria. 2014. "Remitting Wealth, Reciprocating Health? The 'Travel' of the Land from Guinea-Bissau to Portugal." *American Ethnologist* 41 (2): 261–75.

Accheri, Claudio. 2017. "By Migrants for Migrants: The New Faces of Italian Media." Reuters. http://news.trust.org/item/20170127120540-mw22q; accessed October 18, 2019.

Agamben, Giorgio. 2005. *State of Exception*. Chicago: University of Chicago Press.

Agence France-Presse. 2018. "Italy's PM Takes Aim at Migrants and Austerity in Maiden Speech." *The Guardian*, June 6. www.theguardian.com/world/2018/jun/06/italy-prime-minister-giuseppe-conte-migrants-austerity-maiden-speech; accessed October 17, 2019.

Agustín, Laura. 2003. "A Migrant World of Services." *Social Politics* 10 (3): 377–96.

Ahmed, Sara. 2004. "Affective Economies." *Social Text* 22 (2): 117–39.

Albahari, Maurizio. 2015. *Crimes of Peace: Mediterranean Migrations at the World's Deadliest Border*. Philadelphia: University of Pennsylvania Press.

Aldrich, Daniel P. 2012. *Building Resilience: Social Capital in Post-Disaster Recovery*. Chicago: University of Chicago Press.

Alkon, Allison, and Julie Guthman, eds. 2017. *The New Food Activism: Opposition, Cooperation, and Collective Action*. Berkeley: University of California Press.

Alpes, Maybritt J., and Alexis Spire. 2014. "Dealing with Law in Migration Control: The Powers of Street-Level Bureaucrats at French Consulates." *Social & Legal Studies* 23 (2): 261–74.

Andersson, Ruben. 2015. *Illegality, Inc.: Clandestine Migration and the Business of Bordering Europe*. Berkeley: University of California Press.

Andretta, Massimiliano. 2017. "Neoliberalism and Its Discontents in Italy: Protests without Movement?" In *Late Neoliberalism and Its Discontents in the Economic Crisis: Comparing Social Movements in the European Periphery*, ed. Donatella della Porta, 201–41. London: Palgrave Macmillan.

Andretta, Massimiliano, and Donatella della Porta. 2015. "Contentious Precarious Generation in Anti-Austerity Movements in Italy and Spain." *OBETS: Revista de Ciencias Sociales* 10 (1): 37–66.

ANSA. 2018. "Food, Music, Art and Sport for Refugee-Italian Dialogue." InfoMigrants. www.infomigrants.net/en/post/9588/food-music-art-and-sport-for-re fugee-italian-dialogue; accessed October 18, 2019.

ANSAmed. 2014a. "Immigration: 'Italy Saves Us Then Abandons Us' Activist Says." ANSAmed. www.ansamed.info/ansamed/en/news/nations/italy/2014 /08/11/immigration-italy-saves-us-then-abandons-us-activist-says_053cb97f -1615-4349-b4fb-3d2a0b55022e.html; accessed October 17, 2019.

——. 2014b. "Immigration: Renzi, EU Must Care for Mediterranean." ANSAmed. www.ansamed.info/ansamed/en/news/sections/politics/2014/05/05 /immigration-renzi-eu-must-care-for-mediterranean_6332f3f5-2baf-4110-b7 78-e81dd3e9251f.html; accessed October 17, 2019.

——. 2016. "Oxfam Says 28 Child Migrants Disappear Each Day in Italy." ANSAmed. www.ansamed.info/ansamed/en/news/sections/generalnews/2016 /09/08/oxfam-says-28-child-migrants-disappear-each-day-in-italy_6c9d8949 -b20f-440c-b3c2-7391fe17312e.html; accessed October 18, 2019.

——. 2020. "Migrants: 'Sardines' Launch Social Campaign 'Stay Human.'" ANSAmed. www.ansamed.info/ansamed/en/news/sections/politics/2020/03 /04/migrants-sardines-launch-social-campaign-stay-human_d60a86db-3b96 -42f9-ab1f-406605e1c189.html; accessed March 5, 2020.

Anzaldúa, Gloria. 1987. *Borderlands/La Frontera: The New Mestiza*. San Francisco: Aunt Lute Books.

Arampatzi, Athina. 2017. "The Spatiality of Counter-Austerity Politics in Athens, Greece: Emergent 'Urban Solidarity Spaces.'" *Urban Studies* 54 (9): 2155–71.

Arce, Alberto, and Norman Long. 2000. *Anthropology, Development, and Modernities: Exploring Discourses, Counter-Tendencies and Violence*. London: Routledge.

Arendt, Hannah. [1963] 2006. *On Revolution*. New York: Penguin Books.

Arie, S. 2013a. "Has Austerity Brought Europe to the Brink of a Health Disaster?" *British Medical Journal* 346: f3773.

——. 2013b. "Health Effects of Greece's Austerity Measures Are 'Worse than Imagined,' Report Researchers." *British Medical Journal* 346: f2740.

Associated Press (AP). 2017. "Italy Law Gives Comprehensive Care for Minor Migrants." *News 24*. www.news24.com/World/News/italy-law-gives-compre hensive-care-for-minor-migrants-20170330; accessed October 18, 2019.

Ayuso-Mateos, J. L., P. P. Barros, and R. Gusmao. 2013. "Financial Crisis, Auster-ity, and Health in Europe." *Lancet* 382 (9890): 391–92.

Ballinger, Pamela. 2007. "Borders of the Nation, Borders of Citizenship: Italian Repatriation and the Redefinition of National Identity after World War II." *Comparative Studies in Society and History* 49 (3): 731–41.

Barbata Jackson, Jessica. 2020. *Sicilians, Race, and Citizenship in the Jim Crow Gulf South*. Baton Rouge: Louisiana State University Press.

Bartolo, Pietro, and Lidia Tilotta. 2018. *Tears of Salt: A Doctor's Story*. New York: Norton.

Bassel, Leah, and Akwugo Emejulu, eds. 2017. *Minority Women and Austerity: Survival and Resistance in France and Britain*. Bristol: Policy Press.

Basu, Sanjay, Megan A. Carney, and Nora Kenworthy. 2017. "Ten Years after the Financial Crisis: The Long Reach of Austerity and Its Global Impacts on Health." *Social Science & Medicine* 187: 203–7.

Bazurli, Raffaele. 2019. "Local Governments and Social Movements in the 'Refugee Crisis': Milan and Barcelona as 'Cities of Welcome.'" *South European Society and Politics* 24 (3): 343–70.

BBC News. 2015. "An African Migrant's Story: 'Libya Is Too Dangerous.'" BBC News Online. www.bbc.com/news/world-europe-32391752; accessed October 17, 2019.

——. 2018. "Italy Migrants: Matteo Salvini Calls for End to Sicily 'Refugee Camp.'" BBC News Online. www.bbc.com/news/world-europe-44346084; accessed October 17, 2019.

Benton, Adia, and Yarimar Bonilla. 2017. "Rethinking Public Anthropologies in the Digital Age: Toward a New Dialogue." *American Anthropologist* 119 (1): 154–56.

Ben-Yehoyada, Naor. 2017. *The Mediterranean Incarnate: Region Formation between Sicily and Tunisia since World War II*. Chicago: University of Chicago Press.

Berlant, Lauren. 2004. *Compassion: The Culture and Politics of an Emotion*. New York: Routledge.

——. 2007. "Slow Death (Sovereignty, Obesity, Lateral Agency)." *Critical Inquiry* 33 (4): 754–80.

Berry, Maya, Claudia Chavez Arugelles, Shanya Cordia, Sarah Imhoud, and Elizabeth Velasquez Estrada. 2017. "Toward a Fugitive Anthropology: Gender, Race, and Violence in the Field." *Cultural Anthropology* 32 (4): 537–65.

Bianchi, Georgia E. 2011. "Italiani nuovi o nuova Italia? Citizenship and Attitudes towards the Second Generation in Contemporary Italy." *Journal of Modern Italian Studies* 16 (3): 321–33.

Biehl, João. [2005] 2013. *Vita: Life in a Zone of Social Abandonment*. Berkeley: University of California Press.

Bocci, M., and F. Tonacc. 2013. "Due milioni in fuga dalle cure non hanno i soldi per il ticket" [Two Million Leaving from Care Do Not Have the Money for the Ticket]. *La Repubblica*, April 25. http://inchieste.repubblica.it/it/repubblica /rep-it/inchiesta-italiana/2013/04/25/news/quattro_milioni_in_fuga_dalle _cure_non_hanno_pi_i_soldi_per_il_ticket-57450028/; accessed December 19, 2016.

Boehm, Deborah. 2012. *Intimate Migrations: Gender, Family, and Illegality among Transnational Mexicans*. New York: New York University Press.

Boris, Eileen, and Rhacel Parreñas. 2010. *Intimate Labors: Cultures, Technologies, and the Politics of Care*. Stanford, CA: Stanford University Press.

Borsatti, Luciana. 2014. "Immigration: Documentary on Italy's CIEs, 'The Last Frontier.'" ANSAmed. www.ansamed.info/ansamed/en/news/sections/politics /2014/03/05/Immigration-documentary-Italy-CIEs-last-frontier_10186137 .html; accessed October 17, 2019.

Bou, Enric. 2020. "Food and the Everyday in Spain: Immigration and Culinary Renovation." *Bulletin of Spanish Studies*. DOI:10.1080/14753820.2020.1699344.

Buondonno, Giuseppe. 2020. "Molti volti a Ballarò." *Il Manifesto*. https://ilmanif esto.it/molti-volti-a-ballaro/; accessed February 25, 2020.

Brand, H., N. Rosenkötter, T. Clemens, and K. Michelsen. 2013. "Austerity Policies in Europe—Bad for Health." *British Medical Journal* 346: 3716. DOI:10 .1136/bmj.f3716.

Cabot, Heath. 2014. *On the Doorstep of Europe: Asylum and Citizenship in Greece*. Philadelphia: University of Pennsylvania Press.

———. 2016a. "'Contagious' Solidarity: Reconfiguring Care and Citizenship in Greece's Social Clinics." *Social Anthropology* 24 (2): 152–66.

———. 2016b. "The European Refugee Crisis and the Crisis of Citizenship in Greece." *Migration and Citizenship: Newsletter of the American Political Science Association* 4 (2): 29–33.

Calavita, Kitty. 2005. *Immigrants at the Margins: Law, Race, and Exclusion in Southern Europe*. Cambridge: Cambridge University Press.

Caldwell, Melissa. 2004. *Not by Bread Alone: Social Support in the New Russia*. Berkeley: University of California Press.

———. 2017. *Living Faithfully in an Unjust World: Compassionate Care in Russia*. Berkeley: University of California Press.

Calhoun, Craig. 2010. "The Idea of Emergency: Humanitarian Action and Global (Dis)Order." In *Contemporary States of Emergency: The Politics of Military and Humanitarian Interventions*, edited by Didier Fassin and Mariella Pandolfi, 29–58. New York: Zone Books.

Camilli, Annalisa. 2018. "Non è vero che c'è un'invasione di migranti in Italia." *Internazionale*. www.internazionale.it/reportage/annalisa-camilli/2018/06/18/immigrazione-luoghi-comuni-italia; accessed October 17, 2019.

Campesi, Giuseppe. 2018. "Between Containment, Confinement and Dispersal: The Evolution of the Italian Reception System before and after the 'Refugee Crisis.'" *Journal of Modern Italian Studies* 23 (4): 490–506.

Caratathis, Anna. 2015. "The Politics of Austerity and the Affective Economy of Hostility: Racialised Gendered Violence and Crises of Belonging in Greece." *Feminist Review* 109: 73–95.

Caritas. 2015. "Al via progetto 'Rifugiato a casa mia.'" Caritas Italiana. www.carit as.it/pls/caritasitaliana/v3_s2ew_consultazione.mostra_pagina?id_pagina=6146; accessed October 18, 2019.

Caritas Agrigento. 2015. "Yes, We Host." Caritas Diocesana Agrigento. www.carita sagrigento.it/en/un-rifugiato-a-casa-mia/; accessed October 18, 2019.

Carney, Judith, and Richard Nicholas Rosamoff. 2009. *In the Shadow of Slavery: Africa's Botanical Legacy in the Atlantic World*. Berkeley: University of California Press.

Carney, Megan A. 2013. "Border Meals: Detention Center Feeding Practices, Migrant Subjectivities, and Questions on Trauma." *Gastronomica: Journal of Critical Food Studies* 13 (4): 32–46.

———. 2014. "Bodies on the Line: Fighting Inhuman Treatment with Hunger in Immigrant Detention." *Access Denied: A Conversation on Unauthorized Im/migration and Health*. http://accessdeniedblog.wordpress.com/2014/05/04/bodies-on-the-line-fighting-inhumane-treatment-with-hunger-in-immigrant-detention-megan-carney/.

———. 2015. *The Unending Hunger: Tracing Women and Food Insecurity across Borders*. Berkeley: University of California Press.

———. 2016. "'Back There We Had Nothing to Eat': Mexican and Central American Households in the U.S. and Transnational Food Security." *International Migration* 55 (4): 64–77.

———. 2017a. "'Sharing One's Destiny': Effects of Austerity on Migrant Health Provisioning in the Mediterranean Borderlands." *Social Science & Medicine* 187: 251–58.

———. 2017b. "Sickness in the Detention System: Syndemics of Mental Distress, Malnutrition, and Immigration Stigma in the United States." In *Stigma Syndemics: New Directions in Biosocial Health*, edited by S. Lerman, B. Ostrach, and M. Singer, 119–40. Lanham, MD: Lexington Press.

———. 2020. "'No Crisis Is an Island': On Migration, Pandemic, and Everyday Struggles in Sicily." *American Ethnologist Online*. https://americanethnolo gist.org/features/pandemic-diaries/introduction-intersecting-crises/no-cri sis-is-an-island-on-migration-pandemic-and-everyday-struggles-in-sicily; accessed December 4, 2020.

Carney, Megan A., Ricardo Gomez, Katharyne Mitchell, and Sara Vannini. 2017. "Sanctuary Planet: A Global Sanctuary Movement for the Time of Trump." *Society and Space.* http://societyandspace.org/2017/05/16/sanctuary-planet -a-global-sanctuary-movement-for-the-time-of-trump/; accessed June 14, 2017.

Carney, Megan A., Cecilia Menjívar, and Laia Soto Bermant. n.d. "Immigrant 'Deservingness' and the Enforcement of Law among Street-Level Actors in the US and the EU." Unpublished manuscript.

Carney, Megan A., and Bayla Ostrach. 2020. "Austerity, Not COVID-19, Strains National Healthcare Systems." Somatosphere. http://somatosphere.net/2020 /austerity.html/; accessed June 8, 2020.

Carter, Prudence L., and Sean F. Reardon. 2014. "Inequality Matters." W. T. Grant Foundation, New York. https://ed.stanford.edu/sites/default/files/inequality matters.pdf; accessed June 14, 2017.

Casati, Noemi. 2017. "How Cities Shape Refugee Centres: 'Deservingness' and 'Good Aid' in a Sicilian Town." *Journal of Ethnic and Migration Studies.* DOI: 10.1080/1369183X.2017.1354689.

CENSIS. 2012. "Il ruolo della sanità integrativa nel Servizio sanitario nazionale" [The Role of Integrative Health in the National Health Service]. www.osser vatorionazionalefamiglie.it/images/altrepubb/documenti/2012/il_ruolo_del la_sanit_integrativa_nel_servizio_sanitario_nazionale_-_sintesi_dei_risulta ti.pdf; accessed December 19, 2016.

Ceuppens, Bambi, and Peter Geschiere. 2005. "AUTOCHTHONY: Local or Global? New Modes in the Struggle over Citizenship and Belonging in Africa and Europe." *Annual Review of Anthropology* 34: 385–407.

Chauvin, Sebastien, Blanca Garcés-Mascareñas, and Albert Kraler. 2013. "Working for Legality: Employment and Migrant Regularization in Europe." *International Migration* 51 (6): 118–31.

Chavez, Leo R. 2012. "Undocumented Immigrants and Their Use of Medical Services in Orange County, California." *Social Science & Medicine* 74 (6): 887–93.

Chavez, Leo R., Belinda Campos, Karina Corona, Daina Sanchez, and Catherine Belyeu Ruiz. 2019. "Words Hurt: Political Rhetoric, Emotions/Affect, and Psychological Well-Being among Mexican-Origin Youth. *Social Science & Medicine* 228: 240–51.

Chin, Rita. 2017. *The Crisis of Multiculturalism in Europe: A History.* Princeton, NJ: Princeton University Press.

Chinchilla, Norma Stoltz, Nora Hamilton, and James Loucky. 2009. "The Sanctuary Movement and Central American Activism in Los Angeles." *Latin American Perspectives* 36 (6): 101–26.

Chubb, Judith. 1982. *Patronage, Power, and Poverty in Southern Italy: A Tale of Two Cities.* Cambridge: Cambridge University Press.

Clancy-Smith, Julia. 2010. *Mediterraneans: North Africa and Europe in an Age of Migration, c. 1800–1900*. Berkeley: University of California Press.

Cole, Jeffrey. 1997. *The New Racism in Europe: A Sicilian Ethnography*. Cambridge: Cambridge University Press.

Cole, Jeffrey, and Sally Booth. 2007. *Dirty Work: Immigrants in Domestic Service, Agriculture, and Prostitution in Sicily*. Lanham, MD: Lexington Books.

Cole, Jennifer, and Christian Groes. 2016. *Affective Circuits: African Migrations to Europe and the Pursuit of Social Regeneration*. Chicago: University of Chicago Press.

Colen, S. 1995. "'Like a Mother to Them': Stratified Reproduction and West Indian Childcare Workers and Employers in New York." In *Conceiving the New World Order: The Global Politics of Reproduction*, ed. Faye D. Ginsburg and Rayna Rapp, 78–102. Berkeley: University of California Press.

Commaroff, Jean, and John Commaroff. 2011. *Theory from the South: Or How Euro-America Is Evolving toward Africa*. Boulder, CO: Paradigm Publishers.

Coutin, Susan. 2010. "Confined Within: National Territories as Zones of Confinement." *Political Geography* 29 (4): 200–208.

Cox, Robert Henry. 1998. "The Consequences of Welfare Reform: How Conceptions of Social Rights Are Changing." *Journal of Social Policy* 27: 1–16.

Czajka, Agnes. 2013. "The Potential of Sanctuary: Acts of Sanctuary through the Lens of Camp." In *Sanctuary Practices in International Perspective*, edited by Randy Lippert and Sean Rehaag, 43–56. London: Routledge.

D'Angelo, Alessio. 2019. "Italy: The 'Illegality Factory'? Theory and Practice of Refugees' Reception in Sicily." *Journal of Ethnic and Migration Studies* 45 (12): 2213–26.

Davis, Dána-Ain. 2019. "Trump, Race, and Reproduction in the Afterlife of Slavery." *Cultural Anthropology* 34 (1): 26–33.

De Genova, Nicholas. 2002. "Migrant 'Illegality' and Deportability in Everyday Life." *Annual Review of Anthropology* 31: 419–47.

———. 2016. "The European Question: Migration, Race, and Postcoloniality in 'Europe.'" *Social Text* 34 (3): 75–102.

———. 2017. "Introduction: The Borders of 'Europe' and the European Question." In *The Borders of "Europe": Autonomy of Migration, Tactics of Bordering*, ed. Nicholas De Genova, 1–35. Durham, NC: Duke University Press.

———. 2018. "The 'Migrant Crisis' as Racial Crisis: Do Black Lives Matter in Europe?" *Ethnic and Racial Studies* 41 (10). DOI: 10.1080/01419870.2017.136 1543.

De Genova, Nicholas, and Nathalie Peutz, eds. 2010. *The Deportation Regime: Sovereignty, Space, and Freedom of Movement*. Durham, NC: Duke University Press.

Degiuli, Francesca. 2016. *Caring for a Living: Migrant Women, Aging Citizens, and Italian Families*. Oxford: Oxford University Press.

Dekker, Rianne, and Godfried Engbersen. 2013. "How Social Media Transform Migrant Networks and Facilitate Migration." *Global Networks* 14 (4): 401–81.

Del Castillo, Adelaida. 2007. "Illegal Status and Social Citizenship: Thoughts on Mexican Immigrants in a Postnational World." In *Women and Migration in the U.S.-Mexico Borderlands: A Reader*, edited by Denise A. Segura and Patricia Zavella, 92–105. Durham, NC: Duke University Press.

De León, Jason. 2015. *The Land of Open Graves: Living and Dying on the Migrant Trail*. Berkeley: University of California Press.

De Vogli, Roberto, and Jocelynn T. Owusu. 2015. "The Causes and Health Effects of the Great Recession: From Neoliberalism to 'Healthy De-Growth.'" *Critical Public Health* 25 (1): 15–31.

De Vogli, Roberto, Alessio Vieno, and Michela Lenzi. 2013. "Mortality due to Mental and Behavioral Disorders Associated with the Great Recession (2008–10) in Italy: A Time Trend Analysis." *European Journal of Public Health* 24: 419–21.

Doomernik, Jeroen, and María Bruquetas-Callejo. 2016. "National Immigration and Integration Policies in Europe Since 1973." In *Integration Processes and Policies in Europe*, edited by B. Garcés-Mascareñas and R. Penninx, 57–76. IMISCOE Research Series. New York: Springer.

Dossa, Parin. 2014. *Afghanistan Remembers: Gendered Narrations of Violence and Culinary Practices*. Toronto: University of Toronto Press.

Durkheim, Émile. [1897] 1951. *Suicide: A Study in Sociology*. Ed. G. Simpson and J. A. Spaulding. New York: Free Press.

Edwards, Adrian, and Medea Savary. 2016. "Mediterranean Death Toll Soars in First 5 Months of 2016." UNHCR. www.unhcr.org/news/latest/2016/5/574d b9d94/mediterranean-death-toll-soars-first-5-months-2016.html; accessed October 17, 2019.

Eggerman, Mark, and Catherine Panter-Brick. 2010. "Suffering, Hope, and Entrapment: Resilience and Cultural Values in Afghanistan." *Social Science & Medicine* 71 (1–2): 71–83.

European Union (EU). 2010. "Action Plan on Unaccompanied Minors (2010–2014)." European Commission, Brussels.

European Union Committee. 2016. "Operation Sophia, the EU's Naval Mission in the Mediterranean: An Impossible Challenge." UK Parliament website. https://publications.parliament.uk/pa/ld201516/ldselect/ldeucom/144/14402 .htm; accessed October 17, 2019.

EURES. 2019. "Labour Market Information: Sicily." EURES: European Job Mobility Portal. https://ec.europa.eu/eures/main.jsp?catId=402&countryId=I T&acro=lmi&lang=en&regionId=ITG&nuts2Code=ITG1&nuts3Code=&regio nName=Sicilia; accessed October 17, 2019.

EUROSTAT. 2016. "First Instance Decisions by Outcome and Recognition Rates, 3rd Quarter 2016." https://ec.europa.eu/eurostat/statistics-explained/index

.php/File:First_instance_decisions_by_outcome_and_recognition_rates,_3
rd_quarter_2016.png; accessed October 17, 2019.

———. 2020. "Asylum Applications by State of Procedure." https://ec.europa.eu
/eurostat/web/products-datasets/-/sdg_10_60; accessed January, 20, 2020.

Fassin, Didier. 2005. "Compassion and Repression: The Moral Economy of
Immigration Policies in France." *Cultural Anthropology* 20: 362–87.

———. 2011. "Policing Borders, Producing Boundaries. The Governmentality of
Immigration in Dark Times." *Annual Review of Anthropology* 40: 213–26.

Fassin, Didier, and Richard Rechtman. 2009. *The Empire of Trauma: An
Inquiry into the Condition of Victimhood*. Princeton, NJ: Princeton University Press.

Fekete, Liz, Frances Webber, and Anya Edmond-Petit. 2017. *Humanitarianism:
The Unacceptable Face of Solidarity*. London: Institute of Race Relations.

Feldman-Savelsberg, Pamela. 2016. *Mothers on the Move: Reproducing Belonging
between Africa and Europe*. Chicago: University of Chicago Press.

Fiore, Teresa, and Ernest Ialongo. 2018. "Introduction: Italy and the Euro-
Mediterranean 'Migrant Crisis': National Reception, Lived Experiences, E.U.
Pressures." *Journal of Modern Italian Studies* 23 (4): 481–89.

Fiume, Giovanna. 2006. "A Changing Sicily: Homage to Jane and Peter Schneider." *Journal of Modern Italian Studies* 11 (1): 37–60.

Fleming, Crystal. 2017. *Resurrecting Slavery: Racial Legacies and White Supremacy in France*. Philadelphia, PA: Temple University Press.

Flores, William Vincent, and Rina Benmayor. 1997. *Latino Cultural Citizenship:
Claiming Identity, Space, and Rights*. Boston: Beacon Press.

Fonte, Maria. 2013. "Food Consumption as Social Practice: Solidarity Purchasing
Groups in Rome, Italy." *Journal of Rural Studies* 32: 230–39.

Foucault, Michel. 1980. *Power/Knowledge: Selected Interviews and Other Writings, 1972–1977*. New York: Pantheon Books.

Frisina, Annalisa, and Camilla Hawthorne. 2018. "Italians with Veils and Afros:
Gender, Beauty, and the Everyday Anti-Racism of the Daughters of Immigrants in Italy." *Journal of Ethnic and Migration Studies* 44 (5): 718–35.

Fullin, Giovanna, and Emilio Reyneri. 2011. "Low Unemployment and Bad Jobs
for New Immigrants in Italy." *International Migration* 49 (1): 118–47.

Garth, Hanna, and Ashanté Reese. 2020. *Black Food Matters: Racial Justice in
the Wake of Food Justice*. Minneapolis: University of Minnesota Press.

Gasparetti, Fedora. 2012. "Eating tie bou jenn in Turin: Negotiating Differences
and Building Community among Senegalese Migrants in Italy." *Food and
Foodways* 20 (3–4): 257–78.

Geddes, Andrew. 2008. "Il Rombo dei Cannoni? Immigration and the Centre-
Right in Italy." *Journal of European Public Policy* 15 (3): 349–66.

Gettleman, Jeffrey. 2017. "Loss of Fertile Land Fuels 'Looming Crisis' across
Africa." *New York Times*, July 29, 2017.

Giglioli, Ilaria. 2017. "Producing Sicily as Europe: Migration, Colonialism and the Making of the Mediterranean Border between Italy and Tunisia." *Geopolitics* 22 (2): 407–28.

Gill, Lesley. 2009. "The Limits of Solidarity: Labor and Transnational Organizing against Coca-Cola." *American Ethnologist* 36 (4): 667–80.

Gilmore, Ruth Wilson. 2007. *Golden Gulag: Prisons, Surplus, Crisis, and Opposition in Globalizing California*. Berkeley: University of California Press.

Giordano, Cristiana. 2008. "Practices of Translation and the Making of Migrant Subjectivities in Contemporary Italy." *American Ethnologist* 35 (4): 588–606.

———. 2014. *Migrants in Translation: Caring and the Logics of Difference in Italy*. Berkeley: University of California Press.

———. 2018. "The Funnel Effect." LIMN. https://limn.it/articles/the-funnel-effect/; accessed September 21, 2018.

Glick Schiller, Nina. 2016. "The Question of Solidarity and Society: Comment on Will Kymlicka's Article 'Solidarity in Diverse Societies.'" *Comparative Migration Studies* 4 (6). DOI:10.1186/s40878-016-0027-x.

Gomez, Ricardo, and Sara Vannini. 2015. *Fotohistorias: Participatory Photography and the Experience of Migration*. Charleston, SC: CreateSpace.

Gonzales, Roberto G., and Leo R. Chavez. 2012. "'Awakening to a Nightmare': Abjectivity and Illegality in the Lives of Undocumented 1.5-Generation Latino Immigrants in the United States." *Current Anthropology* 53 (3): 255–81.

Gramsci, Antonio. 1971. *Selections from the Prison Notebooks*. New York: International Publishers.

———. 1978. *Selections from Political Writings (1921–1926)*. Trans. and ed. Quintin Hoare. London: Lawrence and Wishart.

Grasseni, Cristina. 2013. *Beyond Alternative Food Networks: Italy's Solidarity Purchase Groups*. London: Bloomsbury.

Grassilli, Mariagiulia. 2008. "Migrant Cinema: Transnational and Guerrilla Practices of Film Production and Representation." *Journal of Ethnic and Migration Studies* 34 (8): 1237–55.

Gray, Breda. 2013. "Catholic Church Civil Society Activism and the Neoliberal Governmental Project of Migrant Integration in Ireland." In *Religion in the Neoliberal Age*, edited by F. Gautheir and T. Martikainen, 69–90. Farnham: Ashgate.

———. 2015. "The Politics of Migration, Church, and State: A Case Study of the Catholic Church in Ireland." *International Migration Review* 50 (2): 315–51.

Greenhalgh, Susan, and Megan A. Carney. 2014. "'Bad Biocitizens? Latinos and the U.S. 'Obesity Epidemic.'" *Human Organization* 73 (3): 267–76.

Grosglik, Rafi, and Julia Lerner. 2020. "Gastro-Emotivism: How MasterChef Israel Produces Therapeutic Collective Belongings." *European Journal of Cultural Studies*. DOI:10.1177/1367549420902801.

Guglielmo, Jennifer, and Salvatore Salerno. 2003. *Are Italians White? How Race Is Made in America*. New York: Routledge.

Guthman, Julie, and Melanie DuPuis. 2006. "Embodying Neoliberalism: Economy, Culture, and the Politics of Fat." *Environment and Planning D: Society and Space* 24 (3): 427–48.

Gutierrez, C. Paige. 1992. *Cajun Foodways*. Jackson: University Press of Mississippi.

Hacker, Karen, et al. 2011. "The Impact of Immigration and Customs Enforcement on Immigrant Health: Perceptions of Immigrants in Everett, Massachusetts, USA." *Social Science & Medicine* 73 (4): 586–94.

Hale, Charles. 2002. "Does Multiculturalism Menace? Governance, Cultural Rights and the Politics of Identity in Guatemala." *Journal of Latin American Studies* 34 (3): 485–524.

Hall, Stuart. 2000. "Conclusion: The Multi-Cultural Question." In *Un/Settled Multiculturalisms: Diasporas, Entanglements, Transruptions*, ed. Barnor Hesse, 209–41. New York: St. Martin's Press.

Han, Clara. 2012. *Life in Debt: Times of Care and Violence in Neoliberal Chile*. Berkeley: University of California Press.

Harvey, David. 2005. *A Brief History of Neoliberalism*. Oxford: Oxford University Press.

Hatton, Timothy J., and Jeffrey G. Williamson. 2006. "Refugees, Asylum Seekers, and Policy in Europe." NBER Working Paper No. 10680.

Hawthorne, Camilla. 2017. "In Search of Black Italia: Notes on Race, Belonging, and Activism in the Black Mediterranean." *Transition* 123: 152–74.

Hayes-Conroy, Allison, and Elizabeth L. Sweet. 2015. "Whose Adequacy? (Re)Imagining Food Security with Displaced Women in Medellín, Colombia." *Agriculture and Human Values* 32: 373–84.

Heidbrink, Lauren. 2014. *Migrant Youth, Transnational Families, and the State: Care and Contested Interests*. Philadelphia: University of Pennsylvania Press.

Heller, Chaia. 2013. *Food, Farms, and Solidarity: French Farmers Challenge Industrial Agriculture and Genetically Modified Crops*. Durham, NC: Duke University Press.

Hendriks, Martijn. 2018. "Does Migration Increase Happiness? It Depends." Migration Policy Institute. www.migrationpolicy.org/article/does-migration-increase-happiness-it-depends; accessed October 17, 2019.

Henley, Alexandra. 2016. "The Culinary 'Food Chain': Private and Personal Chefs Negotiate Identity and Status in the Culinary Profession." In *Gender and Food: From Production to Consumption and After*, edited by V. Demos and M. Texler Segal, 219–41. Advances in Gender Research 22. Bingley, UK: Emerald Group Publishing.

Hermanin, Costanza. 2017. "Immigration Policy in Italy: Problems and Perspectives." IAI Working Papers 17. www.iai.it/sites/default/files/iaiwp1735.pdf.

Herzfeld, Michael. 1987. *Anthropology through the Looking Glass: Critical Ethnography in the Margins of Europe*. Cambridge: Cambridge University Press.

———. 2007. "Small-Mindedness Writ Large: On the Migration and Manners of Prejudice." *Journal of Ethnic and Migration Studies* 33: 255–74.

Heyer, Kristin. 2012. *Kinship across Borders: A Christian Ethic of Immigration*. Washington, DC: Georgetown University Press.

Heyman, Josiah McC. 2016a. "Conclusion." In *After the Crisis: Anthropological Thought, Neoliberalism, and the Aftermath*, ed. James G. Carrier, 175–89. London: Routledge.

———. 2016b. "Discussion of Frontiers of Fear: Immigration and Insecurity in the United States and Europe." *Journal of Ethnic and Migration Studies* 42 (4): 693–96.

Hikichi, Hiroyuki, Toru Tsuboya, Jun Aida, Yusuke Matsuyama, Katsunori Kondo, S. V. Subramanian, and Ichiro Kawachi. 2017. "Social Capital and Cognitive Decline in the Aftermath of a Natural Disaster: A Natural Experiment from the 2011 Great East Japan Earthquake and Tsunami." *Lancet Planetary Health* 1 (3): E105–E113.

Himmelgreen, David, N. Romero-Daza, E. Cooper, and D. Martinez. 2007. "'I don't make the soups anymore': Pre- to Post-Migration Dietary and Lifestyle Changes among Latinos Living in West-Central Florida." *Ecology of Food and Nutrition* 46 (5–6): 427–44.

Holmes, Seth. 2013. *Fresh Fruit, Broken Bodies: Migrant Farmworkers in the United States*. Berkeley: University of California Press.

Holmes, Seth, and Heide Castañeda. 2016. "Representing the 'European Refugee Crisis' in Germany and Beyond: Deservingness and Difference, Life and Death." *American Ethnologist* (43) 1: 12–24.

Hoover, Elizabeth. 2017. *The River Is in Us: Fighting Toxins in a Mohawk Community*. Minneapolis: University of Minnesota Press.

Horsti, Karina. "Temporality in Cosmopolitan Solidarity: Archival Activism and Participatory Documentary Film as Mediated Witnessing of Suffering at Europe's Borders." *European Journal of Cultural Studies* 22 (2): 231–44.

Human Rights Watch. 2016. "Italy: Children Stuck in Unsafe Migrant Hotspot." www.hrw.org/news/2016/06/23/italy-children-stuck-unsafe-migrant-hotspot#; accessed October 18, 2019.

———. 2020. "Italy: Halt Abusive Migration Cooperation with Libya." www.hrw.org/news/2020/02/12/italy-halt-abusive-migration-cooperation-libya#; accessed March 5, 2020.

Inoue, Sachiko, Takashi Yorifuji, Soshi Takao, Hiroyuki Doi, and Ichiro Kawachi. 2013. "Social Cohesion and Mortality: A Survival Analysis of Older Adults in Japan." *American Journal of Public Health* 103 (12): E60–E66.

International Monetary Fund (IMF). 2016. "IMF Executive Board Concludes

2016 Article IV Consultation with Italy." www.imf.org/external/np/sec/pr/20
16/pr16329.htm; accessed August 8, 2016.

International Organization of Migration (IOM). 2013. "Assessment Report: Health Situation at EU Southern Borders—Migrant Health, Occupational Health, and Public Health." Brussels.

———. 2016. "Mediterranean Migrant Arrivals in 2016: 350,573; Deaths: 4,699." http://reliefweb.int/report/greece/mediterranean-migrant-arrivals-reach-350 573-deaths-sea-4699; accessed August 8, 2016.

———. 2017. "New Study Concludes Europe's Mediterranean Border Remains 'World's Deadliest.'" www.iom.int/news/new-study-concludes-europes-medit erranean-border-remains-worlds-deadliest; accessed October 17, 2019.

———. 2018. "Mediterranean Migrant Arrivals Reached 171,635 in 2017; Deaths Reach 3,116." https://eea.iom.int/mediterranean-migrant-arrivals-reached-171 635-2017-deaths-reach-3116; accessed January 22, 2020.

Italian Ministry of Labor and Social Affairs. 2016. "I minori stranieri non accompagnati (MSNA) in Italia." www.lavoro.gov.it/temi-e-priorita/immigra zione/focus-on/minori-stranieri/Documents/Report-di-monitoraggio-MSNA -31-dicembre-2016.pdf; accessed June 15, 2017.

Italian National Institute of Statistics (ISTAT). 2016. "Poverty in Italy 2015." www .istat.it/en/archive/poverty; accessed August 11, 2016.

Janowski, Monica. 2012. "Introduction: Consuming Memories of Home in Constructing the Present and Imagining the Future." *Food and Foodways* 20 (3–4): 175–86.

Johnson, Michelle C. 2016. "'Nothing is sweet in my mouth': Food, Identity, and Religion in African Lisbon." *Food and Foodways* 24 (3–4): 232–54.

Kea, Pamela. 2016. "Photography and Technologies of Care: Migrants in Britain and Their Children in the Gambia." In *Affective Circuits: African Migrations to Europe and the Pursuit of Social Regeneration*, edited by Jennifer Cole and Christian Groes, 78–100. Chicago: University of Chicago Press.

Keahey, John. 2011. *Seeking Sicily: A Cultural Journey through Myth and Reality in the Heart of the Mediterranean*. New York: Thomas Dunne Books.

Kersh, Adam, and Joanna Mishtal. 2016. "Asylum in Crisis: Migrant Policy, Entrapment, and the Role of Non-Governmental Organisations in Siracusa, Italy." *Refugee Survey Quarterly* 35: 97–121.

Kessler-Harris, Alice. 2003. "In Pursuit of Economic Citizenship." *Social Politics* 10 (2): 157–75.

Klein, Naomi. 2007. *The Shock Doctrine: The Rise of Disaster Capitalism*. New York: Picador.

Knight, Daniel M., and Charles Stewart. 2016. "Ethnographies of Austerity: Temporality, Crisis, and Affect in Southern Europe." *History and Anthropology* 27 (1): 1–18.

Krause, Elizabeth. 2005. *A Crisis of Births: Population Politics and Family-Making in Italy*. Belmont, CA: Wadsworth.

———. 2018. *Tight Knit: Global Families and the Social Life of Fast Fashion*. Chicago: University of Chicago Press.

Krause, Elizabeth, and Milena Marchesi. 2007. "Fertility Politics as 'Social Viagra': Reproducing Boundaries, Social Cohesion and Modernity in Italy." *American Anthropologist* 109 (2): 350–62.

Lahusen, Christian, and Maria T. Grasso. 2018. *Solidarity in Europe: Citizens' Responses in Times of Crisis*. Cham, Switzerland: Palgrave Macmillan.

Larchanche, Stephanie. 2012. "Intangible Obstacles: Health Implications of Stigmatization, Structural Violence, and Fear among Undocumented Immigrants in France." *Social Science & Medicine* 74 (6): 858–63.

La Repubblica. 2017. "Palermo, messaggio al G7: Il salvataggio simbolico con le barchette di carte." www.repubblica.it/solidarieta/cooperazione/2017/05/24 /news/sicilia_messaggio_al_g7_il_salvataggio_simbolico_con_le_barchet te_di_carta-166300942/?refresh_ce; accessed October 18, 2019.

Lawrence, D. H. 1921. *Sea and Sardinia*. New York: Thomas Seltzer.

Lazzarato, Maurizio. 2012. *The Making of the Indebted Man: An Essay on the Neoliberal Condition*. Amsterdam: Semiotext(e).

Levin, Leslie C. 2009. "Guardians at the Gate: The Backgrounds, Career Paths, and Professional Development of Private US Immigration Lawyers." *Law & Social Inquiry* 34 (2): 399–436.

Lippert, Randy. 2011. *Sanctuary, Sovereignty, Sacrifice: Canadian Sanctuary Incidents, Power, and Law*. Vancouver: University of British Columbia Press.

Lipsky, Michael. 2010. *Street-Level Bureaucracy: Dilemmas of the Individual in Public Services*. 30th Anniversary Expanded Ed. New York: Russell Sage Foundation.

Loh, Penn, and Julian Agyeman. 2017. "Boston's Emerging Solidarity Food Economy." In *The New Food Activism: Opposition, Cooperation, and Collective Action*, edited by Allison Alkon and Julie Guthman, 257–83. Berkeley: University of California Press.

Mackenzie, James. 2014. "Italy's Renzi Calls for Europe to Change Course on Austerity." Reuters. www.reuters.com/article/us-italy-eu-idUSKBN0EZ0PW2 0140624; accessed August 31, 2016.

Magaña, Lisa L. 2003. *Straddling the Border: Immigration Policy and the INS*. Austin: University of Texas Press.

Maggini, Nicola. 2018. "The Social and Political Dimensions of Solidarity in Italy." In *Solidarity in Europe: Citizens' Responses in Times of Crisis*, edited by Christian Lahusen and Maria T. Grasso, 127–68. Cham, Switzerland: Palgrave Macmillan.

Mai, Nicola. 2002. "Myths and Moral Panics: Italian Identity and the Media Representation of Albanian Immigration." In *The Politics of Recognizing Dif-*

ference: Multiculturalism Italian Style, edited by Ralph Grillo and Jeff Pratt. Aldershot: Ashgate.

Mankekar, Purnima. 2002. "'India Shopping': Indian Grocery Stores and Transnational Configurations of Belonging." *Ethnos* 67 (1): 75–97.

Mares, Teresa. 2012. "Tracing Immigrant Identity through the Plate and Palate." *Latino Studies* 10: 334–54.

———. 2019. *Life on the Other Border: Farmworkers and Food Justice in Vermont.* Oakland: University of California Press.

Mauss, Marcel. [1950] 1990. *The Gift: The Form and Reason for Exchange in Archaic Societies.* London: Routledge.

Mazzuccheli, Chiara. 2007. "Ethnic Regionalism in American Literature: The Case of Sicilian/American Writers." *Tamkang Review* 38 (1).

McEwan, Bree, and Miriam Sobre-Denton. 2011. "Virtual Cosmopolitanism: Constructing Third Cultures and Transmitting Social and Cultural Capital through Social Media." *Journal of International and Intercultural Communication* 4 (4): 252–58.

McKee, M., et al. 2012. "Austerity: A Failed Experiment on the People of Europe." *Clinical Medicine* 12 (4): 346–50.

Médecins Sans Frontières (MSF). 2015. "Migration: EU Leaders Orchestrating Humanitarian Crisis on Europe's Shores." www.msf.org/article/migration-eu -leaders-orchestrating-humanitarian-crisis-europe%E2%80%99s-shores; accessed November 5, 2015.

———. 2016. "Asylum Seekers in Italy: An Analysis of Mental Health Distress and Access to Healthcare." www.msf.org/sites/msf.org/files/neglected_trauma_re port.pdf; accessed August 8, 2016.

Menjívar, Cecilia. 2013. "Central American Immigrant Workers and Legal Violence in Phoenix, Arizona." *Latino Studies* 11 (2): 228–52.

Menjívar, Cecilia, and Daniel Kanstroom, eds. 2014. *Constructing Immigrant "Illegality": Critiques, Experiences, and Responses.* New York: Cambridge University Press.

Merrill, Heather. 2014. "Postcolonial Borderlands: Black Life Worlds and Relational Place in Turin, Italy." *ACME* 13 (2): 263–94.

Metzl, Jonathan M., and Helena Hansen. 2014. "Structural Competency: Theorizing a New Medical Engagement with Stigma and Inequality." *Social Science & Medicine* 103: 126–33.

Miglierini, Julian. 2014. "Migrants Tell Migrants: 'Don't Come to Italy.'" BBC. www.bbc.com/news/blogs-eu-27352480; accessed June 14, 2017.

Ministry of Interior (MOI). 2015. "Report on the Reception of Migrants and Refugees in Italy: Aspects, Procedures, Problems. Study Group on the Reception System." Ministry of Interior, Rome. www.libertaciviliimmigrazione.dlci .interno.gov.it/sites/default/files/allegati/rapporto_accoglienza_eng_isbn_ap pendice_rev3b.pdf.

Minkoff-Zern, Laura-Anne. 2019. *The New American Farmer: Immigration, Race, and the Struggle for Sustainability*. Cambridge, MA: MIT Press.

Mintz, Sidney. 2008. "Food and Diaspora." *Food, Culture, and Society* 11 (4): 509–23.

Mitchell, Katharyne. 2017. "Freedom, Faith, and Humanitarian Governance: The Spatial Politics of Church Asylum in Europe." *Space and Polity* 21 (3): 269–88.

Mitchell, Katharyne, and Matthew Sparke. 2017. "Hotspot Geopolitics versus Geosocial Solidarity: Contending Constructions of Safe Space for Migrants in Europe." *Environment and Planning D: Society and Space* 38 (6): 1046–66.

Mohanty, Chandra. 2003. *Feminism without Borders: Decolonizing Theory, Practicing Solidarity*. Durham, NC: Duke University Press.

Mol, Annemarie, Ingunn Moser, and Jeannette Pols. 2010. "Care: Putting Practice into Theory." In *Care in Practice: On Tinkering in Homes, Clinics, and Farms*, edited by Annemarie Mol, Ingunn Moser, and Jeannette Pols, 7–26. London: Transcript-Verlag.

Molé, Noelle J. 2012. "Hauntings of Solidarity in Post-Fordist Italy." *Anthropological Quarterly* 85 (2): 371–96.

Moore, Spencer, and Ichiro Kawachi. 2017. "Twenty Years of Social Capital and Health Research: A Glossary." *Journal of Epidemiology and Community Health*, January 13.

Mudu, Pierpaolo, and Sutapa Chattopadhyay. 2016. *Migration, Squatting, and Radical Autonomy*. London: Routledge.

Muehlebach, Andrea. 2012. *The Moral Neoliberal: Welfare and Citizenship in Italy*. Chicago: University of Chicago Press.

——. 2016. "Anthropologies of Austerity." *History and Anthropology* 27 (3): 359–72.

Mullings, Leith. 1995. "Households Headed by Women: The Politics of Race, Class, and Gender." In *Conceiving the New World Order: The Global Politics of Reproduction*, edited by Faye D. Ginsburg and Rayna Rapp, 122–39. Berkeley: University of California Press.

Murphy, Fiona. 2018. "Seeking Solidarity through Food: The Growth of Asylum Seeker and Refugee Food Initiatives in Ireland." *Studies in Arts and Humanities* 4 (2): 1–13.

Narotzky, Susana. 2013. "The Anthropology of Economic Processes in a Europe in Crisis." *Council for European Studies, Perspectives on Europe* 43 (1): 22–26.

Nastasi, Giuseppe, and Giuseppe Palmisano. 2015. "The Impact of the Crisis on Fundamental Rights across Member States of the EU: Country Report on Italy." Report commissioned by the LIBE Committee, European Parliament. www.europarl.europa.eu/thinktank/it/document.html?reference=IPOL_STU (2015)510018; accessed January 20, 2020.

Negrón-Gonzales, Genevieve. 2014. "Undocumented, Unafraid and Unapologetic: Re-Articulatory Practices and Migrant Youth 'Illegality.'" *Latino Studies* 12 (2): 259–78.

Nelson, Robin G., Julienne N. Rutherford, Katie Hinde, and Kathryn B. H. Clancy. 2017. "Signaling Safety: Characterizing Fieldwork Experiences and Their Implications for Career Trajectories." *American Anthropologist* 119 (4): 710–22.

New Keywords Collective. 2016. "Europe/Crisis: New Keywords of 'the Crisis' in and of 'Europe.'" *Near Futures Online* 1, "Europe at a Crossroads." http://ne arfuturesonline.org/europecrisis-new-keywords-of-crisis-in-and-of-europe/; accessed August 11, 2016.

Oiarazabal, Pedro J., and Ulf-Dietrich Reips. 2012. "Migration and Diaspora in the Age of Information and Communication Technologies." *Journal of Ethnic and Migration Studies* 38 (9): 1333–38.

Oliveri, Federico. 2015. "Subverting Neoliberal Citizenship: Migrant Struggles for the Right to Stay in Contemporary Italy." *ACME* 14 (2): 492–503.

Oparah, Julia Chinyere, and Margo Okazawa-Rey. 2009. *Activist Scholarship: Antiracism, Feminism, and Social Change.* Boulder, CO: Paradigm Publishers.

Orlando, Giovanni. 2015. "Critical Consumption in Palermo: Imagined Society, Class, and Fractured Locality." In *Ethical Consumption: Social Value and Economic Practice,* edited by James G. Carrier and Peter G. Luetchford, 142–63. New York: Berghan.

Osservatorio migrazioni. 2016. "Migrazioni in Sicilia 2015." Istituto Arrupe. www .osservatoriomigrazioni.org/fr/; accessed August 15, 2016.

———. 2018. "V Rapporto migrazioni in Sicilia 2017." Istituto Arrupe. https://isti tutoarrupe.gesuiti.it/wp-content/uploads/sites/34/2018/06/Comunicato-stam pa-V-Rapporto-Migrazioni-in-Sicilia-2017-1.pdf; accessed January 22, 2020.

Ostrach, Bayla. 2017. *Health Policy in a Time of Crisis: Abortion, Austerity, and Access.* New York: Routledge.

Oxfam. 2013. "The True Cost of Austerity and Inequality: Italy Case Study." Oxfam International. ; www.oxfam.org/sites/www.oxfam.org/files/cs-true-co st-austerity-inequality-italy-120913-en.pdf accessed August 8, 2016.

———. 2016. "Children Alone: Pulled from the Sea, Fallen by the Wayside." Oxfam International. www.oxfam.org/en/research/children-alone-pulled-sea-fallen -wayside; accessed June 15, 2017.

Palese, A., et al. 2014. "Financial Austerity Measures and Their Effects as Perceived in Daily Practice by Italian Nurses from 2010 to 2011: A Longitudinal Study." *Contemporary Nurse* 48 (2): 168–80.

Pallares, Amalia, and Ruth Gomberg-Muñoz. 2016. "Politics of Motion: Ethnography with Undocumented Activists and of Undocumented Activism." *North American Dialogue* 19(1): 4–12.

Panter-Brick, Catherine. 2014. "Health, Risk, and Resilience: Interdisciplinary Concepts and Applications." *Annual Review of Anthropology* 43: 431–48.

Parla, Ayse. 2019. *Precarious Hope: Migration and the Limits of Belonging in Turkey*. Stanford, CA: Stanford University Press.

Parvulescu, Anca. 2014. *The Traffic in Women's Work: East European Migration and the Making of Europe*. Chicago: University of Chicago Press.

Pearce, J. 2013. "Financial Crisis, Austerity Policies, and Geographical Inequalities in Health." *Environment and Planning A* 45 (9): 2030–45.

Pérez, Rachel L., and Meredith E. Abarca. 2007. "Cocinas Públicas: Food and Border Consciousness in Greater Mexico." *Food and Foodways* 15 (3): 137–51.

Permoser, J. M., S. Rosenberger, and K. Stoeckl. 2010. "Religious Organizations as Political Actors in the Context of Migration: Islam and Orthodoxy in Austria." *Journal of Ethnic and Migration Studies* 36 (9): 1463–81.

Perry, Keisha-Khan. 2009. "The Groundings with My Sisters: Toward a Black Diasporic Feminist Agenda in the Americas." *Scholar and Feminist Online* 7 (2): 1–8.

———. 2014. "State Violence and the Ethnographic Encounter: Feminist Research and Racial Embodiment." In *Bridging Scholarships and Activism: Reflections from the Frontlines of Collaborative Research*, edited by Bernd Reiter and Ulrich Oslender, 151–70. East Lansing: Michigan State University Press.

Petrini, Carlo. 2004. *Slow Food: The Case for Taste*. New York: Columbia University Press.

Pfeiffer, James, and Rachel Chapman. 2010. "Anthropological Perspectives on Structural Adjustment and Public Health." *Annual Review of Anthropology* 39: 149–65.

Pine, Adrienne. 2013. "Revolution as Care Plan: Ethnography, Nursing, and Somatic Solidarity in Honduras." *Social Science & Medicine* 99: 143–52.

Pinelli, Barbara. 2015. "After the Landing: Moral Control and Surveillance in Italy's Asylum Seeker Camps." *Anthropology Today* 31 (2): 12–14.

Porter, S. 2013. "Capitalism, the State and Health Care in the Age of Austerity: A Marxist Analysis." *Nursing Philosophy* 14 (1): 5–16.

Portillo, Shannon. 2010. "How Race, Sex, and Age Frame the Use of Authority by Local Government Officials." *Law & Social Inquiry* 35 (3): 603–23.

———. 2011. "The Paradox of Rules: Rules as Resources and Constraints." *Administration & Society* 44 (1): 87–108.

Povoledo, Elisabetta. 2014. "Palace of Squatter Is Symbol of Refugee Crisis." *New York Times*, June 15. www.nytimes.com/2014/06/15/world/europe/palace-of-squatters-is-a-symbol-of-refugee-crisis.html?_r=1; accessed November 5, 2015.

Pratt, Jeff C. 2002. "Political Unity and Cultural Diversity." In *The Politics of Recognizing Difference: Multiculturalism Italian-Style*, edited by Ralph Grillo and Jeff Pratt. Aldershot: Ashgate.

Proglio, Gabriele. 2018. "Is the Mediterranean a White Italian-European Sea? The Multiplication of Borders in the Production of Historical Subjectivity." *Interventions* 1–22.

Quesada, James, Laurie K. Hart, and Philippe Bourgois. 2011. "Structural Vulnerability and Health: Latino Migrant Laborers in the United States." *Medical Anthropology* 30 (4): 339–62.

Rabben, Linda. 2016. *Sanctuary and Asylum: A Social and Political History.* Seattle: University of Washington Press.

Rakopoulos, Theodoros. 2014. "The Crisis Seen from Below, Within, and Against: From Solidarity Economy to Food Distribution Cooperatives in Greece." *Dialectical Anthropology* 28: 189–207.

———. 2015. "Solidarity Economy in Contemporary Greece: 'Movementality,' Economic Democracy, and Social Reproduction during Crisis." In *Economy for and against Democracy*, ed. Keith Hart, 161–81. New York: Berghahn.

———. 2016. "Solidarity: The Egalitarian Tensions of a Bridge-Concept." *Social Anthropology* 24 (2): 142–51.

———. 2017. *From Clans to Co-ops: Confiscated Mafia Land in Sicily.* Oxford: Berghahn.

Reese, Ashanté. 2019. *Black Food Geographies: Race, Self-Reliance, and Food Access in Washington, D.C.* Chapel Hill: University of North Carolina Press.

Regione Siciliana. 2020. "I focus della storia." http://pti.regione.sicilia.it/portal /page/portal/PIR_PORTALE/PIR_150ANNI/PIR_150ANNISITO/PIR_Sch ede/PIR_Ifocusdellastoria; accessed January 22, 2020.

Ribeiro, Gustavo Lins. 2004. Commentary on "Mafia, Antimafia, and the Plural Cultures of Sicily." *Current Anthropology* 46 (4): 501–20.

Riccio, Bruno. 2002. "Toubab and Vu Cumpra: Italian Perceptions of Senegalese Transmigrants and the Senegalese Afro-Muslim Critique of Italian Society." In *The Politics of Recognizing Difference: Multiculturalism Italian-Style*, edited by Ralph Grillo and Jeff Pratt. Aldershot: Ashgate.

Robb, Peter. 2007. *Midnight in Sicily.* New York: Picador.

Rodotà, Stefano. 2014. *Solidarietà: Un'utopia necessaria.* Rome-Bari: Laterza.

Rorato, Laura. 2020. "'New Italians' and Intercultural Citizenship: Challenging Hegemonic Visions of Migration, Childhood and Identity through Fiction." *European Journal of Cultural Studies.* https://doi-org.ezproxy4.library.arizo na.edu/10.1177/1367549420902807; accessed February 25, 2020.

Rovisco, Maria. 2013. "Towards a Cosmopolitan Cinema: Understanding the Connection between Borders, Mobility and Cosmopolitanism in Fiction Film." *Mobilities* 8 (1): 148–65.

Rozakou, Katerina. 2012. "The Biopolitics of Hospitality in Greece: Humanitarianism and the Management of Refugees." *American Ethnologist* 39 (3): 562–77.

———. 2017. "Access to a Hot Field: A Self-Reflexive Account of Research in the

Moria Camp, Lesvos." *Border Criminologies* (blog). www.law.ox.ac.uk/resear
ch-subject-groups/centre-criminology/centreborder-criminologies/blog/2017
/11/access-hot-field; accessed October 17, 2019.

Sagona, Alice. 2018. "Palermo, l'integrazione si fa mangiando: Ex migranti diven-
tati cuochi 10 e lode." *Corriere della Sera*. https://viaggi.corriere.it/viaggi/even
ti-news/palermo-lintegrazione-si-fa-mangiando-ex-migranti-diventati-cuochi
-10-e-lode/?fbclid=IwAROwTALzhX-VKp-2G_VcXeYRqvSk5oJryaoeZV_gDZ
jajgF1I3QFT8AyVxE&refresh_ce-cp; accessed October 18, 2019.

Sanchez, G., and L. Achilli. 2020. "Stranded: The Impacts of COVID-19 on
Irregular Migration And Migrant Smuggling." Policy Briefs. Migration Policy
Centre. https://cadmus.eui.eu//handle/1814/67069.

Sandoval, Chela. 2000. *Methodology of the Oppressed*. Minneapolis: University of
Minnesota Press.

Sassatelli, Roberta. 2019. "Introduction: Food, Foodways, and Italianicity." In
Italians and Food, ed. Roberta Sassatelli, 1–15. New York: Springer.

Schneider, Anne, and Helen Ingram. 1993. "Social Construction of Target
Populations: Implications for Politics and Policy." *American Political Science
Review* 87 (2): 334–47.

Schneider, Jane. 1998. *Italy's "Southern Question": Orientalism in One Country*.
Oxford: Berg.

Schneider, Jane, and Peter Schneider. 2003. *Reversible Destiny: Mafia, Antimafia, and the Struggle for Palermo*. Berkeley: University of California Press.

———. 2004. "Mafia, Antimafia, and the Plural Cultures of Sicily." *Current
Anthropology* 46 (4): 501–20.

Sciascia, Leonardo. 1994. *Sicily as Metaphor: Conversations presented by Marcelle Padovani*. Trans. James Marcus. Marlboro, VT: Marlboro Press.

Sen, Arijit. 2016. "Food, Place, and Memory: Bangladeshi Fish Stores on Devon
Avenue, Chicago." *Food and Foodways* 24 (1–2): 67–88.

Smith, Christian. 1996. *Resisting Reagan: The US Central America Peace Movement*. Chicago: University of Chicago Press.

Snyder, Susanna. 2012. *Asylum-Seeking, Migration, and Church*. Burlington,
VT: Ashgate.

Soto Bermant, Laia. 2017. "The Mediterranean Question: Europe and Its Pre-
dicament in the Southern Peripheries." In *The Borders of "Europe": Autonomy
of Migration, Tactics of Bordering*, ed. Nicholas De Genova, 120–40. Durham,
NC: Duke University Press.

Speed, Shannon. 2005. "Dangerous Discourses: Human Rights and Multiculturalism in Neoliberal Mexico." *PoLAR: Political and Legal Anthropology Review*
28 (1): 29–51.

———. 2016. "States of Violence: Indigenous Women Migrants in the Era of
Neoliberal Multicriminalism." *Critique of Anthropology* 36 (3): 280–301.

Squire, Vicki, and Jennifer Bagelman. 2012. "Taking Not Waiting: Space,

Temporality, and Politics in the City of Sanctuary Movement." In *Citizenship, Migrant Activism, and the Politics of Movement*, edited by Peter Nyers and Kim Rygiel, 146–64. New York: Routledge.

Stanley, Flavia. 2008. "On Belonging in/to Italy and Europe: Citizenship, Race and the Immigration 'Problem.'" In *Citizenship, Political Engagement, and Belonging: Immigrants in Europe and the United States*, edited by Deborah Reed-Danahay and Caroline B. Brettel, 43–60. New Brunswick, NJ: Rutgers University Press.

Steavenson, Wendell. 2018. "'Our Island Is Like a Mosaic': How Migrants Are Reshaping Sicily's Food Culture." *The Guardian*, June 17. www.theguardian .com/world/2018/jun/17/our-island-is-like-a-mosaic-how-migrants-are-resha ping-sicilys-food-culture?fbclid=IwAR1zlEYQyRCRV5sUWIlvjv2feOd8Y8_hy ohU80Bz-7K8DF67K9-0040ZjT0; accessed October 18, 2019.

Stoler, Ann Laura. 2011. "Colonial Aphasia: Race and Disabled Histories in France." *Public Culture* 23 (1): 121–56.

Stuckler, David, and Sanjay Basu. 2013. *The Body Economic: Why Austerity Kills*. New York: Basic Books.

Talavera, Victor, Guillermina Gina Núñez-Mchiri, and Josiah Heyman. 2010. "Deportation in the U.S.-Mexico Borderlands: Anticipation, Experience, and Memory." In *The Deportation Regime: Sovereignty, Space, and the Freedom of Movement*, edited by Nicholas De Genova and Nathalie Peutz, 166–95. Durham, NC: Duke University Press.

Ticktin, Miriam. 2011. *Casualties of Care: Immigration and the Politics of Humanitarianism in France*. Berkeley: University of California Press.

Tondo, Lorenzo. 2016. "How the Mafia Makes Millions Out of the Plight of Migrants." *Time*. https://time.com/4134503/mafia-millions-migrants/; accessed October 17, 2019.

———. 2020. "Matteo Salvini Trial for Kidnapping Authorised by Italian Senate." *The Guardian*, February 12. www.theguardian.com/world/2020/feb/12/mat teo-salvini-trial-for-kidnapping-authorised-by-italian-senate#maincontent; accessed March 5, 2020.

Tuckett, Anna. 2015. "Strategies of Navigation: Migrants' Everyday Encounters with Italian Immigration Bureaucracy." *Cambridge Journal of Anthropology* 33 (1): 113–28.

———. 2016. "Moving On: Italy as a Stepping Stone in Migrants' Imaginaries." *Focaal: Journal of Global and Historical Anthropology* 76: 99–113.

Tuhiwai Smith, Linda. 1999. *Decolonizing Methodologies: Research and Indigenous Peoples*. London: Zed Books.

United Nations High Commissioner for Refugees (UNHCR). 2015. "Global Trends." www.unhcr.org/en-us/statistics/unhcrstats/576408cd7/unhcr-global -trends-2015.html; accessed June 15, 2017.

UNICEF. 2017. "At Least 200 Children Lost at Sea Trying to Reach Italian Shores

So Far This Year." www.unicef.org/media/media_96066.html; accessed June 30, 2017.

UNIPA. 2019. "Migrare: Appeal to the Europe of Enlightenment." Università degli studi di Palermo. www.unipa.it/redazioneweb/.content/documenti/Appe al-to-the-Europe-of-Enlightenment_English.pdf; accessed October 17, 2019.

van der Zee, Renate. 2017. "He Fought the Mafia and Won. Now This Mayor Is Taking on Europe over Migrants." *The Guardian*, April 18. www.theguardi an.com/global-development-professionals-network/2017/apr/18/he-fought -the-mafia-and-won-now-this-mayor-is-taking-on-europe-over-migrants; accessed October 17, 2019.

Van Mol, Christof, and Helga de Valk. 2016. "Migration and Immigrants in Europe: A Historical and Demographic Perspective." In *Integration Processes and Policies in Europe*, edited by B. Garcés-Mascareñas and R. Penninx. IMISCOE Research Series. New York: Springer.

Vassalo Paleologo, Fulvio. 2012. "Diritti sotto sequestro: Dall'emergenza umanitaria allo stato di eccezione." Rome: Aracne.

Vavvos, Andreas, and Sofia Triliva. 2018. "The Neoliberal Myth of Austerity: Debt and Solidarity in the Forefront of Public Space." *Journal of Social and Political Psychology* 6 (2): 315–30.

Vélez-Ibañez, Carlos. 1996. *Border Visions: Mexican Cultures of the Southwest United States*. Tucson: University of Arizona Press.

Vicarelli, G., and E. Pavolini. 2015. "Health Workforce Governance in Italy." *Health Policy* 119: 1606–12.

Virdee, Satnam, and Brendan McGeever. 2016. "Racism, Crisis, Brexit." *Ethnic and Racial Studies* 41 (10): 1802–19.

Voci di Confine. 2018. "Chi Siamo." www.vocidiconfine.com/chi-siamo/; accessed October 18, 2019.

Wekerle, Gerda. 2004. "Food Justice Movements: Policy, Planning, and Networks." *Journal of Planning Education and Research* 23: 378–86.

Willen, Sarah S. 2007. "Toward a Critical Phenomenology of 'Illegality': State Power, Criminalization, and Abjectivity among Undocumented Migrant Workers in Tel Aviv, Israel." *International Migration* 45 (3): 8–38.

———. 2014. "Lightning Rods in the Local Moral Economy: Debating Unauthorized Migrants' Deservingness in Israel." *International Migration* 53 (3): 70–86.

———. 2019. *Fighting for Dignity: Migrant Lives at Israel's Margins*. Philadelphia: University of Pennsylvania Press.

Willen, Sarah, Jessica Mulligan, and Heide Castañeda. 2011. "Take a Stand Commentary: How Can Medical Anthropologists Contribute to Contemporary Conversations on 'Illegal' Im/migration and Health?" *Medical Anthropology Quarterly* 25 (3): 331–56.

World Bulletin. 2014. "500 Minors Escape Migrant Centers in Italy." www.world

bulletin.net/europe/500-minors-escape-migrant-centers-in-italy-h133943
.html; accessed October 18, 2019.

Zimmerman, Mary K., Jacquelyn S. Litt, and Christine E. Bose. 2006. *Global Dimensions of Gender and Carework*. Stanford, CA: Stanford University Press.

Zincone, Giovanna. 2006. "Italian Immigrants and Immigration Policy-Making: Structures, Actors and Practices." IMISCOE Working Paper. https://ec.europa .eu/migrant-integration/librarydoc/italian-immigrants-and-immigration-po licy-making-structures-actors-and-practices.

Index

Page numbers followed by *f* indicate figure and by *n* indicate note.